Robert Sempill

The Sempill Ballates

A series of historical, political, and satirical Scotish poems, ascribed to Robert

Sempill. 1567-1583. To which are added poems by Sir James Semple of Beltrees,

1598-1610

Robert Sempill

The Sempill Ballates
A series of historical, political, and satirical Scotish poems, ascribed to Robert Sempill.
1567-1583. To which are added poems by Sir James Semple of Beltrees, 1598-1610

ISBN/EAN: 9783337068622

Printed in Europe, USA, Canada, Australia, Japan

Cover: Foto ©ninafisch / pixelio.de

More available books at **www.hansebooks.com**

THE
𝔖empill 𝔅allates.

A SERIES OF

HISTORICAL, POLITICAL, AND SATIRICAL SCOTISH POEMS,

ASCRIBED TO

ROBERT SEMPILL.

M.D.LXVII.—M.D.LXXXIII.

TO WHICH ARE ADDED

POEMS BY SIR JAMES SEMPLE OF BELTREES,

M.D.XCVIII.—M.DC.X.

NOW FOR THE FIRST TIME PRINTED.

EDINBURGH:
THOMAS GEORGE STEVENSON.

M.DCCC.LXXII,

Preface.

HEN the First and only collected Edition of "The Poems of the Sempills of Beltrées" [Sir James, Robert, and Francis], was published in the year 1849, it was remarked that "A Collection of the Poems of Robert Sempill,—an author of so much ability and reputation,—is certainly a desideratum in Scotish Litera-ture, which the Publisher may at no distant period endeavour to supply." Since that time various matters occurred which prevented such an endeavour from being carried out. The chief cause was the rather sudden and unexpected death, on the 22nd April 1863, at the age of fifty-two years, in London, of my friend and well-wisher, WILLIAM BARCLAY DAVID DONALD TURNBULL, ESQ., Advocate, who had undertaken for me the duty of Editor. Many of the "Ballates" were copied by MR. TURNBULL during his residence in London, and amid his engagements, either as a Barrister-at-Law of Lincoln's Inn or as a student of history at the State Paper Office. But there were several others of them which he found at that time difficult of access.* However, through the kind assist-

---

* A very interesting Memoir of Mr. Turnbull, with Notices of the Sale of his highly valuable *(Second)* Library, and that of his various Bibliographical labours, from the pen of John Gough Nichols, Esq., appeared in "The Herald and Genealogist for January 1864." It was afterwards "Reprinted with some corrections," and circulated separately. His remains are interred in the grounds of the Episcopal Church at the Dean Bridge, Edinburgh.

ance of JOSEPH WALTER KING EYTON, ESQ. F.S.A. of Elsham
Road, Kensington, London, and that of DAVID LAING, ESQ.,
LL.D., Librarian to the Society of Writers to the Signet,
Edinburgh, copies of all these have since been obtained, and
the other difficulties overcome. This Collection, or series of
Historical, Political, and Satirical Poems, Ballads, and Pas-
quinades, is of the highest interest and curiosity. The pieces
of which it is composed were originally issued as BROADSIDES
and SMALL TRACTS, printed in BLACK-LETTER, between the
years 1567 and 1591, chiefly during the reign of the Earl of
Murray as Regent for Mary Queen of Scots and her son James
the Sixth. They have now been here brought together and
REPRINTED in a uniform style, without the slightest alteration,
and thereby made accessible to Antiquaries for the FIRST TIME.
No doubt these " Ballates " have been characterized as "gross,
illiberal, and obscene ;" but they are not unworthy of preservation.   Every writing coeval with the great and momentous
occurrences of the SIXTEENTH CENTURY must be regarded as
interesting, more especially if in any instance historical reality
can be contrasted with popular belief. Many of these BLACK-
LETTER BROADSIDES, describing the death of the King Henry
Darnley, and the Assassination of the " Good Regent"
Murray, &c., were scattered amongst the people, and the ex-
asperation of the two parties in the state became daily more
incurable.   On the rarity of these Broadsides it is superfluous
to enlarge.   In many, if not in most, instances they are
UNIQUE.   Few or no Duplicates of them are to be met with in
Public or Private Libraries ; a circumstance for which it is
easy to account, if we reflect that they were seldom printed in
a form calculated for preservation.   Several of the Poems are
ANONYMOUS ; but they are not the less interesting and curious

as expressing the sentiments of contemporaries, and may thus be considered as contributions to the history rather than the poetry of the age.

Of ROBERT SEMPILL, to whom the Authorship of the "Ballates illustrative of Public Affairs about the close of the Regency of James Earl of Murray," has been attributed, little or nothing is known. He has been described as "a copious and voluminous versifier of wars," and also as being "one of the most persevering and most unsuccessful of the period." He is represented to have been "Robert, Fourth Lord Sempill, a Scotish Peer;" but his identity at this moment remains as doubtful as ever it did. Certain it seems, however, that none of the Lords Sempill were poets; and although it is altogether extraordinary that the identity of an author of so much ability and reputation as Robert Sempill should have been lost sight of, still it is nevertheless true that it has hitherto eluded all research. Lord Sempill professed the Roman Catholic Religion, while the poems of Robert Sempill contain the most unequivocal proofs of having been written by a Protestant and very zealous Presbyterian. There is some reason to believe that Robert Sempill was a Captain in the Army; he speaks of himself as being present at the "Sege of Edinburgh Castle." His poems are said to be "indecent and unpoetical," and his "Legend of the Bischop of St Androis Lyfe," is spoken of as "a compound of vulgarity, passion, and malevolence," and also "as a most persevering, gross, and illiberal attack on the character of Dr. Patrick Adamson, who was a scholar, a man of talents, and a prelate of ingenuity and of erudition, but was not free from the glaring errors into which churchmen are sometimes betrayed by the fatal allurements of ambition. He became" it is added, "successively Minister of Paisley, Chaplain to the

Regent, and Archbishop of St. Andrews. These honours were not obtained without loud impeachments of his consistency and sincerity. And when the Archbishop was rapidly sinking into poverty and contempt, Sempill employed himself in the composition of this cruel invective." * On the other side, THOMAS DEMPSTER, in his "Historia Ecclesiastica Gentis Scotorum : sive, De Scriptoribus Scotis 1627," (*page* 602,) Edinburgh, (Bannatyne Club), 1829, represents Robert Sempill as exhibiting the combined excellencies of Propertius, Tibullus, Ovid, and Callimachus. His Panegyric is too remarkable to be omitted :—

" SEMPLE, claro nomine poeta, cui patrius sermo tantum debet, ut nulli plus debere eruditi fateantur : felix in eo calor, temperatum judicium, rara inventio, dictio pura ac candida, quibus dotibus Regi Jacobo carissimus fuit. Scripsit Rhythmos vernacule lib. 1. Carmina amatoria, ut Propertii sanguinem, Tibulli lac, Ovidii mel, Callimachi sudorem, aequasse plerisque doctis videatur, lib 1."

In " Robert Birrel's Diary 1532-1605," printed in the " Fragments of Scotish History," Edited by John Graham Dalyell, and published in 1798, it is recorded that there was in "1568 The 17 of Januarii, a play made by Robert Semple, and played before the Lord Regent, and divers uthers of the Nobilitie." There have been several conjectures as to this Play and its author, with little satisfactory result. It was probably a very simple representation of some historical scene or transaction, such as we can imagine the life of the execrable Bothwell to have gratefully furnished before such a company. However, it is generally supposed to have been " A verie excellent and delectable Comedie, intituled Philotos." It was

---

* "Lives of the Scotish Poets," 1810, and " The History of Scotish Poetry," 1861, by Dr. David Irving, *passim*.

first printed at Edinburgh by Robert Charteris in 1603. Another Edition appeared in 1612; and a reprint of the First Edition, edited by Dr. Irving, was presented to the Members of the Bannatyne Club by John Whitefoord Mackenzie, Esq., Edinburgh, in 1835.

JOHN KNOX, in a letter to Thomas Randolph, 3rd May 1564, remarks that—" Boht youris ar cumen to my handis with your bow, for the which I hartelie thank you. Rollettis tydingis are as yit buried in the breastis of two within this realme, butt Maddye telleht ws many newes : ' The mess shall up, the Bischope of Glaskier and Abbot of Dunfermling come as Ambassadouris from the General Counsall, my Lord Bothwell shall follow, with power to putt in execution whatsoever is demanded, and our Soveraine will have done; and then shall Knox and his preaching be pulled by the earis, etc.' Thus with ws ravis Maddye * every day ; but heirupon I greatlie pans not."

SEMPILL appears to have been in such a rank of life as not to be above ordinary rewards for his services, as on the 12th of Feburary 1567–8 there is an entry in the Lord High Treasurer's Books of £66, 13s. 4d. " to Robert Semple." And Alexander Montgomery, (Author of " The Cherrie and the Slaye"), in a sonnet addressed to Robert Hudson, specifies Sempill as not exempted from the too common misfortunes of poets :—

" Ye knaw ill guyding genders mony gees,
    And specially in Poets : for example,
Ye can pen out tua cuple and ye pleis,
    Yourself and I, old Scott and Robert Semple."

---

* " Maddye," a name in common use at all time, and occurring in some of the Ballads of Robert Sempill; one, for instance, ends—" Quod Maddie, Prioress of the kaill-market." Richard Bannatyne, in his Memorials, 1570, also speaks of " Madie in our fisch merkat," &c.—*John Knox's Works,* Collected and Edited by David Laing. Vol. VI. p. 541. Letter lxxviii, Edinburgh, Thomas George Stevenson, 1864.

On the 19th April 1567, an Act was passed, " Anentis the Makaris and Vpsettaris of Plackardes and Billis," viz.,—" For-samekle as be ane licentious abuse enterit laitlie and cum in practize within this Realme, Thair hes bene placardes and billis and ticquettis of defamatioun sett vp vnder silence of nycht in diuerse publict places alswiell within Burgh as vtherwyse in the Realme. To the sclander reproche and infamye of the Quenis Maiestie and diuerse of the Nobilitie. Quhilk disordour gif it be suffereit langer to remaine vnpunist may redound nocht onlie to the gret hurt and detriment of all nobillemen in thair gud fame, privat calumpniatoris having be this means libertie to bakbyte thame. Bot als the commone may be inquietit and occasioun of querrell takin vpounis fals and vntrew sclander ffor remeid quhairof the Quenis Maiestie and thre estaitis of parliament statutis and ordainis that in tyme cuming quhair ony sic Bill or placard of Defamatioun beis fundin affixt or tint the persounis first seand or findand the samin sall tak it and incontinent distroy it sua that no forder knawlege nor copy pas of the samin. And gif he failzeis thairin and that thairthrow owther the writting beis copyit or proceidis to forder knawlege amang the pepille. The first sear and finder thairof salbe punist in the samin maner as the first Inventar, writtar, tynar, and vpsettar of the samin gif he wer apprehendit. That is to say the defamearis of the Quene vnder the pane of Deid and to extend vpounn all vtheris to Imprisonment, at the Quenis grace plesour and for-der to be punist at hir hienes plesour according to the qualitie of the persoun is sua defamit."

In the " Diurnal of Remarkable Occurrents that have passed within Scotland, 1513-1575," published by the Bannatyne Club in 1833, it is recorded that " Vpoun the twantie nyne [nynetene ?] day of Apryle 1567, our souerane ladie com with the nobilitie to the parliament, and come to the tolbuith ; . . . . and certane Actis wes maid thairefter. . . . . The third was twitching certane tickettis and wreittingis, put vp efter the slauchter of the King, defaming diuerse personis without assurance thairof, that nane suld set thame vp, write nor dyte thame, or gif thaj saw thame, thaj suld distroy thame, and na copyse to be tane thairof ; with certificatioun gif thaj be fund in doand the samin, thaj suld be pvneist as principall doaris thairof." . . .

In " The Autobiography and Diary of Mr. James Melvill, Minister of Kilrenny, in Fife, 1556-1610," (Wodrow Society Edition, 1842), it is recorded that while he was at Montrose in the year 1570, " Ther was also ther a post, (a carrier or messenger, John Finheavin), that frequented Edinbruche, and brought ham Psalme Buikes and Ballates ; namlie, of Robert Semple's making, wherin I tuik pleasour, and lernit sum thing bathe of the esteat of the countrey, and of the missours and cullors of Scottes ryme."

David Calderwood, in his " History of the Kirk of Scotland," records under date 1582, that " Robert Sempill was takin out of his bed tymouslie in the morning, upon Tuisday, the 5th of June, by William Stewart, Arran's Brother, and was sent to Kinneill the nixt morning, because it was alledged he had receaved letters frome the Earle of Angus," And again, under date 1584, remarks that Bishop Adamsone's " Behaviour in his journey to, at, and from Londoun, is sett doun in a certan poem made by Robert Sempell, a Scotish Poet, intituled, " The Legend of the Lymmar's Life." The summe is, he pretended he was to goe to the well of Spaw ; but his intent was no farther than England. As he went by Yorke, he caused Johne Harper, a Scotish tailyeour, tak off frome the

merchants a doublet and breaches of Turkie taffatie ; promised
payment when he returned back, alledging that the Scotish
merchants at Londoun would give him as muche money as he
desired. But he returned another way, and so the tailyeour
was disappointed of his seven pund sterline. After he gott
presence, he stayed two months, but gott never presence
again. He frequented the French ambassader's hous, where
he gott his fill of good white wine. He would have borrowed
frome the Frenche ambassader an hundreth pund ; but the ambassader was advertised by one of his servants, that he had
borrowed frome his mother in Parise fyfteene crownes, and
frome other neighbours lesse or more, but never payed a groat
again. Yitt the ambassader gave him ten punds sterline
knitt in a napkin nuike, saying he might spaire no more for
the present. He borrowed likewise from Scotish merchants
at Londoun, and cousened them, speciallie Gilbert Donaldsone
and Patrik White. He alledged that he had sent some
letters of great importance with Patrik White. The said
Patrik tooke oathe he saw no suche thing ; yitt he was forced to
leave the land, and so was he paid for his 300 merk   Another
merchant gave him ten pund sterline, to purchase him licence
to transport fortie last of English beare. He went to Secretar
Walsinghame, and purchased a licence, alledging it was to
serve his owne hous at home ; but he gave the licence to
another man, frome whom he tooke twentie pund sterline. He
borrowed frome the Bishop of Londoun a gowne to teache in.
The bishop lent him a gown of grograne silk, weill lynned with
costlie furrings ; but [Adamsone] restored it not againe. He
begged hackneyes, bookes, &c., from bishops, and payed them
after the same maner. When he was to gett presence of the
queene, this famous ambassader pissed at the palace wall. The

porter was so offended at his incivilitie, that he beate him with a battoun."*

According to Dempster, Robert Sempill died in 1595.

In an "Essay on the Poets of Renfrewshire," by WILLIAM MOTHERWELL, prefixed to "The Harp of Renfrewshire," published in 1819,† we are informed that "The Poets of Renfrewshire have neither been few in respect of numbers, nor contemptible in regard to merit. Although none of them have ever risen far above mediocrity, yet their performances have been such as to entitle their names to an honourable place amongst the minor bards of Scotland, and to preserve them from the death of total oblivion. As yet nothing like a compendious account, not even so much as a catalogue of these *makers* has been given, albeit the same is much wanted to fill up some little chasms in the history as well of our ancient, as our modern, stock of national biography and literature. . . . With regard to the *older Poets* of this county, little can be said, for the best of all possible reasons, because little is known. Those of what may be called the *middle period*, are scarcely known at all, except by name and the inimitable pieces they have bequeathed to a forgetful and ungrateful posterity. Of the *late Poets* this Shire has produced enough in all conscience has been written; but whether much to the purpose or not, is a question easier propounded perhaps than conveniently answered. . . . . Contemporaneous with Montgomerie (*Author*

* Calderwood's History (Wodrow Society Edition), Vol. IV. p. 61. Edinburgh, 1843.

† "The Harp of Renfrewshire: a Collection of Songs and other Poetical Pieces, (many of which are original), accompanied with Notes, Explanatory, Critical, and Biographical, and a Short Essay on the Poets of Renfrewshire. [Edited by William Motherwell.] 18mo, Paisley 1819. *Reprinted*, small 8vo, Paisley, 1872."

of the Cherrie and the Slae) was his friend ROBERT SEMPILL a more voluminous, but by no means so good or so popular a poet. It has been said elsewhere, that this Robert Sempill was a titled personage; but it is right to mention in this place, that Dr. Irving is decidedly hostile to such an opinion, and treats the whole matter as a mere figment of an idle imagination. 'One of the most persevering and unsuccessful versifiers of this period,' says he, 'was Robert Sempill, whom a late writer (Sibbald), who amuses himself with perpetual conjectures, ridiculously supposes to have been a Scottish Peer.— The eulogium which Dempster has bestowed on Sempill's genius, is highly extravagant, and must have been conceived without any previous acquaintance with his writings; he represents him as exhibiting the combined excellencies of Propertius, Tibullus, Ovid, and Callimachus. Some pieces of this poetaster are to be found in the *Evergreen;* and Mr. Dalyell has lately republished others from the original editions. They are equally indecent and unpoetical.' With every mark of deference to the opinions of a writer who seldom dogmatises rashly, and who has by his labours done so much for the memories of Scotland's poets, we at the same time are compelled to dissent as widely from him on this point, as he seems to do from Sibbald and Dempster.

"It is to be observed, that albeit the Doctor contradicts Sibbald, he does not disprove his position, nor even attempt to shake it by any investigation whatever which might throw more light on the subject matter of dispute. Mere assertions are to be received with extreme caution, when unaccompanied with their proofs. As for our simple selves, we see nothing ridiculous at all in Sibbald's supposition; but on the contrary every reason to make us believe it perfectly correct. According to Douglas's Peerage and Crawfurd's History of Renfrewshire, Robert, the fourth Lord Sempill, succeeded to his grandfather in 1571, and died at an advanced age in 1611. Sempill the poet wrote all his works between the years 1565 and 1573 : for in Birrell's diary occurs the following notice : ' 1568 Jan. 17. A play was made by Robert Sempill, and performed before the Lord Regent and divers others of the nobility ;' which play Sibbald imagines in all likelihood to be Philotus ; and in Ames' Typography of Great Britain, it appears that ' The Sege of the Castel of Edenburgh,' was ' imprintit be Robert Lepreuick, anno 1573.' By Dempster, the death of Sempill is fixed in 1595, but this discrepancy is over-ruled by the fact that this author was at a distance from his native country when he wrote, and could not therefore be very conversant with, or correct in obituaries, and must of necessity have trusted greatly to vague and uncertain rumours regarding these particulars in the biographies of the celebrated men of his age. Here then we have two individuals bearing the same name, and living at the same period. That these two are one person, we have little hesitation to affirm ; and with the simple affirmation of this fact we might rest satisfied inasmuch as the Doctor is concerned, because one opinion is quite as good as another, when both happen to be unsupported by any evidence in their favour, and none of them are unplausible in themselves. It is admitted at once, that there is no direct mention made in any writer of Sempill the poet being Lord Sempill, or that that nobleman was the same person with the said poet : and the reason of this is obvious, because none of Sempill's contemporaries were his biographers, and the incidental notices, gleaned from various quarters respecting him, relate to his literary character, not to his lineage and family connections. Moreover, it never hath been the custom to give poets any titles, save those which serve to mark their peculiar excellencies : all other trappings are derogatory to the might and majesty of the simple sirnamo. No one, even in our own days, when speaking in general terms of Byron as a great poet, thinks of saddling his discourse with the epithet *Lord*.   The sirname is enough to let him who bears it be known without this puny prefixture of worldly rank. Now if it should so happen, that everything respecting the birth of this great man were lost, and all the Magazine histories of him and other trash burned to a scroll, and nothing save fragments of his poems were extant, and a few remarks of some critics contemporary with him upon his genius were all that reached to distant posterity, it is very likely that a long-headed wiseacre of that generation, would split his lordship into two halves—one whereof, to be Lord Byron, son of such a one—and the other, Byron a poet, of whose birth nothing was known.

" Such a one might write a very plausible sentence or two, after this fashion :—' One of the most celebrated poets of his day, was Byron.   His works would appear to have been numerous and excellent, but of them few remnants now survive, and such as I have seen, are so mutilated and imperfect, that it is impossible to say anything definitive upon their merits or defects.   It has been alleged by some, but without any foundation in truth, that Byron was of noble extraction ; and others have gone so far as to say, he really was titled, than which nothing can be more ridiculous.   True, there was a Lord Byron coeval with him, but I find no clue whatever in the history of these times that can lead me to suppose they were one and the same person.   Had they been so, such a circumstance would never have been overlooked by the historian,

I therefore hold those who cling to this opinion as fools.' And who would dare to beard or contradict so authoritative a wise one?

" What is now assumed with regard to Byron, has happened to Sempill, Surely there is nothing ridiculous in supposing, that a Nobleman might write poems as well as a Squire of low degree. And yet it is with the ridiculousness of this supposition Dr. Irving is at odds. He may know, or at least he ought to do, that with a very few exceptions, none save Noblemen, Courtiers, and Clerical dignitaries, were the poets, philosophers, historians, and literary factotums of that age. Education then was not, as is the case now, diffused through every rank and condition of society, but confined exclusively to the higher classes or professional orders. Without one having some real or pretended claim to genteel, if not noble birth, it is questioned if they then would even have been admitted to any terms of familiarity with the great, whatever their talents were or labours had been. Feudalism, to be sure, was in that age shaken to its base, but its ramparts were not cast to the ground; and where it appears in any formidable shape, a mortifying distance is always maintained between the magnates of the land and the other members of the body politic.

" Although the poetry of Sempill cannot be eulogised to the extent which Dempster has done, neither can it be so far depreciated as Irving has attempted to do. He wrote in the spirit of the times; and it is unfair to measure him by the standard of taste established now. We much suspect that the Dr. has but sparingly looked into them, and been in the main as much at fault while speaking of them, as he supposes Dempster to have been on a like occasion. This far we can safely say, namely, that they will bear comparison with similar productions of the same period, and not be greatly the loser by the experiment.

" The poetic vein that began in Lord Sempill, was continued in the person of his cousin-german, Sir James Sempill of Belltrees, author of the '*Packman's Pater Noster*' and by him transmitted to Robert Sempill, the author of the celebrated '*Epitaph on Habbie Simson*,' Piper of Kilbarchan, until it terminated in the person of Francis Sempill, his son, author of these popular songs: '*Scho rase and loot me in*'—'*Maggy Lauder*,'—'*The blythsum Bridal*,' &c., &c., and of a poem, entitled '*The Banishment of Poverty*,' &c.

" Anything more than this catalogue of names our limits forbid us to give. It is to be regretted, that the manuscripts of Francis Sempill are irretrievably lost. They fell into hands which knew not their value, and it is to be feared out of them they will never be recovered. Respecting the Sempills, considerable information will be found in two small periodical publications, entitled *The Paisley Repository and Annual Recreations*, printed in 1812. 'Bating some inaccuracies in the matter, and sundry inelegancies of style, the information contained in them will be useful to those desirous of knowing more about this distinguished family, more especially in regard to Francis Sempill, of whom several anecdotes were related, and who appears to have been rather of a *harum scarum* disposition."

Notwithstanding Mr. Motherwell's very specious arguments, the great question still remains to be solved—Who was Robert Sempill, the Scotish Poet of 1567-1595?

It has not been considered requisite to prefix to this Collection any Disquisition as to the times and state of the parties,— Kingsmen and Queensmen,—during the period embraced by

these " Ballates."   Neither could it be expected that Biographical notices should be given of the Lives and Characters
of Mary Queen of Scots, King Henry Darnley, the Regent
Murray, Lord Methven, Sir William Kirkcaldy of Grange, or
of the Archbishop of St. Andrews.   All such are already well
known to the most cursory reader of Scotish History.   Mary
Queen of Scots was married to Prince Henry, Duke of Albany,
Lord Darnley, on Monday, the 29th of July 1565, in the
Chapel of Holyrood.   Henry Lord Darnley was murdered
on Monday, the 8th of February 1566, at the Kirk of Field.
James Stewart, (natural son of King James V. by Margaret,
daughter of John, Fifth Earl of Mar,) Earl of Murray or Moray,
" the Good Regent," was assassinated by James Hamilton of
Bothwellhaugh on the 23rd of January 1569-70, at Linlithgow,
in the thirty-seventh year of his age.   " His funeral, which
was a solemn spectacle, took place on the 14th of February,
in the High Church of St. Giles, at Edinburgh, where he was
buried in St. Anthony's aisle, ' his head placed south, contrair to ordour usit ; the sepulchre laid with hewin wark
maist curiously, and on the head ane plate of brass.'   The
body had been taken from Linlithgow to Stirling, and thence
was transported by water to Leith, and carried to the palace of
Holyrood.   In the public procession to the church it was accompanied by the magistrates and citizens of Edinburgh, who
greatly lamented him.   They were followed by the gentlemen
of the country, and these by the nobility.   The Earls of
Morton, Mar, Glencairn, and Cassillis, with the Lords Glam-
mis, Lindsay, Ochiltree, and Ruthven carried the body ; before it came the Lairds of Grange, and Colvil of Cleish ;
Grange bearing his Banner, with the Royal Arms, and Cleish his
coat armour.   Both of them on horseback.   The servants of

his household followed, making great lamentation.   On enter-
ing the church the bier was placed before the pulpit, and John
Knox preached the funeral sermon over the remains of his friend,
taking for his text, ‘ Blessed are the dead that die in the Lord,’
which drew tears from the eyes of all present.” *   Henry
Stewart, Second Lord Methven, was killed at Brochtoun
(Broughton) by a shot from the Castle of Edinburgh on the
3rd of March 1571-2.   John Erskine, Earl of Mar, was
chosen Regent of Scotland on the 6th of September 1571, and
died at Stirling on the 28th of October 1572.   Sir William
Kirkcaldy of Grange surrendered the Castle of Edinburgh to
the English on the 29th of May 1573.   On the 3d of
August following he was tried, and almost immediately after
sentence, brought from Holyrood drawn in a cart back-
ward as a spectacle to the people, and executed in the presence
of an immense concourse of spectators at the market cross of
Edinburgh.   His body was quartered, and his head placed
over the Castle gate.   Patrick Cousteane, Coustane, Constance,
or Constantine, afterwards Adamsone, Archbishop of St.
Andrews, died on Saturday the 19th of February, 1592.

   Robert Lekprevick, the Printer of the “ Ballates” appears to
have been in business at the Nether Bow, Edinburgh, during the
years 1561 to 1570 ; in Stirling and St. Andrews from 1571 to
1573, and again in Edinburgh from 1573 to 1581.   In 1574,
he “ was summoned to underly the law for printing in the
moneth of Januar last bypast, in the yeere of God, 1573 yeeres
thereby, a little Booke, called, a ‘ Dialogue or mutual talking
betwixt a Clerk and a Courteour,’ compiled, made, and set furth
by Mr. Johne Davidsone, regent for the time within Sanct

* “ Diurnal of Occurrents in Scotland, 1513-1575,” and “ Tytler’s History
of Scotland, &c., 1828-1843,” *passim.*

Leonard's Colledge, in Sanct Andrewes,' * to the reproache
and slaunder of our Soverane Lords Regent and Secreit
Counsell. . . . . He compeered, was convict by an assise, and
thereafter, committed to waird in the Castell of Edinburgh."
Interesting notices of various works issued from his press are
given in " Ames's Typographical Antiquities, by Herbert,
1785-90."

At the sale of the very fine Library of DAVID CONSTABLE,
ESQ., Advocate, Edinburgh, on the 12th December 1828, there
was knocked down,—as the phrase is,—for the sum of £2, 12s.,
a LARGE PAPER COPY of the volume entitled, " Scotish Poems
of the Sixteenth Century, (*with the Cancels*), 1801," having
bound in at the beginning of it a Letter to MR. ARCHIBALD
CONSTABLE, the Publisher, from the celebrated Critic and An-
tiquary, MR. JOSEPH RITSON. This very fine—nay, *unique*—
copy is now in the possession of JOHN WHITEFOORD MACKENZIE,
ESQ., Edinburgh. We subjoin the following extract from MR.
RITSON's letter, as affording a notable instance of how a
writer may speak out when he is in earnest, and as showing
that the bile, engendered in the heat and bitterness of contro-
versy, is not at all allayed by " abstinence from animal food."†

" Gray's Inn,   1801.

" I am sorry to say that i have looked over (for it is impossible that any one should read) your publication of ' Scotish
poems of the sixteenth century,' with astonishment and disgust.

* The Poetical Remains of the Rev. John Davidson, 1573-1595, were for the
first time collected, and Forty Copies printed, with a Biographical Account
of the Author, by James Maidment, Edinburgh, [John Stevenson], 1829.

† Poor Joseph very shortly afterwards met with more than his match in
this way. It is pretty generally known that he wrote and published a volume
recommending " abstinence from animal food," and the merciless castigation
which he in consequence received from the pen of Mr. Brougham, in the
second volume of the *Edinburgh Review*, was said to have hastened his death.

b

To rake up the false, scandalous, and despicable libels, against the most beautyful, amiable, and accomplished Princess that ever existed ; whose injurious treatment, misfortunes, persecution, imprisonment, and barbarous murder, wil be a lasting blot in the national character to the end of time, and which were, as they deserved, apparently devoted to everlasting oblivion and contempt, to stuf almost an entire volume with the uninteresting lives of such scoundrels as regent Murray and the laird of Grange, to publish, in short such vile, stupid, and infamous stuf, which few can read, and none can approve, is a lamentable proof of a total want of taste or judgement, a disgrace to Scotish literature, degrades the reputation of the editor, and discredits your own. I must be free to tel you, that i wil not suffer such an infamous and detestable heap of trash to pollute and infect my shelves : it is therefor under sentence of immediate transportation, though much more fit for some other situation than a gentleman's library, or even a bookseler's shop.   I confess, at the same time, that the libel against the Tulchan bishop, though excessively scurrilous, has much merit, and would have been admissible in any collection of a different description."

In the sale of the Library of R. H. Bright, Esq., London, 1845, Lot 296, "Ballads," which sold for £525, contained *nine* of " Sempill's Ballates," ranging from 1567 to 1570.

As SUPPLEMENTAL to the " Sempill Ballates" I have given in an Appendix a few others which are believed to have been the production of one of the " Sempills of Beltrees."   These were unknown to me when I published their Poems in 1849.   I have also inserted a Poem by ALLAN RAMSAY, which he intended to have prefixed to " The Ever Green, being a Collection of Scots Poems, wrote by the Ingenious before 1600," published in 1724, as being worthy of preservation, not so much in regard to any merit the lines possess, but as expressing his sentiments respecting the merits of some of our "early makers," he having been the first to recommend them to public notice. It has not been included in any edition of his works.

I hope the reader, when he dips into these "Ballates," will not be displeased with this reflection, "That he is stepping back into the times that are past and that exist no more." I do not expect that they will please everybody ; nay, the critical reader must needs find several faults, for I confess that there will be found among them two or three pieces whose antiquity is their greatest value ; still I am persuaded there are many others that merit more of approbation than of censure and blame.

I cannot conclude without expressing in an especial manner my very grateful thanks to J. W. K. EYTON, ESQ., F.S.A., Elsham Road, Kensington, London, for his exceeding kindness and liberality in furthering this publication, and for his cordial co-operation in procuring for me copies of many of the " Ballates." I also gratefully acknowledge the kind assistance rendered by DAVID LAING, ESQ., LL.D., Edinburgh, whose knowledge of Scotish antiquities is only equalled by the liberal zeal with which he communicates the results of much reading and research. His description of the various "Ballates," and his information as to where copies of them were to be found, were truly of great importance, and saved much time and expense. To my esteemed friend, DR. WILLIAM STEVENSON, Professor of Divinity and Ecclesiastical History, Edinburgh University, my thanks are equally due for his kind advice and suggestions during the progress of the " Ballates" through the press ; and to MR. ALEXANDER GIBB, for his careful compilation of the Glossary.

To the Council of the Society of Antiquaries of London, I beg sincerely to tender my grateful thanks for the very kind and handsome manner in which they afforded me free access to their valuable collections, by which means I have been enabled, with the assistance of MR. GEORGE GATFIELD, MS. Department, British Museum, London, to revise and compare the proof sheets with the Original Black-Letter Broadsides, &c., in the possession of the Society, the State Paper Office, and that of the British Museum. To other friends and supporters who very readily assisted me in my editorial labours, I have to tender the assurance of my grateful remembrance.

It is here proper to mention, that having considered that the printing of the present Collection of Ballates would be attended with considerable risk, emolument is not to be expected ; but I undoubtedly do not wish to make any pecuniary sacrifice. In limiting the number of copies, the object has been to secure for such persons as may be induced to become purchasers, the certainty of not seeing the work exposed at book-sales, or included in a list of " Really Cheap Books" at a third of its original cost. It is not besides likely that any work, the publication of which is simply to preserve literary or poetical remains of an antiquarian character, would become popular, or that its circulation would be extended beyond those individuals who have a taste for such matters. To multiply copies, therefore, would produce no beneficial result. These are the reasons which have induced me to limit the IMPRESSION of this rather singular Collection strictly to THREE HUNDRED COPIES.—Two Hundred and Sixty on Small Paper, crown octavo, and Forty on fine Large Paper, demy octavo.

𝔗. 𝔊. 𝔖.

EDINBURGH, *July* 1872.

In Memoriam.

I HAVE now the painful duty of recording, that since the preceding pages were printed, and which had been approved of by my esteemed and very kind friend, J. W. K. EYTON, ESQ., he has gone to his rest, having died on Thursday, the 1st of August 1872, at his residence, 27 Elsham Road, Kensington, London, in the fifty-third year of his age, in the full enjoyment of the profound respect and admiration of his friends, and the affectionate love of his family.

The following admirable tributes to his memory,— by his old friends, Mr. TIMMS and Mr. W. J. THOMS,— I have deemed well worthy of being reprinted and recorded here :—

I. *Extracted from the* "BIRMINGHAM DAILY POST," *5th August, 1872.*

"THE LATE MR. J. W. K. EYTON.—Not only our Shropshire readers, but many of our older local readers too, will

learn with deep regret that Mr. Joseph Walter King Eyton,
F.S.A., died at his residence, Elsham Road, Kensington, on
Thursday, August 1st, in the 53d year of his age. Mr. Eyton
was a son of the late Rev. John Eyton, rector of Wellington
(Salop), and was not only a member of the most ancient of the
county families of Shropshire, and a worthy descendant of an
honourable line resident in Shropshire from Norman days, but
he had general as well as personal claims to the honour in
which he was held by all who knew him. Although neither
an author nor a public man, he exercised no small influence in
many of the best works of his day. In the compilation of
that unrivalled county history, entitled the ' History of Shropshire,' by his brother (the Rev. R. W. Eyton, M.A.), the late
Mr. Eyton greatly assisted by his knowledge, and industry,
and taste. In the book-world his name will ever be famous
as the collector of the choicest and most perfect library ever
formed by a private purchaser—every book being the best or
rarest—procured with generous liberality, and chosen with
consummate taste. The 'Eyton sale,' in fact, marks an era
in bibliography, as the Roxburgh and Heber and Daniel sales
have done, and the best books of all classes derive a special
value from having passed through Mr. Eyton's hands. So
large was his knowledge, and so perfect his taste in all matters
of printing, paper, and bookbinding—of each of which he had
the choicest and costliest examples—that he was chosen as
one of the Council of the Society of Antiquaries, and as one
of the Council of the Camden Society, and was ever one of the
most generous patrons of the Archæological Societies and
Printing Clubs during the last thirty years. His munificence
in presenting books to the Library of the Society of Antiquaries, his taste and judgment in reprinting at his own cost,
choice and curious works, his generous patronage of the best
printers and bookbinders who really understood their ' art,'
made him ever popular among some of the most famous bibliographers and the most eminent *literati* of our day. His
assistance was sought wherever real knowledge about books or
printing or paper or binding was needed, and was always
willingly at the service of strangers as well as friends. For
some years Mr. Eyton lived in Birmingham and Leamington,
where, although his manners were so modest, he made himself

numerous friends. For Birmingham itself he ever had a special fondness, and our Reference Library and our Shakespeare Library owe no small portion of their treasures to his knowledge and generosity and care. As a private friend Mr. Eyton was beyond all praise. His ample means were ever at the service of literature and art. He had no purpose in life except the gratification of his friends. His one thought every morning must have been whom to please and how to oblige. In all parts of England he had correspondents, many of whom he had never even seen, but to whom he constantly sent whatever was likely to minister to their pleasures or to gratify their tastes. His matured judgment, his long experience, his knowledge of literature, his friendships with famous men, were always at the command of his correspondents, and he would gladly search all over London to find a book which any friend might want. His generous and noble nature, his courteous and kindly manners, his unbounded yet modest munificence, his untiring devotion to the tastes and pleasures of his friends, his large store of literary knowledge, his intercourse with many famous men, made him always welcome wherever he appeared; but those only who knew him most intimately can fully appreciate his manly modest virtues, or deplore too deeply the irreparable loss which his death has caused in a large circle of grateful friends."

II. *Extracted from* "Notes and Queries," *10th August, 1872.*

" Death of J. Walter K. Eyton, Esq., F.S.A.—Those who shared with us the advantage of knowing Mr. Eyton, will share the deep regret with which we record his death. Mr. Eyton must have been known to all lovers of fine books by the remarkable library which he amassed, the dispersion of which some years ago by Messrs Sotheby created quite a sensation among bibliographers. But great as was Mr. Eyton's knowledge of everything connected with bibliography, printing, binding, &c., he was more remarkable for his kindness and liberality,—

for his readiness, we should rather say his anxiety, to help his literary friends, and his liberal gifts to the Society of Antiquaries and other kindred Societies; and he has left a name which will be treasured with affectionate respect by all who knew him."

The Sale of MR. EYTON's Library, above-mentioned, commenced on the 15th May 1848, in London, and continued for eight days. The total produce was the sum of £2,693, 15s. 6d.

T. G. S.

22 FREDERICK STREET,
EDINBURGH, *16th August 1872.*

Table of Contents.

c

Appendix.

The Sempill Ballates.

1567=1583.

I.—Heir followis ane Ballat declaring the Nobill and Gude inclinatioun of our King.

[A Broadside, printed very closely in three columns, Black
Letter.—STATE PAPER OFFICE.   Scotish Series, Volume
13, (*May*) Number 47.]

TO Edinburgh about vj. houris at morne,
   As I was passand pansand out the way
Ane bony boy was soir makand his mone,
   His sory sang was oche and wallaway,
That euer I sould byde to se that day,
   Ane King at euin with Sceptur Sword and Crown
At morne but ane deformit lumpe of clay,
   With tratouris strang sa cruellie put downe.
Than drew I neir sum tythingis for to speir,
   And said my freind quhat makis the sa way :
Bludie bothwell hes brocht our King to beir,
   And flatter and fraude with dowbill Dalyday.
I studeit still and nathing could I say,
   My minde was full of admiratioun,

1

My bony boy tell me without delay,
    The Kingis maneris forme and fassioun.
¶ Narratioun shir gif I do tell,
    His cruell murther ze will call monsterous :
For in meiknes he did all men excell,
    And vnto na man was he odious,
To meit his marrow he was audatious,
    On sturdie steid with craftie feat of weir,
Mars favourit him as fair Ascanius,
    Æneas Sone that weill ane steid could steir.
☞ In deidis he soulde haue bene lyke Deiphœbus
    Had feinzeit Fortoun fauourit him to Ring :
Or Theseus or gentill Julius,
    In gentill featis ferand for ane King.
Dartis about him swyftlie could he fling,
    And rin ane rais and shortlie turne ane steid :
Cunning of crosbow cutthrot and culuering,
    Ane flaine lat fle with bow in tyme of neid.
☞ In gamis glaid he was rycht weill asswetit,
    Rycht featlie on the fluire alswa could dance
Bot Dalila vnto him was vanlatit,
    Quhilk causit him oft to be sad and pance.
Zit neuer did sho se his maik in France,
    Off royall bluid to fang to be hir feir :
Not her fyrst spous for all his great puissance,
    In portratour and game mycht be his peir.
¶ Cunning of Clergy of musick meruelous,
    The louing leid of Latine could declair :
Sangis set with diuers tunis expres,
    With Instrument maist sweit into the eir.
With hundis hunt he could baith Da and Deir
    The faid also rycht feitlie could he set,
Ane gay gois Halk vpone his hand to beir,
    Ane Falcowne fle to se he thocht delyte.
☞ With Romaine hand he could weill leid ane pen,
    And storyis wryte of auld antiquitie,
Nobill himself, and Nobill of Ingyne,
    And louit weill concord and vnitie,

He swoumit in the fluidis of Poetrie,
    And did exerse the science liberall :
The facund Phrase did vse of oratrie,
    His gude Ingyne was rycht celestiall.
☞ In pulchritude to Paris perigall
    With browis brent and twinkland Cristell eine :
Off face formois and vult heroycall,
    He mycht haue bene ane marrow to ane Quene,
At ten houris on Sonday lait at euin,
    Quhen Dalila and Bothwell bad gudnycht :
Off hir finger fals sho threw ane Ring,
    And said my Lord ane taikin I zow plycht.
¶ Scho did depairt than with ane vntrew traine,
    And than in haist ane culuering they leit crak :
To teiche thair feiris to knaw the appoint tyme,
    About the Kingis lugeing for to clap.
To dance that nycht they said sho sould not slak,
    With leggis lycht to hald the wedow walkane
And baid fra bed vntill sho hard the crak,
    Quhilk was ane signe that hir gude Lord was slane.
☞ And Maddie meinis sho did in Setoun sing
    Full weill was her that day that sho was fre :
And into joy and out of tray and tene,
    So frely fred from all aduersitie.
O Stewartis stout ha benedicitie.
    War ze not Royis in this Regioun
And ay did vse Justice and equitie,
    And now zour glas of honestie is run.
☞ Unles ze now sharplie shuit out zour handis
    And trewlie try the gyltie of this blude :
Ze wilbe repuite Lowreis ouer all landis,
    And fais to Christ deit on the Rude.
My Lordis thairfoir I think for zow gude,
    The tresoun try and puneis equallie :
Lat not your landis defylit be with blude,
    And gif ze do God shaw his Maiestie.
¶ Quhen Davie deit our Quene rycht potentlie
    Into this Realme did rais ane ryall rout :

Out of this Regioun Lordis gart sho flie,
    Tresoun to try sho was that tyme maist stout,
But sho is slak to try this tresoun out,
    And to him Dauy was na perigall :
Dauy and his, thair state was wont shone clout,
    Our cumly King was of the blude royall.

For dowbill Dauy sho did zow expell,
    Think on thairfoir quhill ze haue sic ane cryme,
And ze defend the cruell Jesabell
    Than Baallis Priestis will cal zow verray kynde
Now euerie Dowglas of ane hartsum mynde,
    Thinke on dame Margaret sumtyme in the towre,
And of young Charles prudent of Ingyne.
    I pray God lat them se ane ioyfull houre.

¶ O ze that dois profes Godis worde deuyne,
    Se that ze sclander not his haly Name :
Remember Jesus Judas put to pyne,
    For slak regaird of Godlynes and blame.
God he is all that layis ane stumling stane,
    Quhilk may the cause be of our britheringis fall,
Restoir againe zour foule polluted fame
    Gif ze fauoure Christ Jesus trew Gospell.

The buik of Josua as I did reid,
    And thairin ane exampill did I find
How Acan tuik the excommunicat guid
    All Israell war threitnit for that sin.
The fauour of God be na way could he win,
    Quhill trewlie tryit war faultouris of the faill :
Quhome Josua in flambis fell did burne
    And then did ceis God's wrath celestiall.

Gif God was wrath at ane small pegrall stouth.
    And for ainis fault ane multitude did shoir,
Gif diligence to mak the giltie couth,
    Or he will do to zow as he befoir.
Ze knaw zour cryme is wors ane greit daill moir,
    Nor hunders twa of sicklis silver fyne,
To pull ane King fra his hie potent gloir
    Quhome God did place be ordinance dewyne.

☞ O ze that to our Kirk hes done subscriue
    Thir Ecanis try alsweill traist I may
Gif ze do not the tyme will cum belive
    That God to zow will rais sum Josuay,
Quhilk sall zour bairnies gar sing wallaway,
    And ze your selfis be put downe with shame :
Remember on the ugsum latter day
    Quhen ze rewaird sall ressaif for zoure blame.

☞ I ken rycht weill ze knaw zour dewtie,
    Gif ze do not purge zow ane and all,
Than sall I wryte in prettie poetrie
    In Latine leid in style Rethoricall.
Quhilk throw all Europe sall ring lyke ane bell,
    In the contempt of zour malignitie,
Fy fle fra Clitemnestra fell
    For sho was neuer lyke Penolopie.

☞ With Clitemnestra I do not fane to fletche,
    Quhilk slew hir spous the greit Agamemnon :
Or with ony that Mynos wyfe dois matche,
    Semiramus quha brocht hir gude Lord downe.
Quha dow abstene fra litigatioun,
    Or from his paper hald aback the pen :
Except he hait our Scottis Natioun,
    Or than stand vp and traitouris deidis commend.

¶ Now all the wois that Ouid in Ibin
    Into his pretty lytill buik did wryte,
And mony mo be to our Scottis Quene,
    For sho the cause is of my wofull dyte.
Sa mot hir hart be fillit full of syte,
    As Herois was for Leanderis deth :
Hirself to slay for wo quha thocht delyte,
    For Henryis saik to lyke, our Quene war laith.

¶ The doloure als that peirsit Diddis hart,
    Quhen King Enee from Carthage tuik the flycht.
For the Quhilk cause vnto ane brand sho start
    And slew hirself quhilk was ane sory sycht.
Sa mot sho die as did Creusa brycht,
    The worthie wyfe of dowchtie Duik Jason :

Quha brint was in ane garment wrocht be flycht
    Off Medea throw incantation.
☞ Hir lauchter lycht be lyke to trim Thysbie,
    Quhen Pyramus sha fand deid at the well :
In langour lyke vnto Penolopie,
    For vlyssis quho lang at Troy did dwell :
Hir duilsum deith be wars than Jesabell,
    Quhome throw ane windo suirlie men did thraw.
Quhais blude did laip the cruell hundis fell,
    And doggis could hir wickit bainis gnaw.
¶ War I ane hund, o gif sho war ane hair,
    And I ane cat and sho ane lyttill mous
And sho ane bairne and I ane wylde wod bair,
    I ane firrat and sho Cuniculous.
To hir I sal be ay contrarius,
    Quhill to me Atropus cut the fatell threid :
And feill deithis dartis dolorus,
    Than sall our Spiritis be at mortall feid.
☞ My Spirit hir Spirit sal douke in Phlegethon
    Into that painfull fylthie flude of hell :
And thame in Styx and Lethee baith anone,
    And Cerberus that cruell hund sa fell.
Sall gar hir cry with mony zout and zell,
    O. wallaway that euer sho was borne
Or with tresoun be ony maner mell,
    Quhilk from all blis sould cause hir be forlorne.
¶ War John Bochas on lyue as he is deid,
    Worthy workis wold wryte in hir contempt :
Alsweill of tresoun as of womanheid,
    Thairto his pen wald euer mair be bent.
Hir for till shame and bludie Bothwell shent,
    And wold the counsall craif his warysoun,
The quhilk King James the fyrst in Parliament,
    Gaif to his Father for ane hie tresoun,
☞ Quha did forfault him of his land and rent,
    And his leuing annext to the Crown :
And to hir shame, and to hir greit contempt,
    Quhen that he come vnto ane strange natioun.

Than sould he mak declaratioun,
    The causis all of his sory banishment,
To be for trasoun done vnto the Crowne,
    Gif I do lie reid the Act of Parliament.
¶ My bony boy thy murning dois me harme,
    Bot thy sweit figureit speiche dois me delyte
In poetrie I traist zow be na barne,
    Quhilk dois reheirs the Poetis auld indyte.
At thir traytouris I find thow hes dispyte,
    And I ane Menstrell is and can sing :
Wald thow in Poetrie thy mater wryte
    In thair dispyte thy scellat sall I ring.
☞ Albeit my hart be fillit full of syte,
    And mony troublis tumbland in my mynde,
Zit vnder neth this hauthorne sal I wryte
    Or my forwereit body preis to dyne
In Poetrie narratioun of the cryme,
    Quhilk thow may sing except that thow be red,
In Inglis toung quhan will gif place and tyme,
    And than in Latine leid I think to spred,
¶ My veirsis prompt in style Rethoricall,
    Quhilk pass sall to the Tane of Tartarie
And Peirs sall erthe and air Etheriall,
    The wickit works done in Britannie.
My bony boy quod I fair mot the fa
    With that he rais and reikit me this bill :
And tuik gude nycht and shuik our handis twa,
    Sa we departit soir against my will

¶ Finis.

◉ Imprentit at Edinburgh be Robert Lekprevik.

8 THE SEMPILL BALLATES.

II.—Heir followis the Testament and Tragedie of vmquhile King Henrie Stewart of gude memorie.

[British Museum.—Cottonian MSS. Caligula, C. 1. f. 17.
—Scotish Poems of the Sixteenth Century, collected by
John Graham Dalyell, Edinburgh 1801.]

Henry Stewart, vmquhile of Scotland King,
Sumtyme in houpe, with reuerence to Ring:
Within this Realme in dew obedience,
Traisting with ane attoure all eirdlie thing
Quha was the ruite quhair of I did spring,
In honour to liue, be kindelie allyance:
Putand in hir sic faith and confidence,
Ingland I left, seducit be ignorance;
Scotland I socht, in houpe for to get hir,
Quhilk I may rew, as now is cum the chance,
And vthers learne be me experience:
In tyme be war, fra ainis the work missit her.

Sumtyme sho thocht, I was sa amiabill,
Sa perfyte, plesand, and sa dilectabill:
Lancit with luif, sho luid me by all wycht,
Sum tyme to shaw effectioun fauorabill,
Gratifeit me with giftis honorabill,
Maid me ze knaw, baith Lord, Duik, Erle and Knycht:
Sum tyme in mynde sho praisit me sa hycht,
Leifand all vther, hir bedfellow brycht
Chefit me to be, and maid me zour King:
Than was I thocht happy into menis sycht,
And puir anis did pryse thair maker of mycht
That send thame ane Stewart sa kindelie to Ring.

Thus quhen sho had auancit me in estate,
Hir for to pleis I set my haill consait:

Quhilk now is cause of my rakles ruyne,
-Hir *licherous* luife quhilk kindlit ouer hait,
Cauld hes it cuild, and sylit me with dissait
Plungeit my corps into this present pyne,
Not onelie zow Lordis causand me to tyne,
Bot als allace fra my trew God declyne,
Quhome I imbrasit, for plesoure of hir Mes
Justlie thairfoir, I haue deseruit this fyne,
Quha for hir saik denyit the God deuine
That did me bring fra plesoure to distres.

Backwart fra God my Spirite fra sho wylit
Daylie with darknes my sycht sho ouersylit,
My Princelie pretence began to decay,
Vaine houpe in hir my ressoun exilit,
My truethles toung my honoure defylit
My doing in deid sho gart me deny,
Fra credite I crakit, kyndnes brak ray,
No man waid trow the worde I did say,
My leigis me left, persauand hir Ire
Ingland I left, and help was away
God maid hir scurge to plaigue me for ay,
Be war the scurge he cast not in the fyre

Thus was I than to doloure destinat,
Miserabill man and Prince infortunat,
Quhomlit in sorow and plungeit in cair :
Sum tyme in mynde with anger agitat,
Sum tyme in Spirit pansiue and fatigat,
Musand the meine mycht meis hir euer mair,
Sum tyme with doloure drewin in dispair,
Wariand the warld, welth and weilfair,
Deid I desirid hir falset to fle,
Sum tyme in mynd thinkand the contrare,
Sum vncouthe vaiage I purpoisit prepare,
Bot not sa vncouth as was prepairit for me.

Into the tyme of this my extasie,

Quhen I was in this fearfull fantasie,
With *feinzeit* fair, and *wylie* wordis discreit,
Scho come to me with greit humilitie :
Lamentand sair my greit calamitie,
My langsum lyfe, and sair tormentit Spirite,
Promittand with ane faithfull hart contreit,
In tyme to cum, with reuerence me treit
To my degre, in honoure, luife and peace,
Traistand into hir *wylie* wordis sweit,
My hairt and lyfe into hir handis compleit,
I put, and past vnto the Sacrifice.

Quhat sall I wryte, how I was troublit thair,
I wat it wald mak ony haill hairt sair.
For to reuolue my tristsum tragidie,
How that thay boucheouris blew me in the air,
And stranglit me, I shame for to declair :
Nouther to God, nor honoure hauand Ee,
I houpit weill to haue na ennymie,
Into this Realme fra my natiuitie,
Thair was na man, quhome to I did offend,
Dissauit far I fand the contrarie,
Off Tygeris quholpis fosterit in tyrannie,
Ane treuthles troup hes drewin me to this end

O faithless flock, denuide of godlyness,
O Serpentis seid, nurisheit in wickitnes,
Fosteraris of falset, huirdome and harlatrie,
Mantenaris of murther, witchecraft expres,
Tresoun amang zow dois daylie incres :
Lawtie is banist, Justice and equitie.
Quhat sall I wryte of zoure wyle vanitie :
On falset is foundit zoure haill felicitie,
Zour Castellis nor townis, sall not zow defend,
God hes persauit zour infidelitie,
And schortlie will plaigue zour crewell tyrannie,
Off zour schort solace sorow salbe the end.

Quhat hairt so hard for petie will not bleid!
Quhat breist can beir bot man lament my deid!
Quhat toung sa thrall in silence suir can rest!
To se ane saule in sorow sowsit but feid,
Ane saikles Lambe, ane innocent but dreid,
Taine be consent of thame he luiffit best:
Furth of his bed with doloure to be drest,
By thrawart malice and murther manifest,
Jugeit by Law, and hangit syne but dome,
Sair it was to se zoure Prince with murther prest:
Sairar I say him in his place possest,
The deid that did, than Burrio, now Brydegrome.

O wickit *wemen* vennomus of natuire,
Serpentis of kynde, thocht cumlie seme zour statuire
Vnstabill ioy, full of aduersitie,
In mynde malicious attoure all creatuire,
Quhais malice taine, for euer dois induire:
Teichit be experience, sa may I testifie,
Zoure craftie consaitis cloikit with flatterie,
And mylde meiknes sylit with subtilitie
Ar Medeais helters to bring vs in zour net,
Gude deidis of auld gois furth of memorie,
The ruite of euill remaines but remedie,
Ay in zoure mynde sum vengance quhill ze get.

For Dawyis deid in *Maryis mynde* sa prentit
Consauit haitrent, daylie mair augmentit,
Meik war his wordis, thocht greit was his greuance
Oft at command, to mak hir weill contentit,
In pouertie and paine my self fra court absentit
Paine could not pleis hir, nor zit obedience,
Persaue of *lust* the malice and mischance,
Quhair *Venus* anis gettis in hir gouernance,
Sic sylit subiectis felterit in hir snair:
Wisdome is exilit, and prudent puruoyance,
Nobilnes and honour, defacit be ignorance,
And vertew banist, fra shame pas shed of hair.

This sentence trew we may persaue in deid,
In sindrie authouris quha lykis for to reid,
In luiffis raige, as storyis dois reheirs,
The crewell work of wretheit womanheid,
We may persaue in Scylla to succeid :
For Minos luife, hir Father gaif na grace,
Deianira hir husband Hercules,
For Nessus saik, maist crewellie allace
Brocht to mischeif, for all his vassalage,
And Clytemnestra for Egistus face,
Agamemnon the mychtie King of Greice,
Hir husband slew, so vyle was hir vsage.

Off Ancus Martius we reid the greit mischance
Quha rang in Rome in proude preheminance,
Slaine be Lucinio at Tanaquillis procuire,
Samson also for manheid and prudence,
All Israell that had in gouernance :
Dalila desauit in vnder couertoure :
Quhairfoir lat men be war and keip thame suire,
Fra wemenis vennome, vnder faithles figure,
And gif na wyfe thair counsall for to keip,
For as the woirme that workis vnder cuire
At lenth the tre consumis that is duire,
So wemen men, fra thay in credite creip.

I speik not but pruise, quhilk I may sairlie rew,
Quhat lyfe did thoill, my deid dois try it trew,
My fragill fortowne, sa faithles hes bene heir,
Wald God the day that I thee Scotland knew,
Atropus the threid had cut, lachesis drew,
So sould not felt the change of fortownes cheir,
My Kingdome cair, my wealth was ay in weir,
My state vnstabill, me drew fra Godis feir,
My plesosre prikis my paine ay to prouoke.
My solace sorow sobbing to asteir,
My ryches, powertie, power to empire,
My *wratchit wyfe* hes now put out the smoke.

Quhat warldlie joy in earth may lang induire,
Or quhat estate may heir him self assuire ?
For to conse rue his lyfe in sicernes,
Quha may sustene the perrillous auentuire ?
Off fals fortowne inconstant and vnsuire :
Or quhair sall men find steidfast stabilnes ?
All warldlie blis is mixt with bitternes,
Springand with ioy, endand with wretchitnes,
As heir my end reheirsit dois record,
Quhairfoir let Princes pryde thame not expres
In warldlie welth in pomp nor worthynes,
Bot stablishe thair strenth, with Dauid on the Lord.

In earth thairfoir sen nocht is parmanent,
My soule to God I leif omnipotent,
My Bab and Childe vnder the counsallis cuire,
To zow my Lordis of my deid Innocent,
For to reuenge I leif in Testament,
My saikles bluid, my murther and iniure,
Thocht Princes wald be falset zow alluire,
Hurt not zour honouris, the samin to smuire,
First luik to God, syne to zour libertie,
Think weill suppois my death ze wald induire,
Gif Rubbers Ring na subiect salbe suire
Mair nor the sheip in Foxes companie.

¶ Finis.

Imprentit at Edinburgh be Robert Lekpreuik.
Anno Do. 1567.

NOTE.—The words printed in *Italics* are crossed in the original.

III.—The Complaynt of Scotland.

[In Major Pearson's Collection.   Printed on one side, without
    date, place, or printer's name.   Black Letter.   Commu-
    nicated by Joseph Ritson to the Gentleman's Magazine,
    where it is reprinted, November 1791.—Scotish Ballads
    and Songs.   Edited by James Maidment, Edinburgh,
    1859.]

DEW all glaidnes, sport, and play,
        Adew fair weill, baith nycht and day—
        All thingz that may mak mirrie cheir,
        Bot sich rycht soir in hart and say,
            Allace to Graif is gone my deir.

¶ My lothsum lyfe I may lament,
With fixit face and mynde attent,
In weiping wo to perseueir,
And asking still for punischement,
    Of thame hes brocht to graif my deir.

¶ But lang allace I may complaine,
Befoir I find my deir againe,
To me was faithfull and Inteir,
As Turtill trew on me tuke paine :
    Allace to graif is gone my deir.

¶ Sen nathing may my murning mend,
On God maist hie I will depend
My cairfull cause for to vpreir :
For he support to me will send
    Althocht to graif is gone my deir.

¶ My hauie hap, and piteous plycht,
Dois peirs my hart baith day and nycht,
That lym nor lyth I may not steir,
Till sum reuenge with force and mycht
    The Cruell murther of my deir.

¶ This cureles wound dois grief me soir,
The lyke I neuer felt befoir
Sen Fergus first of me tuke steir,
For now allace decayis my gloir
    Throw cruell murther of my deir.

¶ O wickit wretche infortunat,
O Sauage seid Insatiat,
Mycht thow not frantik fule forbeir
To sla with dart Intoxicat,
    And cruellie deuoir my deir.

Wa worth the wretche, wa worth thy clan
Wa worth the wit that first began
This deir debait for to vpsteir,
Contrare the Lawis of God and man,
    To murther cruellie my deir.

¶ Throw the now Lawles libertie
Throw the mischeif and crueltie
Throw the fals men thair heidis vpbeir
Throw the is baneist equitie,
    Throw the to graif is gone my deir.

Throw the ma Kingz than ane dois ring
Throw the all tratourz blyithelie sing,
Throw the is kendlit ciuill weir,
Throw the murther wald beir the swing,
    Throw the to graif is gone my deir.

¶ Throw the is rasit sturtsum stryfe,
Throw the, the vitall breith of lyfe
Is him bereft, did with the beir :
Quhen Gallow pin, or cutting knyfe
    Suld stranglet the, and saift my deir.

¶ Ungraitfull grome, sic recompence,
Was not condigne to thyne offence,

With glowing gunne that man to teir,
From doggis deith was thy defence:
　　To the sic mercie schew my deir.

¶ O curssit Cain, O hound of hell,
O bludie bairne of Ishmaell,
Gedaliah quhen thow did steir,
To vicis all thow rang the bell,
Throw cruell murther of my deir.

¶ Allace my deir did not foirsie,
Quhen he gaif pardone vnto the
Maist wickit wretche, to men sinceir
Quhat paine he brocht and miserie,
　　With reuthfull ruine to my deir.

¶ But trew it is, the godly men
Quhilk think na harme nor falset ken,
Nor haitrent dois to vtherz beir,
Ar sonest brocht to deithis den:
　　As may be sene be this my deir.

¶ Thairfoir to the I say no moir,
But I traist to the King of Gloir,
That thow and thyne sall zit reteir
Zour Campz with murning mynde richt soir,
　　For cruell murther of my deir.

¶ O nobill Lordis of Renoun,
O Barronis bauld ze mak zow boun
To fute the feild with fresche effeir,
And dintis douse, the pryde ding doun
　　Of thame that brocht to graif my deir.

¶ Reuenge his deith with ane assent,
With ane hart, will, mynde, and Intent,
In faithfull freindschip perseueir:
God will zow fauour, and thame schent,
　　Be work or word that slew my deir.

¶ Be crous ze commouns in this cace,
In auenture ze cry allace,
Quhen murtherars the swinge sall beir,
And from zour natiue land zow chace,
　Unles that ze reuenge my deir.

¶ Lat all that fische be trapt in net,
Was counsall, art, part, or reset
With thankfull mynde and hartie cheir
Or zit with helping hand him met
　Quhen he to graif did bring my deir.

¶ Defend zour King and feir zour God,
Pray to auoyde his feirfull rod,
Lest in his angrie wraith austeir
Ze puneist be baith euin and od,
　For not reuenging of my deir.

¶ And do not feir the number small,
Thocht ze be few, on God ze call
With faithfull hart, and mynde sinceir,
He will be ay zour brasin wall,
　Gif ze with speid reuenge my deir.

¶ Remufe all sluggische slewth away,
Lat lurking Inuy clene decay,
Gar Commoun weill zour baner beir,
And peace and concorde it display :
　Quhen ze pas to reuenge my deir.

¶ With sobbing sych I to zow send
This my complaynt with dew commend
·Desiring zow all without feir,
Me pure Scotland for to defend
　Sen now to graif is gone my deir.

¶ Finis.

IV.—Heir followis ane Exhortatioun to the Lordis.

[STATE PAPER OFFICE.—Scotish Series, Volume 13, (*June*) Number 62.]

M Y Lordis now gif ze be wyse,
    Knaw weil the grace y^t God hes send zow
    Gif to that leuing Lord all pryse,
    Pray that from dainger he defend zow,
And na way lat zoure fais offend zow
But gif zow counsell and curage,
Bauldlie togidder all to bend zow,
That ze do nouther swerue nor swage.

Think it is nouther strenth nor fors
That hes set zow a fuite befoir,
Think weill that nouther men nor hors
Off sic ane act sould get the gloir :
Bot he that ringis euer moir
Hes luikit on zoure quarell rycht,
Gif him all thankis now thairfoir,
And pryse his name with all zour micht.

I grant zour interpryse was gude,
Zour purpose worthy till allow,
Bot I considder how it stude
And how the cais is cumin now
Had they keipit thame self fra zow,
And langer taryit in thair strenth,
Thocht zour curage was gude I trow
Ze had zit irkit at the lenth.

Think weil thair wit was thame bereft
Quhen fulishlie thay tuik the plane
Think thay war to thair foly left,
Quhen thay in feild come zow agane.
Think weill ze aucht for to be faine,

But bluid to win the upperhand
Quhair nouther man was hurt nor slane
To get the Jewell in zour hand.

Sen ze it haue thairof be suie,
Or els ze ar rycht far to blame
Gif ze hir till eschaip enduire,
Think ze sall haue baith skaith and shame
Quha babishlie bourdis with his dame
It war weill wairit he gat his quhippz,
Think neuer agane to dwell at hame,
Gif ze lat ga that is in zour grippis.

Gif sho had not cum in the feild,
For to defend the tratoure kene,
And not laubourit with speir and sheild
His wickit quarrell to sustene,
Ze had done wrang as sum men mene
Hir to withald agane hir will,
Bot now quhill trew tryell be sene
Sho moste be keipit or all will spill.

Pas fordwart in zour interpryse,
Reuenge in haist the cruell act :
Spair not to gif thame all ane syse
Quhome ze beleif the King did sact.
Be bauld and na way turne abak,
Spair nouther midling greit nor small
With wysdome syne gude tryall tak
And cause sum ane confes thame all.

Proclaime that all quha ocht dois knaw
To mak probatioun euident,
With diligence thay cum and shaw
In oppin and in place patent.
That sinners shortlie may be shent,
And gude men fred from all defame :
Sen God hes to zow power lent,
Gif ye be lashe ye ar to blame.

The heid traytoure quhair euer he be
Gif ye haue fors se ye persew,
Thocht he fra hoill to hoill do fle
At last he can not weill eschew.
Lat him be slaine your King that slew,
Bring ainis his fylthie lyfe till end :
Quha wickitlie this beir did brew
Wa worth the tyme that sho him kend.

Syne on your self ye tak gude keip,
And lat na ennimeis heir resort :
Be walkryfe and fall not on sleip,
Baith day and nycht gar walk your poIt,
Lat gude quarrell your hartis comfort :
The wark is greit ye haue in hand,
Think weill it is not play nor sport
Bot outher man ye die or stand.

For Godis saik aboue all thing,
Keep clene your handis fra wrangus geir
Gif ye wald haue his trew blissing,
Schaw first that ye the Lord do feir.
Exerce your selfis in gentill weir,
And fle from fylthie auarice,
Quhilk is as I in Scriptuire leir
The verray ruite of euerie vice.

Zour brether of the Nobill race,
With all meiknes desyre concur,
And your querrell in this cace,
Quhilk I dout not will be ane spur.
So that your pride cause thame nor stur
Bot your gude gyding thame alluire :
To cause thame enter mak ane duire,
Gif ye do swa ye may be suire.

Tak Godis quarrell als in hand,
And purge vs from Ipocrasie,
And than ye sall haue in your band

The townis and communitie.
Prouyde als for the Ministerie,
Reforme the Justice gif ye can,
Than sall tryumph your memorie
Above all sen this Realme began.

Sen Fergus first come in this land,
Sic gude beginning neuer was sene,
That gentilnes at thair awin hand
Sa just ane quarrell did sustene.
Reuoltis hes bene ma nor fyftene,
And Princes in strang presoun set :
Quhair all from bluid was keipit clene
Skantlie can I exampill get.

Think than ye wil preforme the work
That now dois your beginning blis,
And thocht your ennimies seme stark
He will cause thame thair purpose mis
That all war ane faine wald I wis,
Bot zit thocht sum againis zow faill
This actioun haill sa honest is,
With Godis grace it sall preuaill.

Lat na man throuch yow harmit be
And than ye sall na hartis tyne,
Gif euerie ane his awin degre
Excluid na man out of his lyne.
Set all at rest and efter syne
With all the rest concur togidder,
To mak ane ordour gude and fyne,
As your wisdomis can best considder.

Keip weil your Prince & for him pray
That God indew him with his grace,
That he incres may day be day :
To be the best of all his race.
The trew Religioun syne imbrace

Fra vice to vertew tak the traine,
His pepill weill in perfyte peace
And lang in helth with thame remaine.

All vitious wycht fra him exclude,
Be walkryfe wyse and diligent :
Gif ony be wald him na gude
Lat thame na way be thair present.
To teich him vertew tak gude tent
Lat not his zoutheid be infectit
Greit is the gift God hes yow lent
Sair sall ye rew hif ye neglect it.

And thus yow sportlie till exhort,
My Lordis all I thocht it gude :
For men of-tyme of meinest sort
That raknit war of ressoun rude.
Seing the cais and how it stude,
Hes geuin gude counsall to the wyse,
Sa wald I now and to conclude
God blis yow and your interpryse.

Finis.

Imprentit at Edinburgh be Robert Lekpreuik.
Anno Do. 1567.

V.—Ane Exhortatioun derect to my Lord Regent and to the Rest of the Lordis accomplisis.

[STATE PAPER OFFICE.—Scotish Series, Volume 14. (*August*)
   Number 72.]

IAN   with hir Court of Poyetis cleir,
        Qu § is land now plesandly dois sing
        In sin   gis that plesoure is to heir
        For io   nes our fair zoung tender King.

§ Torn out in the original.

Quho   hes set aboue vs for to Ring
Will §   l quhat I am, hes tane on hand,
Sa b   ure, rashely in thair Court to thring
By th   comission, lyke Johne vpaland.

T § aine thair plesand flowre of Poyetrie
With rurall termis and sentences denude
Of trym figuris and painted oratrie
From art poetick heir I it exclude.
Desyrand zour Lordshippes to be sa gude
To mark the sentence rather nor the style
And take it in gude pairt thocht it be rude,
Will God the nixt sall haue ane sharper fyle.

To call to mynde I think not necessair,
The warkes of God within this cuntrie shawin
Within thir seuin zeiris or lytill mair
Sen Christis trumphet throw this land was blawin.
Unto baith pure and riche it is weill knawin,
And als zour selfes my Lordis may cleirly se
That God wil haue the pride of man doune thrawin
Thocht he war neuer exalted so hie.

Zit with myself considdering the estate
Off zow my Lord Regent quhome God preserue
And all the rest, I thocht gude to repeate
Sum thingis that to zoure interprise mycht serue.
Knawing that man is reddy for till swerue,
Without continuall admonitionis be
Man of his awin nature is so proterue
Thairfoir I pray youre Lordeshippes beir with me.

How potent was that horint byke of hell
Into this land quhen God did zow vpsteir
It is weill knawin, ze will confesse zour sell
Zour strenth to thairis on na way mycht be peir.
Zit God Almychtie did zour baner beir

§ Torn out in the original.

And all thair mycht and prydfull pomp ouerthrew
Because the Lord of Hostis they did not feir
Thairis did decay, and ay zoure honour grew.

Quhill that, allace, ze begouth to neglect
The gloir of God and sa did seik zour sell,
The maist pairt I mein, that did infect
From feruencie within proces ze fell.
Quhilk Godis seruandz from tyme to tyme did tel,
And shew that God wald not sic thingis ouerse.
Ze gaif deif earis, bot God did zow compell
To find his worde effectuall to be.

Ze knaw my minde I neid not be mair plane
Ze se all warldly gloir for to be stidder,
Quhen God is greuit than he spairis nane
King Quene and Lord thay pas into ane fidder.
Thairfoir I warne zow ane and all togidder
To put zour stay vpone the leuing Lord,
And all his warkis into this land considder
Continuing in obeying of his word.

Ze doing this ze neid not for till feir
Deu. 28.   The boisting of zour ennemeis without,
The Lord will blis zow baith in peace and weir
Levi. 26.   And all zour enemeis rudely ruit out.
Ze sall haue freindis of them that dwellis about,
Jos. 24.   Bot gif that ze grow slak or negligent
The clene contrare sall cum to pas but dout
Thairfoir I pray zow to zour selfis tak tent.

Sa lang as Juda in King Asais dayis,
2 Chr. 15.   Did seik the Lord with all thair hartis desyre
Baith King and people prosperit in thair wayis
2 Chr. 16.   Bot ho §   ne Asa Benhadad did hyre.
That ho   battell mycht with him conspyre
And vsit meanis as God did not allow

§ Torn out in the original.

The Propheit threitnit, during his impyre
That war and battell sould his land pas throw.

Als by King Saull I think ze may attend,
Not for till spair quhome God commandis to slay
Gif that ze do I say behauld the end
n. 15. Reid quhat the buik of Kingis of him dois say.
Siclyke of Salamon behauld the way
n 11. And als Jehu with mony vther ma
That throuchly with the Lord walkit not ay
n. 10. Thocht thay begonth weill, luik ye do not sa.

Fall to stoutly all fantnes set asyde
And throw this land mak reformation,
Remember thir exampllis tyme and tyde
Quhilkis war amang the Jewis nation.
24. Quhairof partly is maid narration
Dissave not vs pure people of this land
Quha with ane gredie expectation
Lukis for gude reformation at your hand.

To heidis politick se ze geue na care
r. 17. Into reforming of this pure cuntrie
Bot Godis buik se that with zow ye beare,
With godlie men of wit and feruencie.
Abuif all thingis haue syc in cumpanie
34. Obeying thame quhen they command a rycht
Without respect of blude or dignitie,
Ze doing sa the Lord sall mak yow wycht.

From offices se that ye first depois
But feid or fauour of kinred or blude,
All wickit papistis, proud and Christis fois
And Jak on baith the sydis will neuer do gude.
All ignorantis and sic men ye exclude,
Syne plat me godly men into thair place
r. 17. Quha equally can Judge the people rude,
And rychtly reule ouer thame in eueric cace.

Let na Idolator your handis eschaip
7. Or ocht that dois Idolatrie mantene
Leif nathing that belangis to the Paip
Unrutit out as it had neuer bene.

23. Anis of thay Locustis mak this cuntrie clene
Zour foulishe pietie did thame spair befoir,
Thairfoir ye fand thame prickis vnto your ene
And gif ye spair thame yit sall find thame moir.

15. Nixt principallie I pray yow set your cure
For till relief the greit penuritie
Off laubouraris and of your tennentis pure
Quha sair opprest hes bene in this cuntrie.
This mony zeir by the Nobilitie
Let thame anis knaw the defference betwene
Zow and the Papistis, by your charitie
Quhilk heirtofoir amang yow was not sene.

Thir thingis to do luik no way ye neglect
Gif ye think lang in honour for till ring
Bot principallie I pray yow to eiect
Ane cursit byke that cheiflie dois maling.
In Abirdene of Sophistis the welspring
And in thair place put learnit men of God
I pray God blis James Stewart our young King
And mak him rychtly reule vs with his rod.

To thee my Lord Regent I turne my sang
I pray thee now for till be circumspect
In thy default se that na thing be wrang,
For Godis seruandis thair eyis to thee direct.
Thinking on na wayis that thow will neglect
The gloir of God in Scotland to vpreir
Seing he hes the rasit for that effect,
That the Lord Jesus baner thow should beir.

To yow my Lordis als I direct my pen
Proceid into your godlie interpryse,

As ye begouth curagiously lyke men
For quhy greit help into your handis lyis.
Thairfoir stoutlie se ye assist and ryse
Hauing Godis gloir alwayis befoir your eine
Than sal ye be haldin hardie and wyse
Sa lang as men sall on the earth be seine.

Finis.

⊶⊶⊰⊱⊷⊷

VI.—Ane Declaratioun of the Lordis Iust Quarrell.

[BRITISH MUSEUM.—Cottonian MSS.—Caligula C. 1. f. 10—
STATE PAPER OFFICE.—Scotish Series, Vol. 14, (*August*,)
Number 73. — Scotish Poems of the Sixteenth Century,
collected by John Graham Dalyell, Edinburgh, 1801.]

NOT lang ago as I allone did walk,
    Intill ane place was plesand to behauld :
    Twa leirnit men in priuie I hard talk,
        And eich of thame his taill in ordoure tauld
I vnderstuid thair sentence quhat thay wald,
    And thocht it gude to put in memorie
Thair Names als as efter ze sall se.

The taine him self Philandrius did call,
    Quha in vertew and manheid tuik delyte :
The tother feirfull semt to be at all,
    Erideilus he did his Name indyte
Off mony thingis thay did togidder flyte,
    But I tuik tent aboue all vther thing
Quhen they spak of this Realme and gouerning.

Erideilus sayis it dois merwell me,
　　Quhat causit hes the Lordis of Scotland
Tak on ane enterpryse of sic folie,
　　Againe the Quene and againis hir husband :
Mycht thay not weill ilk ane in his awin land
　　In quyetnes leifit in peace and rest,
Guyding his awin as him had lykit best.

To quhome Philandrius did answer mak,
　　And said that men war not deuyst onlie :
Without all cair thair awin plesure to tak,
　　Bot to foirse the weill of that countrie
Reularis of quhilk, the Lord will that thay be,
　　Quhilk charge (he sayis) thay can not weill refuse,
Les schamefullie thair office thay abuse.

Behalding than the actis execrabill,
　　That in this countrie hes committit bene,
The schame the lack the bruit abbominabill :
　　That saikles men with sorow did sustene,
Ane priuat hart it mycht prik vp with tene,
　　To seik redres and mend that cairfull caice
Far mair the nobillis of the Royall raice.

To se the King fyrst lychtlit schamefully,
　　And not chereist in chalmer nor in hall :
Syne murdreist downe causeles and crewelly,
　　Off that tresoun na tryall taine at all.
Thay quhome the bruit did trewlie traytouris call,
　　Greitest in Court and chereist all thair best,
Quhat Lordis hart culd luik on this and lest.

To se ane monstuire full of fylthynes,
　　Aboue the rest heich mountit vp in gloir
Baith Prince and Realme and all power posses.
　　Ane gled ay gaipand guid men to deuoir,
Quhat hart sa hard bot this sycht sould mak soir,
　　Quha rychtly than dar thir men reprehend :
Sic greit mischeif quha menis till amend,

To se the Quene furth rydand on the plaine,
   Reft lyke ane huire with ruffians shamefullie,
And thocht that sum think that was bot ane traine,
   Hir awin wryting dois contrar testifie,
In France Ingland and mony strange countrie :
   Pleinzeand that sho was rauyssit by hir will
Quhat Nobill hart mycht se this and sit still.

To reif, to murther and wyle licherie,
   The fourt forfault is eikit euin fra hand :
To testifie that Law and honestie
   With sic ribaldis can not ring in ane land,
The Quene is cuplit with ane wyffis husband
   And farther zit he quha the King did sack,
But Law the Quene dar into mariage tak.

Besyde all this thair durst na vertuous wycht,
   In presence of that proud tyran appeir :
Bludy boucheouris and throtcutters on nycht,
   War only hard, and only had the steir.
The Nobill men durst not the Court cum neir,
   The royall hous refuge to honest men
Was maid ane bordell and ane theifis den.

Our prettie Prince the peirle of all this land,
   With duilfull deid thay socht for to deuoir :
That riche relick and thresour of Scotland,
   Destroy as thay his father did befoir.
Quhat duilfull mynde mycht dewlie this deploir,
   In sic dainger to se that innocent
For our releif quhome God had till vs sent,

Quhat Nobill hart could langer this induire ?
   Quhat common breist did not for sorrow burst ?
Quhat godly man of himself could be suire ?
   Quhat stranger thocht bot this countrie was curst ?
Quhat preachour this repreif, I pray zow durst :
   Quhat chaist woman wyssit not to be deid,
To se sic vice set vp in vertewis steid.

Gif it was sa, than quha can worthylie
  Exalt and prais, and magnifie the Name
Off thir Nobillis quha durst couragiouslie
  Haziard thame self to saif vs all fra shame.
Thair laud, thair honour, and tryumphand fame,
  Salbe disperst in dispyte of Inuy,
Quhen faceles fuillis sall not be settin by.

Erideilus than answer maid againe,
  Thy talk he sayis is treuth and veritie :
Bot sit sum douts thair is of quhilk rycht faine,
  Gif laser lat I wald resoluit be,
And fyrst tuiching the Queni's libertie :
  For mony thinkis thir Barronis ar to bauld.
In strait keping a Princes for to hauld.

Philandrius to answer than him sped,
  And this he said Eridielus vntill :
Gif that a freind with fayis away war led
  Be wickit craft syne tystit war till ill.
Thocht he couet in that stait to byde still,
  Zit in that caice his freindis of dewtie
Sould wis his weill and seik his libertie.

And gif his fantasie war sa far infectit,
  That to the treuth he could not bent his eir.
He sould not be in foly zit neglectit
  Bot fairnes than sould mixit be with feir,
And gif all this could him na wysedome leir
  Than acht he be of all puissance denude,
To do na euill gif he could do na gude.

Than sen that bowdin bludy beist Bothwell,
  Hes trayterously in myrk put downe our King :
His wyfe the Quene syne rauyssit to him sell,
  In fylthie lust throw cullour of wedding.
Thocht sho be witcheit wald in ruttery ring,
  The Nobillis sould nether of thir enduire,
That lowne to leif, nor hir to be his huire.

And gif the poysone in her hart be sonkin,
   That sho will not consent he puneist be :
Gif with his fylthie lust sho be sa dronkin,
   That sho forzet office and honestie
Than man her Nobillis of necessitie,
   Cut of hir force quhill tresoun be reuehgeit,
And this confusioun in ane ordour changeit.

In priuat personnis sayis Eridielus,
   I vnderstand thy taill is trew in deid :
Bot in Princes it is mair perrillous,
   And few examplis thairof can I reid.
And in sic caice the subiectis all had neid,
   Haill to concur with ane authoritie
Sic concurrence in Scotland nane I se.

Philandrius sayis brother than considder,
   How fyrst began all dominatiounis :
Quhen ruid pepill assemblit thame togidder.
   And maid thair Kingis be creatiounis.
In votis than war variatiounis,
   I trow rycht few was chosin be the haill,
Bot he was King quhais pairtie did preuaill.

Rycht sa gif Princes sa thame self abuse,
   That of force subiectis man put to thair hand :
Guid men sould not than to reforme refuse,
   Thocht all at ainis concur not on thair band.
Naimly gif Justice on thair partie stand,
   And maist consent gif quha wald rackin rycht,
Sen God hes gein to thame baith strenth and mycht.

Zea thocht it war ane King for to depose,
   For certaine crymis I think the subiectis may,
Or fylthy faultouris fast in prisone close,
   Rather than lat ane haill countrie decay :
Thay sould not sturre thocht sum men wold say nay
   To ane purpose the haill will neuer conclude,
Thay haue aneuch, hes force and quarrell gude.

May thay not put ane ordoure to the heid :
   Quha in beginning did the heid vp mak
May thay not set ane better in the steid,
   Gif it fra vice can not be callit bak.
Les this be done Realmes will ga to wrak,
   Namely quhen that the cryme is sa patent
That nouther misters Juge nor argument.

As gif ane King his pepill wald betray,
   And him and thame baith bring to seruitude :
He sould in this reformit be I say,
   Naimly be Nobillis and be men of gude.
The Baliols cause considder how it stude,
   Quhat rycht had Robert Bruice him to expell ?
Because to Ingland he subiect him sell.

And now gif I durst speik without respect,
   To huirmaisters, to murderers of Kingis :
To throtcutters our Realme was made subiect,
   Quha in thair malice proudely zit malingis.
Lat Nobill hartis considder all thir thingis,
   Thay sall weill find that this puire natioun,
Greit mister had of reformatioun.

Sic fylthie lust in Sardanapalus,
   Sic crueltie Nero did not ring :
Sic brutishe lyfe in Heliogabalus
   Sic traytour mynde to slay his Lord and King,
In feinzeit Phocas breist did neuer spring :
   Sic beistly bowgrie Sodome hes not sene
As rang in him quha rewlit Realme and Quene.

And sould the Nobill Barronis of this land
   In hoilis lurk and this mischief behauld,
Quhair is the wittis wont to reule Scotland ?
   Go reid the buik, repeit the storyis auld,
King Euenus was keipit in strang hauld
   And deit thair Conarus was inclosit,
Fist being dewlie for his fault deposit.

For wickit lyfe imprisont was Ferquhaird,
  Quha slew him self of proude melancolie,
Donald the fyft he gat the same reuaird :
  And Ethus did in prisone priuate die.
And gif ze list to go fra this countrie,
  In euerie land examplis dois abound
Gif thay be socht thay may be eithlie found.

For sic misordour proude Tarquinius
  Was the last King that euer did ring in Rome,
For lyke crymes the tyran Claudius :
  Losit his stait and gat deid for his dome.
To speik of Nero now I haue na tome,
  Off Commodus, Caius and Caracall,
It war to lang for to discriue the fall.

Quhat sorow into Naples than was sene,
  Quha knawis the story cleirly thair may reid,
Quhen Charlis dochter Jeane that catiue Quene :
  Baith honestie forzet and womanheid.
Hir husband and hir cousing put to deid,
  Syne with his Burrio band ane new mariage,
Allace this sample seruis ouer weill our age.

And zit the Lord he leit hir not eschaip,
  Bot of hir tuik ane punishement conding :
Quha fyrst hir husband hangit in ane raip,
  The murtherer syne in his bed did bring.
God maid hir paine aggre with hir guyding,
  As bedfoly to sic mischeif hir led
Euin so sho endit smorit with a bed.

Than to conclude thir Nobillis dois bot rycht,
  Gif thay the Quene keip still in sicker gaird,
Untill that coward Kingslayar on nycht
  For his demeritis get ane iust rewaird.
Than lat thame all concur baith Lord and Laird,

3

Thair Realme and Quene with gude consall to guyde.
Settand all priuate profit far a syde.

Gif thay do this than dar I say ane thing,
  Thair laude and fame sall mont aboue the skyis,
Thair heich renoune sall in all Regioun ring :
  Thair name sall gang quhair euer the Sone do ryse,
Thay salbe repuite hardy wycht and wyse,
  In all storyis thay salbe cleirly kend,
The Leuing Lord bring thame to this gude end.

As this Philandrius did frely talk,
  The tother pairt Erideilus be name,
Rais vp and quyetlie away did stalk,
  And as me thocht he waxit reid for schame,
Quhilk when I saw I rais vp and come hame
  And put in wryt thair disputatioun,
As ze haue hard be this narratioun.

Finis.

Imprentit at Edinburgh be Robert Lekpreuik.
Anno Do. 1567.

∘▸▶▷▓▷◀◂∘

VII. —Ane Ansʳ maid to yᵉ Sklanderaris yᵗ blasphemis yᵉ Regent and yᵉ rest of yᵉ Lordis.

[STATE PAPER OFFICE.—Scotish Series, Volume 14. (*August*)
  Number 74.]

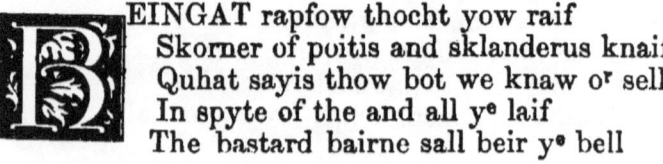

BEINGAT rapfow thocht yow raif
Skorner of poitis and sklanderus knaif
Quhat sayis thow bot we knaw oʳ sell
In spyte of the and all yᵉ laif
The bastard bairne sall beir yᵉ bell

Outher thow art ane papist loun
Hepburne or hoitbag Hammiltoun
Gif thie be tha thow callis thi prince.
War zour richt reknit to yi croun
It myᵗ be laid with litill menss.

Blasphemus baird and beggeris get
The regentis self hes nocht forzet
How gude King Willm wes ane bastard
And yow nocht bot ane carlengs pett
Ane daft fule or ane drunken dastard.

And forthermoir gif yow wald flyte
Be weill avisit quhome yow bakbyte
Recant and sweir yow said it nocht
For he sall prosper in dispyte
Off ye and yame yat wald it noᵗ.

Revoik ye wyndie words vane
Ze knew mair quhen ye King wes slane
Spit out and speik mair and ze pleis
Wist I quhome wᵗ to flyte agane
The mater sould be war to meiss

To flyte wᵗ ye and fyle my lippis
The sone ye mone sould haif the clippis
For all ye quentance with the quene
Thay hound ye to ye hangmanis grippis
Quhair mony better man hes bene

Sweingeoʳ cum sweir ye saikles sone
Deny ye evill yat yow hes done
Againis ye man yat maid na falt
Allege lunatyke to ye mone
Or yan abone ane mask of malt

Euir ye mair yow wald be trowit
The les yi lounrie is allowit

Returnand to ye turpitude
Thow sould haif waige durst yow awow it
The gallowis for ye gratitude

Maist lyke sum myllare of ane myll
Had maid ye mater of ye bill
Outher sum cuiks or keching clerks
Be doand fule-face flite yi fill
Men may nocht ding all doggs yat barks

Palzart war nocht o' faith defendit
Pure commonn weill and knaifrie endit
Than you my᷑ writte in gennerall
All detouris ar bot discommendit
That speiks dispite in speciall

In fechting man yow maid yi vant
That yow sould sla ye Innocent
But caus or cryme of ony querrell
Bot knew I the yow sould recant
Or yan thy pallat ly in parrell

Luik ye first of everie verss
Hangman gif yow can reherss
Mark weill my name & set ane day
In fechting war yow never so ferss
Thow salbe marrowit and I may

ffinis quod Maddie gar mak ye boun
To all ye papistis of yis toun.

[Robert Symple ys the dooer hereoff.]
Note by Sir William Drury.

VIII.—¶ The Kingis Complaint.

[BRITISH MUSEUM.—Roxburghe Ballads.   Volume 3.]

WITH hauie hart on Snadoun hill,
    Ane zoung King I hard schoutand schill
With reuthfull rair he did record :
    Prayand as I haif writ this bill
        Judge and Reuenge my cause O Lord.

    ☞ He sayis this causles I not craif
Nor he is now gone to his graif
My commoun weill that maist decorde,
Na merwell albeit my hart claif
    For sorrow of his deith O Lord.

    ¶ Hard is my chance all tyme and houris
And harder to my Gouernouris,
Ze hardest (bot wo am I forde)
To him hes felt of deith the schouris
    And only for thy cause O Lord.

    ☞ Quhen I was not zit ane zeir auld,
Bothwell that bludy Bouchour bauld,
My Father cruelly deuorde,
He him betrayit and his blude sauld
    Judge and Reuenge my cause O Lord.

    ¶ Than Father slaine, Mother was schёt
My Gudschir flemit Incontinent,
My self to poysoun it was schorde,
Me to betray was summis Intent
    Judge and Reuenge my cause O Lord.

    ☞ Than vp thow rasit to reule my Ring,
In to my tender yeiris zing,
My faithfull freind that maid him forde,
James Regent my Uncle ding,
    Judge and Reuenge my cause O Lord.

¶ He was my buckler and my beild,
He was my Targe, my speir and scheild,
My stait maist hie for to restorde:
He futtit euer mair the feild,
   Judge and Reuenge his cause O Lord.

☞ For me he left Kin, Freind and wyfe,
For me he sufferit dailie stryfe
For me he was haill Indeuorde,
For me now he hes loist his lyfe,
   Judge and Reuenge his cause O Lord.

¶ For me that Nobill of Renoun,
With ane Tyke Tratour Hammiltoun,
Was schot, and throw the body borde
For the mantening of my Crowne
   Judge and Reuenge his cause O Lord.

☞ Peloure thow peirst him, gaif ye peace,
Tratoure to him that gaif the grace,
Behind his bak thy Gunne him gorde:
Quhome thow nor nane of thyne dirst face,
   Judge and Reuenge his cause O Lord.

¶ Lord sen my gratious gyde is gone,
And I am left as Byrd allone,
This thing maist eirnistly I Implorde:
That Instantly thow steir vp one
   For to Reuenge his cause O Lord.

☞ Sen for my saik now he is slane,
Lord for thy grace grant me agane,
That deith my lyfe neuer deuorde,
Quhill that fals tressonabill trane
   Be with my hand Reuengd O Lord.

☞ O Scotland thy Josias trew
That first Idolatrie ouerthrew

He was, and Christs trew Kirk restorde
Throw him in my Realme grace ay grew,
   Judge and Reuenge his cause O Lord.

   ¶ He Abrahamis Faith but feir profest
He Dauidis mercy manifest
With Salomonis wit he was decorde,
Sampsonis strenth to him accrest
   Judge and Reuenge his cause O Lord.

   ☞ Theif and Reuer he did dant,
Justice and vertew he did plant,
Quhair thair was mys he gar remorde,
My faithfull seruand and thy Sanct,
   Judge and Reuenge his cause O Lord.

   ¶ As his Renoun is all ouerblawin,
And now his deith plainly furthschawin,
Sa sall all blyithnes be abhorde
Quhill his Reuenge be als wa knawin,
   Throw thy help and support O Lord.

   ☞ All ze my trew Nobilitie,
That fauourit him, and seruit me,
Lat not his duilfull deith be smorde,
Bot it Reuenge maist cruellie
   For it is the will of the Lord.

   ¶ And quha his deith dois sair regaird
And it to puneis will not spaird
I wow to the in quhome he glorde
Thay sall not mys ane riche rewaird
   For to Reuenge his cause O Lord.

   ☞ Now sall appeir in wark and nature,
Quha is the trew man, quha is the trature.
Quha fittis the feild, quha cuiris not forde,
The trew liege be the Rubiature
   In this cause salbe kend O Lord.

¶ And think that thay that did this deid.
With lyke effect dois seik my heid,
For to be beatin downe and smorde
All Faithfull hartis quyte thair meid,
 And thow Reuenge my cause O Lord.

☞ For surely thair will and Intent
That seikes of me the Gouernment,
Be fraudfull factiounis, I stand forde,
Wald me forfault in Parliament,
 Gif thow withstude thame not O Lorde.

My Coronatioun thay deny
And dois maist spytefully defy
All thame that faithfully restorde
Me to my Crowne and Seignorie
 Thy michtie hand requyte thame Lord.

Last Lord now him of me hes cvre
And in quhais handis I think me sure,
Thy puissant power I Implorde,
That he with me lang dayis Indure
 For to Reuenge his cause O Lord.

With this the Babe he gifis ane rair
Quhilk maid my hart to sich sa sair,
That farther I culd not recorde
Bot with him sall cry euer mair,
 Judge and Reuenge his cause O Lord.

¶ Finis.

IX.—A Ryme in Defence of the Q. of Scotts against the Earle of Murray.

[BRITISH MUSEUM.—Cottonian MSS. Caligula C. 1. p. 274.—
STATE PAPER OFFICE. Scotish Series, Volume 13,
(xi. December 1568,) Number 67.]

TOM TROATH TO THE ENUIOUS.

IF Momus children seke to knowe my name and
where I dwell,
    I am Tom Troath and my aboade I list not
it to tell
For wise men loue not to enquyre, who where, but what
is said
And holde themselves therewith content till further
proufe be made.

THE DOUBLE DEALINGE OF THE REBELLS IN SCOTLAND.

If tongue could tell or pen could write, the craftie cloaked
case
Or yet the treasons to recyte of this newe Regents grace
Then Tullies stile or Vergills vearse of God sure would
I crave
His shameles acts here to rehearse as he deserues to have
But that were farre aboue my reach and more then well
could be
Sith he all others doeth excell in craft & crueltye.
Yet can I not with silence passe his vices strainge & rare
But that I must set furth the same the truthe least I
should spare
And nowe since that it is my luck vnfittest though I be
This Caco's ofsprings to advaunce as semes to his decree
I pray you take it in good parte whats'euer I shall saye
In setting furth his shameles acts whose shame shall
not decaye.
Yet can I not set furth the same nor in such wise expresse

As fittest were for one past shame and past all godlines
This trayto' tyraunt of our tyme This Sathans seed I
    meane
This Rebell Regent that his prince to mate doeth not
    desdaine
This perfect patterne of deceipt whose high and hawghtye
    minde
Is paste so full of pride that hard it were the like to
    finde
This sinfull seed of lothsome life this bastard past all
    grace.
At Glocester that Trayto' vile a perfect paterne chase.
Who to obteyne that Kingly seate of this most woorthy
    land
His brothers sonnes his Nephewes dere to guyde they
    toke in hand
The lambes alas vnto the wolfe to guyde comitted were
Who murdered them to haue their place as storyes well
    declare
But shall I say this trayto' nowe at him did learne his lore
Who doeth surpasse his wilie wit a thowsand folde and
    more
A scholler sure of pregnant wit and apt for such a place
Who trayned vp was in the schole of lyeinge Sathans
    grace
Where he hath learnd a finer feate then Richard earst
    did see
To doe the deede and laye the blame on them that
    blameles be
For he and his companions take agreeing all in one
Did kill the Kinge and laye the blame the sakelesse
    Queene vpon.
And that this deede to each mans sight might seme to
    be most plaine
They drewe her from her spowse that night by craft &
    subtill trayne
And feyned that her suckinge Sonne was in great daunger
    brought

Wherfore with speed to visit him the messenger be
    sought
With subtill shifte so feately wrought was cause men
    thought it trewe
That she of purpose parted thence & of the murder knewe
For if that boeth at once had bene ther murder at that
    tyme
Then might each babe with half an eye haue spyed who
    did the cryme
And this suspicion to increase they found a newe
    devise.
That Bothwell chiefest murderer was tryed by asise
And found not guilty by his peeres of whome the
    chiefest be
Such as the Kings death did conspire and knewe as well
    as he.
They cleared him eke by parliamente a traytour false
    & vile
That they their good and vertuous Queene might soner
    so beguyle
And when that he was cleared boeth by sise and parla-
    ment
To marry then they went about to have her to consent
They sayd that she the realme & they should so most
    safest be
From daunger of all cevill strife & outward enemy.
Alack good Q. what hap hadst thou so oft thy foes to
    trust
Couldst thou not shun these bateinge beasts who then had
    tryed vniust
But I who pray yo^u was the man they willed her to
    take
Forsooth the chiefest murderer whom they most clere
    did make
And that their purpose once begun might come vnto
    an end
They caused Trayto^r Lidington on her still to attend
That this false mache vilian attempt her euery waye

Whose poysoned words so sugred were that she could
      not say Nay
But did consent to ther request suspecting nothing lesse
Then they such false deceipt to meane & vse such
      doables
But when the wofull weding daye was finished & past
Their boyleing malice that laye hid in rageing sort out
      brast
For they that were of Counsell boeth to murdering of
      the Kinge
And to the mariage gan to spread howe Bothwell did
      ye thinge
And how he tooke away the Q. by force against her
      will
And sought himselfe to raigne as Kinge and eke y^e prince
      to spill
But (bastard) nowe the truthe is knowne how y^t thy
      self it was
That sought to spill boeth prince and Q. and to possesse
      their place
But when amongst the simple sort this $rumo^r$ once was
      brought
It ran abrode from place to place more swift than can
      be tho^t
So they not privy to the sleight did think it for most
      sure
That she to wed the murderer the murther did procure
And thus this simple Q. each way was wrapt in wo &
      care
For they that cannot skill of craft are sonest caught in
      snare
And then the Traytor Lidington in treason neuer slack
At hand ye pickpurse still before began to start now back
And fled vnto her fruyteles foes her secrets to bewray
Like will to like the proverb saith you know the old
      said sawe
Then Murray y^e of longe before this murder did devise
Did voyd the land the rather so to blind the simples eyes

And then his fellowe Traytors all the more their cause
to clere

Did rise in armes against their Q. as though she guilty
were

But she to save the sackles bloud not willing to offend

Did leave her power and offred them all things amisse
t'amend

The traytors not therewith content did lead her thence
away

And chainged all her leave attyre into a frock of grey

That done they lead her furth by night vnto Lochleuin
hold

And kept her there in prison close that no man se her
could

Then when they had this brought to passe their trayt^rous
false desire

They sent with speed to Bastard James & willd him to
retyre

Who comeinge home for loue he bare the prince as he
did saye

Did take in hand to rule the realme lest it fell in decay

Howe well this Traytor lovs the Child comytted to his
gward

Is plaine in that the mother dere he kept in Crewell
warde

And causd her thereby forced fact ye present death to
shunne

Her Royall Crowne for to resigne vnto her tender sonne

And make this mynyou Murray eake chiefe Regent of
the land

Vntill the prince of lawfull age the same shall take in
hand

W^{ch} while he would as Richard did if he might haue
his will

His Nephewe younge his sisters sonne by secret meanes
to spyll

And then he would vsurpe the Crowne as next heire to
the same

W^{ch} doeth appeare in that he doeth his father so defame
And saith his brother precontract was in most solomne
    wise
Vnto the Kinge before that he was maried to the Guise
Although that wisemen know the truthe this sorceress
    how she wrought
By rings and wichcrafte from the Q. the Kings minde
    to haue brought
And thus this trayto^r doeth debase the Q. in all he can
That from her grace withdrawe he might the hearts of
    euery man
A Cowle a Cowle for such a greke were fitter for to weare
Then this Apostat deacon should such princely Rule to
    beare
But where is nowe true discipline dare no man take in
    hand
To teach such false Apostate Monks their faults to
    vnderstand
And ncake this base borne Deacon come home to his
    former state
From whence the Lither Lozell fled least he should live
    too straight
But sure no marvell though Gods rodd hath plagued
    this noble dame
That gaue to Monkes should serue in Churche such place
    of worldly fame
Yet he not all vnmindfull of this Ladies gratefull deed
Did purpose with a cruell death to quick her for her nede
But God Almightie in whose hands the harts of princes be
Preserue her from these false attempt & vile captivitye
And when this Noble pray was past this brothers
    bloudy night
He rages like a Tiger fell for sorowe and for spite
So seing that he could not then his Noble Q. to spill
Vpon her faithfull subiects he began to work his will
For some he cast in prison depe no cause at all thereto
And some he thrust out of the realme to work them
    great^r woe

And some he put to cruell death his rage for to fulfill
No meanes he left there vnattempt her subiects lives to
    spill
Yet not content in this great rage on men to play his parte
In spight of God against his Christe he gan to shewe his
    art
And pulled thence boeth bells & lead with iewells many
    one
That he and his companions might more braver therein
    gone
For sure I am that some of them amongst his Trayter-
    ous trayne
Have on their back more lead at once then covereth
    Churches twayne
So that no hardned hearte of brasse but would lament
    right sore
To se prophaneing of each place as serueth God and yore
And when he had this sacrelidge comitted euery where
On loftye Towres & Castles stronge his rage did then
    appere
On Dunbarre first he spued his spite a castle fayre and
    stronge
And there he wrought boeth day and night till it was
    layd alonge
Then uisteth furth and Loghinuar so semely to the
    shewe
He spoyld them first & sackt them then who could more
    cruell doe
The lord of Sterlinges howse likewise did fele ye form^r
    chauce
W^{ch} trayterouslye he did deface his glorie to advaunce
Then Roslin Bower of brave attyre wth Saintclere doth
    possesse
Most shamefully he ransauckt so to work him more
    distresse
Lord Harris lands that Baron bolde who let him of his will
When he was gone throughout the same he did both
    robb & spill

But what should I here longer staye eche place here to
    recyte
Sith few there are but that his rage hath nowe defaced
    quite
When he had wrought his wilfull witt & had his false
    intent
To blinde the eyes of faithfull men he calld a parlament
Where flockt his fellowe Traytors all both Moreton and
    Magill
With Lindsay Marre and Ledington yea Balflour laye
    not still
With other of this fruyteles flock and falsely did invent
That all things there concluded were by full & whole
    consent
Thus sinfull Sathan workt his will through these his
    children dere
That falsehood raignes in steed of right as here it doeth
    appere
Yet haue they not so slilye wrought though Sathan was
    their guide
But that their treason euery deale at last as well espied
For they to some were innocent of this most haynous
    deed
Did catch 4 of the murderers and put to death with
    speed
Whereby they hope to make men think herein that they
    were clere
Sith Justice they did execute on some that guylty were
As Hepburne Daglace Penory too John Hey made vp
    the messe
Wch 4 when they were put to death the treason did
    confesse
And said that Murray Moreton to with others of their
    rowte
Were guylty of the murder vile though nowe they loke
    full stowte
Yet some perchaunce do think that I speake for affection
    here

Though I would so 3000 can herein true witnes beare
Who present were as well as I at the execution tyme
And hard how these in conscience prickt confessed who
did the cryme
Wherefore all princes take good heed let this for warning
stand
And trye before you trust I warne lest check be nere at
hand
But though his check it semes so sure that mate is now
at hand
Yet may his Q. such gward procure as shall his force
withstand
And then she may as he began bid check & mate with
thee
And warne him since his force is done to yeld or els to
flye
To yeld I meane from false attempt & flye such vaine
request
And gward himself wth reasons rule and set his heart
at rest
And spend no more his tyme in vaine such false attempts
to trye
Least if they vse them over oft hele clime I feare to
highe
And thus I reaste & make an end and wish him to
beware
No more such checks & tawnes to give least he be caught
in snare.

Finis q^d Tom Trowth.

X.—Ane Tragedie, in forme of ane Diallog betwix Honour, Gude Fame, and the Authour heirof in ane trance.

[Scottish Poems of the Sixteenth Century, Collected by John Graham Dalyell, Edinburgh 1801.]

IN Januar the thre and twentie day,
Befoir midnycht, in Lythquo as I lay,
Tumbling sum tyme on bed abon the clais,
Now heir, now thair, quhylis doun, quhylis
up I rais ;
Till at the last, in tuinkling of ane ee,
Schir Morpheus the Mair assailzeit me,
With all his sluggische suldarts out of number,
Quhilks led me captiue vnto Maister Slumber,
Quha softly said, Gar keip this pure catiue,
And tak from him his speiche and wittis fiue.
Than come Dame Dreming, all clad in blak sabill,
With sweyning nymphis in cullouris variabill ;
Amangis the quhilks, befoir me thair appeiris
Ane woundit man, of aucht and threttie zeiris,
Paill of the face, baith blaiknit, blude and ble,
Deid eyit, dram lyke, disfigurat was he,
Nakit and bair, schot throw pudding and panche,
Abone the nauil, and out abone the hanche.
Na word he said, quhairthrow I did misknaw him,
Because in sic ane stait I neuer saw him.
I wes agast, and sa begouth to feir,
Bot suddanly with him thair did appeir
Twa graif lyke persounis, of greit maiestie,
And with gude countenance thay said to me :
    We ar cum heir to the, O wofull wycht,
To cause the write that thing thow seis this nycht ;
For we are knit, in band maryit togidder,
And to this woundit wycht father and mother ;
We him begat within thir twentie zeiris,

Thocht deid lyke now he so to the appeiris ;
We brocht him vp, as ovr deir sone and air,
And he to serue vs na traueil did spair ;
Thacht Atropus hes maid his corps decay,
Zit immortall in heuin his saule dois stay,
And, als immortall, he sall with vs rest,
And we with him, sa lang as warld may lest.

Gude Schir, (quod I), and ze also Madame,
Be not offendit that I speir zour name.
How thay call zow, that talkis sa hamely with me,
And quhat is he that first appeirit vnto me,
That woundit man, quhome ze do call zour chylde,
Quhat is zour names, lat se how ar ze stylde ?

Quod thay, My sone, of that we think na schame ;
Honour I am, heir with my spous Gude Fame :
This woundit chylde of ouris thow may lament,
He was thy maister ainis, and zour Regent.

My Maister ainis ! (quod I) : zit is he so.

Nay, nay, (quod thay), he is with vs ago ;
We haif him taine out of that wickit lyfe,
And red him of all miserie and stryfe ;
Because ze wardlingis ar ane cursit clan,
Ze war not worthie of this godly man.

Allace, (quod I), deid lyke he dois appeir.

Be still, (quod thay), and to our sayingis heir :
Speid, speid, go to; tak pen, ink, paper, and wryte
As we, Honour and Gude Fame, sall indyte.

First thow sall wit, he was sone natural
To James the Fyft, zour King and Prince Royal :
Thocht, beand zoung, to kirkis he was promotit,
Zit we his hart with martiall deidis dotit :
For them the Lord sa blissit his affairis,
That furth of Fyfe he chaist his aduersairis,
With help of gentill men and subiectis to him,
The quhilkis war willing all seruice to do him :
Thair we begat him, and maid him our awin,
As he is, was, and sa sall euer be knawin.
Syne, efter that, he passit into France,

Quhair he did vs, and we did him auance:
Than hauing leirnit thair sum Frenche langage,
He brocht agane with vs his pucelage.
Now, to be schort, it war lang to discerne
The godly giftis that this our sone did lerne;
For as in age he daily did incres,
In vertew sa grew he, and lawlynes:
First he did leirne to lufe God aboue all,
And syne his nichtbour with lufe mutuall:
Trew faith he leirnit of gude Abraham,
With hoip and cheritie knit to the same:
He leirnit als of Salomon the wisdome,
How with the feir of God to reule ane kingdome:
Of strang Sampsone he had also the fors,
For to resist Gods foes on fute and hors;
Thocht thir tratours, that drest him in this cace,
Durst not present thair force befoir his face:
He had lykewyse the justice of Jethro,
And als the chastitie of Scipio:
He had of Dauid the beningnitie,
And of Titus the liberalitie.
Quhat wald thow moir? To tell of all his vertus,
For commoun-welthis he did excell Camillus:
Quhen pleisit God to send zow Scottis ye treuth,
The same to further at Leith he was not sleuth;
Reforming first his awin with diligence,
In euerie quarter quhair he had puissence;
Than was he stylit Lord James at that tyde,
To quhome zour Lordis gaif sum reule and gyde.
    Sone efter that, zour Quene ane wedow was,
The quhilk to bring in Scotland he did pas;
In France he went, and brocht that Lady hame,
Quha efterwart agane changit his name;
Bot zit we maryit him, quhen we thocht gude,
Unto ane Lady of hie kyn and blude:
Than did zour Quene mak him baith Erle & Lord
Of Murray land, to quhilk we did accord;
Sa condiscendit all zour Lordis togidder,

That, nixt zour Quene, he suld reule abone vther.
Bot than, allace, he did sum thing without vs,
Howbeit that all his lyfetyme he did dout vs:
He did permit zour Quene to haif ane Mes,
Throw quhilk at lēth scho grew in greit proudnes;
Sa did the Papistis all, athort this land,
Aganis the Lord his will, law, and command,
That ze almaist amang zow wer deuydit,
Wer not be him all wes the better gydit.
Sa lang in court as our sone had the steir,
And that zour Quene wald his gude counsail heir,
Sa lang all thing zeid weill, and wes weill drest,
In quyetnes, peace, policie and rest:
Nane durst rebell on either syde of Forth,
Ouir all this cuntrie, eist, west, south, & north:
The hiest of thame all he maid full law,
That did rebell aganis justice and law.
Than did zour Quene sum tyme with vs abyde;
In France, and Scotland baith, we did her gyde.
Bot at the last, in hir tranquillitie,
Scho did vs all abandoun wantounlie,
And turnit day in nycht, and nycht in day,
All the nycht lang, to sport, sing, dance and play;
Till at the last, baith Cupido and Venus,
Furth of ye court, gart baneis, chais, and stane vs.
Than come Dishonour and Infame, our fais,
And brocht in ane to reule with raggit clais:
Thocht he wes blak, and moriane or hew,
In credite sone, and gorgius clais he grew:
Thocht he wes forraine, and borne in Piemont,
Zis did he Lords of ancient blude surmont:
He wes to hir baith secreit, trew, and traist,
With hir estemit mair nor all the raist.
In yis mene tyme, cam hame yan my Lord Darlie,
Of quhais rair bewtie scho did sumpart farlie,
The fairest sycht, scho thocht, that euir scho saw;
Hir bewtie als did him in hir snair draw.
For to be schort, thay lufit sa togidder,

That thay culd not be hour of day but vther.
At last scho said, and caist in to hir mynde.
Quhat, quhat, sall I be thus with Cupide pynde ?
That will I not, bot go to my purpois ;
Zit first I will my mynde to sum disclois :
Then with gude vult, and visage meik and mylde,
Brother, (quod scho), scho said vnto our chylde,
Will not ze weill that I marie ane man,
Baith of our surname, kynreid, blude and clan ?
Lo this is he standing befoir zour face,
Lustie, gude lyke, and cum of Royall race ;
Him will I marie, and nane vther wycht,
Witnes heirof, to him my treuth I plycht
In your presence, desyring zow lykewyse
That ze be witnes to this interpryse.
Quhat wald thow mair ? without all friends cōsent,
This Lord scho maryit quhen thay were absent,
Quha was bot zoung, and culd not reule the ring,
And thay disperst that suld haif done sic thing.
Sa this stranger, and fallow of na kin,
In Thuring borne, and wes ane menstrells sone,
Begouth to reule, and callit Seinzeour Dauid,
Be quhome zour King and Lords war all dissauid.
It wald be lang on this mater to stand.
Our sone thay chaist syne efter in Ingland,
With sindrie vther Lordis that went vnto him,
The quhilkis wer all of ane opinioun with him.
Be this Dauid zour Lordis did this sustene ;
Be him zour King was lychtlyit with zour Quene :
Be him all thing was reulit in the court ;
For him cum all this cummer, stryfe, and stourt ;
Throw him, in him, be him, zour court was gydit,
Quhill that zour Kind and Lordis culd not abyde it ;
The quhilkis schortly in cōusall did cōfidder,
And with ane mynde thay did consent togidder
Dauid to slay, quhair euer thay mycht haif him.
Concluding thus, on nycht thay did persaue him,
At supper tyme, quhair he was in hir chalmer ;

Than come zour King & sum Lords, with ane glamer,
And reft him from hir, in spyte of his nois,
Syne schot him furth quicklie amang his fois,
Quha stickit him, withouttin proces moir:
Bot all his mischeif come sensyne thairfoir.
Howbeit scho was sone closit vp beliue,
Hir gairdis defendit, and hir self captiue;
Zit culd scho not in hart sic thing forzet,
Bot baid hir tyme, quhill scho hir tyme mycht get.
Than come thir Lords the nixt morne efter hame,
And maist humblie our sone halsit that dame,
Quha was with chylde, & neir sax monethis gone,
And him forgaif, and maid to him hir mone:
Sayand, Brother, allace, had ze bene heir,
I had not cum in this sturt and steir;
My secretar is slane in my presence,
Oh, oh, brother, allace, quhat greit offence!
Madame (quod he) cair not, that is small tynsall;
He wes our fo, and gaif zour Grace euill cousall.
Weill, weill, (quod scho), at leist, brother, lat se
Gif ze can set me at full libertie;
For I am keipit as in presoun heir,
And na servand of myne dar cum me neir.
With hir fair wordis, he sat hir clene at fredome,
Be our aduyse, quhilk was bot lytill wysdome:
For to Dunbar that nycht scho raid in haist,
Behind ane man in poist, as scho war chaist.
Thair come till hir anew of men fra hand,
Quhilks chaist zour Lords sone efter in Ingland,
Quhair thay remanit baneist and absent,
Quhill France and Ingland maid thappoyntment.
This, quhen we thocht ilk thing wes weill aggreit,
Zit wes zour Quenes hart na wayis satisfeit,
Bot with Bothwell scho maid conspiracie,
Seikand the way to cause hir husband die.
Heir we lat pas greit tressounis thay committit,
Quhilks, for schortnes of tyme, we haif omittit.
Bot of zour King, schortly for to declair,

Bothwell with pulder blew him in the air,
At hir requeist: quhilk is ane thing weill knawin,
As sen syne tauld sum seruands of thair awin;
The quhilk Bothwell, for all his fylthie body,
Maryit he was vnto ane nobill Lady;
Bot zit zour Quene, be wrang law falslie forsit,
Maid him and hir from vther be deuorsit.
    Than went our sone schortly in France agane,
Quhair we thre togidder did remane:
Sa, in our absence, maryit scho Bothwell,
Quha did hir husband kill, as thow hard tell.
Of this zour nobills culd not be content;
With burghis and cōmounis forwardts furth thay wēt,
Quhair thay met vther vpon Carberrie hil;
Tuke hir; he fled, and na blude thay did spill.
Than in Lochleuin scho wes put as in waird,
Thocht efterwart scho had ane sleuthfull gaird.
Zit did zour Lords auyse thame of ane thing,
To crowne hir sone zour Prince, & mak him King:
Quhilk act thay did, with his motheris consent,
Confirmit be the Lords in Parliament;
And than, because he wes ouer zoung to gouerne,
Amangis thame selfis wyslie thay did discerne
For to elect our sone, in his absence,
Regent to be vnto zour zoungly Prence:
Than did zour Lords send for him to cum hame:
With him come we, baith Honour and Gude Fame.
All burghs and cōmounis, halelie did yai loif him;
Bot sindrie said, that thay wald haif nane of him:
Sa gydit he, ane quhyle, with paciencc,
Quhill he mycht to his fais mak resistence.
Bot at the last, zour Quene wes lattin furth,
Conuoyit away be sum wes lytill gude worth;
And spedelie to Hammiltoun scho went,
Quhair scho fand men anew incontinent,
The quhilks dispysit vs, Honour and Fame,
Thairfoir all turnit to thair vtter schame.
Our sone and we wer than in Glasgow towne;

To hald the airis in thay parts he wes bowne :
Than come scho fordwart, with hir strenth & fors,
Ma than seuin thowsand, quhat on fute and hors ;
Zea, twa for ane, we think thay wer agane vs :
The towne to leaue, yai thocht than to cōstrane vs :
Bot we the Langsyde hill befoir thame wan,
And be Gods grace, disconfeist yame :   Ilk man
We tuke and slew ; scho fled into Ingland,
Quhair scho is zit, not at hir awin command.
Ovr sone cryit out, Lat na mair blude be sched,
Bot tak and saif the rest that now be fled.
In deid, yat day, yair wes slane in yat place,
Ma Hammiltounis nor ony vther race.
Howbeit the rest of thame, maist gratiouslie,
He did intreit with pardoun and mercie :
Thay him rewardit with ingratitude,
And traterously this nycht hes sched his blude.
    Efter this feild, our sone in Ingland went ;
We left him not, bot wes with him present.
Than did sum Lords lyft vp yair hornis on hie,
Quhilks did withstand zour Kingis authoritie ;
Bot he come hame agane, or euer thay wist,
And zair rebellioun schortly did resist.
Sone efter him, did cum hame my Lord Duke
For ciuil weir : yan euerie man did luke.
Bot God the Lord brocht all sa weill to pas,
That without blude, all weill aggreit was ;
Except my Lords the Duke and Hereis, baith
Wer put in waird, yair wes na vther skaith ;
Quhair thay ar zit, vnto yis tyme and tyde,
And will be thair quhill sum men get ye gyde.
    Sone efter this, to Liddisdaill he went,
Quhairof the theifis, and sic, war not content ;
For to thair chyftanis he maid biggingis bair,
As efterwart thay did repent full sair.
Than come he north schortly, he tuke na rest,
Till all that countrie had componit and drest.
The hiest of thame all, that wald rebell,

He maid him stoup, and als to knaw himsell.
This being done, amang all vther thing,
He maid thame all subscriue vnto the King,
Baith far and neir, of hie and law degree,
Acknawledgeing the Kingis authoritie.
Except Lord Fleming, nane war in this land,
Bot to the Kingis grace had thay geuin thair hand,
    Sa hauing stablischt all thing in this sort,
To Liddisdaill agane he did resort;
Throw Ewisdaill, Esdaill, and all the Daills raid he,
And also lay thre nychtis in Cannabie,
Quhair na Prince lay thir hundreth zeiris befoir;
Na theif durst steir, thay did him feir so soir.
And that thay suld na mair thair thift alledge,
Thre scoir and twelf he brocht of thame in pledge,
Syne wardit yam, quhilk maid ye rest keip ordour;
Than mycht the Rasche bus keip ky on the bordour.
    Quhen he this thocht till haif bene at his eais,
In come on him the Quene of Inglandis fais,
The quhilks to seik he tuke purpois fra hand,
Without delay he gat Northumberland;
He socht him so, and fand him at the last,
And pat him in Lochleuin, quhair he is fast.
    Than went he suddanly to Dunbartane,
In snaw, sleit, drift, wind, froist, hailstanis & rane.
In deid, lyke snaw, thair words wer soft and fair,
Lyke sleit, quhylis scharp, with promysis maist bair;
Lyke dryft also, thay did driue of the tyme,
Till ane fals tratour suld commit this cryme.
Lyke as the froist dois freis vp all fresche watter,
Thay freisit him in Stirling on this mater.
Windie it was, and windie was the sessoun;
As is ye Frèche prouerb, *grand vant, grād tressoū.*
With scharp hailstanis thay schot him traterouslie,
Lyke rane in greit wind, syne fled suddanlie:
Sa may we weill the tyme to deid compair,
For all wes trublit, baith se, land, and air.
    On Sonday than, the quhilk wes zisterday,

Vnto this towne he come, soupit and lay,
Dynit this day, and at aleuin houris,
Thair wes ane knaif of his conspiratouris,
Ane Hammiltoun, within the bischoppis stair,
Quhilk schot him, as thow seis, withouttin mair;
Syne at the bak zet suddanlie he fled;
Sum saw him weill, and followit his hors tred;
Quhilk hors was knawin belaging to Lord Johne,
Quha with the rest this act maid to be done.
Bot to our sone we keipit cumpanie,
Quhilk in our armes within this hour did die.
　　Than deit with him all vertus cardinall,
Than deit with him justice imperiall:
For in his tyme Gods word was trewly preichit,
And in his tyme collegis rychtlie teichit.
Not only lufit he vprychteousnes,
Bot als he hatit vice and vitiousnes:
Not only did he lufe God, and him ken,
Bot als he hatit all vngodly men.
To sessioun als, ilk day he went to se
Gif justice wes thair ministrate trewlie.
The riche and pure, he did alyke regaird;
Puneist the euill, and did the gude rewaird.
He wald not lat the Papists cause ga bak,
Gif it wer just, bot wald be for him frak:
He wald not thoill the proud oppres the pure,
Sa far as he had regiment and cure:
He did disdane pryde and ambitioun:
He lufit men meik of conditioun:
He did disdane all foull and fylthie word,
In ony sort, outher in eirnist or bourd:
Maist diligent he wes to ryn athort,
To gif the wedow and fatherles confort:
Maist diligent to heir the pure mānis bill,
And gif answer according to Gods will.
Sober he wes in meit, in drink, and claithis;
He wald not thoill blaspheming, nor na aithis.
Reddy to heir, quhen ony man spak to him,

Mistraisting not yat ony wald vndo him.
Peace and concord, ouer all for to meintene,
The pure durst leif yair bestiall on the grene.
For slauchter, mercy wald he neuer grant;
Baith murtheraris, theifis, and vitches he did dant.
For to be schort, lay all zour heidis togidder,
Gif ze can find amang zow sic ane vther.
   Get vp! (quod thay), it is almaist midnycht:
With yat, all thre, thay went out of my sycht.
   Because ane man wes knoking at the zet
Quhair I did ly, and had myself forzet;
Sa rais I vp, all clad in bute and spur:
Quhais yat (quod I) yat knokis at the dur?
I, zour gude freind and nychtbour, answerit he;
Gar oppin the zet, gude brother, now lat se.
Brother, (quod I), how dois my Lord, I pray zow?
Departit, oh! (quod he), and deid, I say zow.
Allace! (quod I), I find my dreme ouer trew,
And that, full sair, all Scotland sone will rew.
Than to the palice went I, and zeid in;
Thair weiping vocis hard I making din.
Within the chalmer I went quhair he departit,
Quhilk sycht to se, God wait, maid me sair hartit.
Than come I furth agane, and saw my Lady,
Quhais horsis at the foir zet wer alreddy.
To Edinburgh scho went, with hart full soir.
Reuenge his deith, ze Lords! I say na moir.

EPITAPHE.

Heir lyis the corps (gude pepill) of a Prince,
Quhais saule in heuin with God is glorifeit:
James Regent was murdreitt without offence,
Be ane false tratour, sa knawin and notifeit,
Quha wes anis bound to haif bene justifeit.
He gaif him grace, allace, aganis all ressoun.

O Hammiltoun, it schawis weill thou wes feit
Be all that Clan for to commit this tressoun.

Quhat mouit the to do yis insolence,
And mak yat clan sa to be falsifeit,
To quhoe, God knawis, he schew his greit clemîce,
Thocht thou with tressoun hes him gratifeit?
With all gude vertewis he wes amplifeit;
With all foull vice thou hes defylde yair maisoun.
Resetting the, now haif thay varefeit
That thay bene weill contentit of this trasoun.

Indeid, I grant that his greit patience
Aganis him self this deid hes testifeit;
For had he put zow doun with diligence,
Zour tressoun had not this bene ratifeit.
Ze wer anis all in his will signifeit
At the Langsyde, sensyne in euerie sessoun:
Now with greit honour is he magnifeit,
And with greit schame ze sall thoil for this tressoū.

OBIIT XXIII JANUARII,

ANNO DO. M.D.LXIX.

Imprentit at Edinburgh be Robert Lekpreuik.
Anno Do. 1570.

XI.—The Deploration of the Cruell Murther of James Erle of Murray, Umquhile Regent of Scotland, togidder with ane admonitioun to the Hammiltounis Committaris thairof, and to all thair Fortifearis, Mantenaris, or assistence, with ane Exhortatioun to the Lordis and Nobilitie, keiparis and defendaris of our Kingis Grace Maiestie.

[STATE PAPER OFFICE.—Scotish Series, Volume 17, (*February*) Number 17.—LIBRARY OF THE SOCIETY OF ANTIQUARIES OF LONDON.]

QUHILE as with flesche, and blude we go about
The wondrous warkis of God for to discriue
Paus quhil we pleis, we sal not find yame out
Bot sall Judge God, aganis all ressoun striue.
Quhen as he tholis, proude Pelours to depriue
The lyuis from sic, as halelie wes his,
Be Cruell murther, thame reuthles for to riue
The flesche of man can neuer considder this.

Bot quha that wald the mater vnderstand,
He man luke lawer, and enter in the Spreit,
And than he sall persaif, the cause fra hand,
That God wirks na thing bot as a Judge discreit,
Quhen as the pepill with sinnis ar replcit,
Without remors, as thay ar, at thir houris
Than, to that end his plaiges he may compleit,
He takis from thame thair Godly Gouernouris.

¶ And this he blis mony sindrie sortis,
Sum tyme be seiknes, in to thair beddis to be,
Sum slane be tratouris, bot not for thair comfortis,
Bot to that end, thay suld distroyit be.
And rutit furth clene out of memorie,

He tholis sic wickit, proude Conspiratouris,
To execute thair lurking traytorie,
And bring to deith thair godly Gouernouris.

1 Jo. 3. We se also the wickit of the warld,
Still beir the godly, at deidly Indignatioun,
Sum tyme be tratouris, ar Innocentis overharld,
And thocht trew men, haif heir bot tribulatioun.
We suld not haif sic thingis in admiratioun
As gif it wer, ane new thing chansit to man
For sa it was, euin from the first Creatioun,
And still hes bene, sen that this warld began.

This mortall feid, this haitrent and Inuie,
Did first begin, as Gods awin buke dois tell
Gen. 4. As in the Genesis we may plainly spie,
Betuix twa brether, Cain and Abell.
Cain aganis his brother did Rebell,
And suffeit not, to sched his saithles blude
And for this cause, I pray zow mark it well.
His warkis war euill, and faithfull Abells gude.

☞ And of thir twa, this haill warld did descend,
Quhilk neuer can, amangis thame selfis aggrie,
Bot baith thair offspringis may be cleirly kend
Curst Cains Clan, be thair Impietie.
And Abells seid for richt and equitie,
And thus all murtherars ar discendit doun
Of Curst Cain, and his posteritie,
As is the Tyrane and Tratour Hammiltoun.

For luke how Justice was the verray cause
To curst Cain, his brother for to kill,
Sa is it zit, but dout, the only clause
That moues the wickit, vnto thair Raging still.
Thay gloir na thing, bot euer into Ill,
And makis thame euer, but mercy to maligne
And quhen thay may, thair wickit wayis fulfill,
Thay will not thole, ane godly man to Rigne.

¶ The Probatioun heirof.

To preif this part, I plainly mycht propone,
Exemplis seir, maist Notabill and trew,
Bot for thame all, I will bot vse heir one
Of our deir Maister, and Sauiour Christ Jesew.
In quhome na spot of sin, it neuer grew,
Zit nocht theles, the bischoppis mycht not byde him,
Quhill on a Croce, on lenth, and breid him drew,
And hangit vp for spyte, twa theuis besyde him.

For to mak mentioun of the marterdome
Of Gods Prophets, it wer sum thing to lang,
And for to reckin, the reuthles Rage of Rome
Quhair sindrie godly, thay dulefully doun dang.
It wer prolixt, thairfoir I let thir gang,
And to my purpois, bot proces mair proceid
How wickit men, delytis ay in to wrang,
And may not suffer, to haif ane godly heid.

Sen sa it was, that Christ baith God and man,
With his Apostills, and Propheits gat na rest,
Bot euer hatit be Cain, and his clan,
As God's trew word, dois mak it manifest,
We suld not grude, howbeit we be opprest,
As was our Maister, and brethrene vs beforne
Bot be assurit, it will cum for the best,
And better to thame that thay had neuer bene borne.

I mene not heir, that thay suld pas vnpunissit,
For thair trespas, nor neuer sic thing thocht,
For than suld Justice and Law be clene diminissit
Gif thay war spairit, this wickit wark hes wrocht.
That our gude gyde to bailfull beir hes brocht
Lat vs assemble thairfoir with curage stout,
And lat thay tratouris, out throw this land be socht,
And neuer leif thame till thay be rutit out.

Ane Admonitioun to all the Hammiltounis and thair assistaris, counsallaris, and pertakeris of this maist vile and abhominabill Murther.

O Teinfall tratouris, quhy did ze him deuoir ?
Maist schamefullie, that puneist euerie vice,
Quha wes the cheif mantenar of Gods gloir
In to this Realme, and lufit all Justice,
Zour bailfull blude can neuer pay the price
Of his deir deith, wrocht be zour wickitnes.
Wa worth zou Uillanis, that slew that Prince maist wise,
For na cause ellis, bot for his rychteousnes.

For sen ze first in to this Realme began,
Ze wer ay callit for zour tyrannie
Strypis of the Schyre, the maist vnworthie clan
That euer wes bred, or sene in this countrie.
As schawis weill bé zour Genalogie,
For thift and murther, reif and oppressiounis,
With Guldis and Rukis, blasnit equallie
Is the auld armes of the Hammiltounis.

And quha wald seik, ane man but conscience.
Ane Renegat for to deny his Creid,
To tak ane pure man vnder his credence
Syne cut his throt, and toung out of his heid.
To put ane hundreth for to beg thair breid,
And bring Just men vnto confusioun
To do ane horrible, and ane vnworthie deid,
Seik neuer farther than ane Hammiltoun.

Ane midding tuilzour, but manheid at assay,
Ane vailzeand tyrane, ane febill Campioun,
Ane wyfe with Childe, that manfully can slay,
Ane noysum nychtbour, proude in oppressioun.
Ane teinfull tratour of rycht Successioun,
To Crucifie Christ, that compts not a feg,

5

I say to zow for schort conclusioun,
Come neuer ane gude byrde of the Deuillis eg,

How horriblie ze spuilzeit vnder nycht
In his awin hous, maist schamefull for till heir,
And Nobill Lord, James of Torphichen knycht,
He can declair, gif ony man list speir.
Ze left him not, ane Malze nor Deneir,
Syne vnder truste, neir schot him and his wyfe,
And Tymothie wes in ane felloun feir
Bot prasit be God, thay chaipit with thair lyfe.

Our Kingis Grandschir, at Lithquo feild ze slew
Baneist his gudschir, from his kynde heritage,
His Fatheris murther also ze cleirly knew
Myschantly hangit, ane wickit vassalage.
Thir ar zour warks, euin fra zour first barnage,
God wait gif ze be Jalps to hald in stoir
Or bony byrdis, to keip into ane Cage,
Christ keip our King out of zour handis heirfoir.

Ze slew our Regent, because his warks wer gude,
Quha was the Lampe of lycht in to this land,
As houngrie tykis, ze thristit for his blude,
Nu. 25. That sauit zow, quhen ze wer in his hand,
Gal. 5. Quhen ze culd not resist his forcie wand,
Joa. 3. Ane suithfast sentence, heirfoir I sall zow tell
Gen. 9. Pronouncit be God, I lat zow vnderstand,
Apo. 3. All Murtherars thay sall Inherit hell.

¶ **Ane admonitioun to the assistaris, counsallaris, by lyaris, and Reioysaris in this maist detestabill murther.**

Nocht only thay, bot all that sic asisstis
Or fortefeis, or ony wayis mantenis,

Incurris his Curse, now luke Gods buke quha listis
For it is not mans Judgement sa that deims,
And quha that this soir sentence small esteims,
The tyme sall cum, that he sall weip and murne,
Quhen hiddeous Hell with greuous glowand gleims
Baith body and saule for euer mair sall burne.

Moirouer all thay of that Genalogie,
And of that Surname, we mak thame Intimatioun,
Thay salbe repute of this foule cryme gyltie
Quha nocht compeiris to mak Purgatioun,
Farther all thay, geuis consultatioun,
Or thame assistis in to this fylthie fact
And not compeiris to our Conuentioun
Thay salbe halden pertakeris of this act.

Be war heirfoir, and be effrayit of this,
Lat sic tryit tratouris defend thair awin curst cause,
Tyne not zour landis, and els the hevinis blis,
Bot be obeysant to God, and mans Lawis,
And be not flatterit with thair vaine wordis & sawis
For thay can not of this foule fack be clengit,
Thocht man wald wink, zit God yat all thing knawis
He will not leif this vile wark vnreuengit.

The exhortatioun to the Lordis and Nobilitie persewaris of this cruell Murther, and defendaris of our King.

5. God sayis my Lords, he wil be aduersair,
   To bludy boucheris, that stand of him na feir,
   My Lords, thir wordis suld carage zow far mair
   Nor the haill help of man baith far and neir.
   Fall to heirfoir with blyith and mirrie cheir,
   Wear anew, thairfoir heis vp zour hartis,
   And fordwarts marche, sa sall we se and heir
   Quhat lurkand lubers will tak thir Lymmers parts.

Thay fylde the feilds befoir, quhen first yai fauchs
Quhair tha for ane, wer aye number thre,
We trowit from thence, thay suld haif sittin saucht,
And suld haif tyrit of all thair tyrannie.
Bot now allace, the contrare we may se,
Our vaine pietie, hes maid vs this fals traine.
Gods Curse thairfoir lycht on thame all for me,
That euer hes pietie or reuth on thame againe.

Gif ze do nocht Reueuge this fylthie fact
Ze will be schamit, ze may weill vnderstand,
And will be namit, ane fals and febill pack
That euer rang in ony Realme or land.
With curage heirfoir, now be the baner stand,
And wyn for euer honour and Renoun,
Do ze not this, ze ar ane bailfull band
And seruis nocht ells, bot Goddis malesoun.

For Gods Curse, his vengance and maledictioun
Sall neuer from zow, nor fra zour seid depart,
Ze sall sustene maist sorowfull afflictioun,
That euer tholde men, in ony land or airt.
Sic hauie harme sall happen to zour hart
Gif this foule murther with silence be ouerpast,
Thir same tratouris sall mak zour selfis to smart
And salbe zour distructioun at the last.

And gif sa hapnis, ze may rycht weill considder
This plaigue maist Justly, of Gods hands ze craif,
Far better it is thairfoir to ryse togidder
For to reuenge the Murther with the laif.
Nor Gods soir wraith abone zour heidis to haif,
For the ouerseing of sic a fylthie cryme
For Gods plaigues approchis I persaif,
Gif ze prolong, schort quhyle and drift ouer tyme.

Fall to thame fraklie, to fecht thay haif na faces,
Persew thame peirtly, and ze sall se thame fle,

Rune is thair glas, and gone now is thair graces,
In to respect of this foule tratorie,
And quha supportis thame, or dois fortifie,
I hope to God that is the heid of hallous
To se thame hyntit in handis haistelie,
Syne hangit hie, but grace vpon the Gallous.

¶ The makaris Exhortatoun to all men in Generall.

Amend zour lyues, and call on God for grace,
Pray for zour King with hartie Exhortatioun,
Repent our sinnis quhill we haif tyme and space
Detest all vice, and foule abhominatioun.
Than God sall gif vs confort and consolatioun,
Pray for the Nobill Quene of Ingland
Quha in our neid still sendis vs supportatioun,
Hir grace, lang space, may in gude weilfair stand.

¶ So be it.

¶ Imprentit at Edinburgh be Robert Lekpreuik.
Anno Do. 1570.

XIII.—The Regentis Tragedie ending with ane exhortatioun.

[BRITISH MUSEUM.—Roxburghe Ballads.   Volume 3.—STATE
     PAPER OFFICE. Scotish Series, Volume 17. (*February*)
     Number 16.—LIBRARY OF THE SOCIETY OF ANTIQUARIES OF
     LONDON.—A few Copies Privately Printed by W. William-
     son, Esq., 23 Carlton Hill, St. John's Wood, London.
     May 1872, Sm. Quarto.]

AMES, Earle of Murray, Regent of Renoun,
Now lyis deid, and dulefullie put doun,
Murdreist but mercy, murnand for remeid,
Quha lost his lyfe in Lithquo with ane loun,
Giltles God wait betraist into that toun,
Slane with ane schot, and saikless put to deid :
Feit be our fais throw fellonie and feid ;
Hangman to Hary, now Burrio to hir brother,
Weill may this murther manifest the tother !

Quhat leid on lyfe wald nocht lament his lose ?
Wais me to want him, is the commoun voce
For sic ane Prince sall neuer pure man haif,
Tint be ane Tratour, steilling vp ane close,
Possest in purpois, lyfe for lyfe to cose,
Bot na compair, ane Kings Sone to ane knaif,
Sen he is gone agane my will to graif,
Throw all this Realme I dar weill mak this ruse,
Rang nocht his maik sen buryit was the Bruse.

To keip gude reule, he raid and tuke na rest,
Baith South and North, and sumtyme eist & west,
All to decoir our commoun weill ze knaw,
Be quhome lat se wes Pirats sa opprest ?
Or zit the theiffis sa dantonit, dung, and drest ?
Argyle and Huntlie hid thame baith for aw,
And quhen he mycht, he myst nocht in the Law

Twyse on the day, and sleipit nocht in sleuth,
To se na buddis suld beir thame by the treuth.

Of this foule fact suppois our fais be fane,
Zit efter Moysis, Josua come agane,
To gyde the pepill, geuand the gloir to God:
Suld thay succeid that hes him saikles slane ?
Be war with that, I wald ze war not vane,
To haif zour waik anis wirryit with the tod,
Think ze with ressoun thay suld reule the rod,
With double murther maid vs all ado ?
And with our King wald play Cowsauly to ?

Pray gif ze pleis, I warne zow ze haif neid,
To keip our King fra cankrit Kedzochis seid,
That daylie wayis Inuentis to put him doun,
His Grandschir slane at Lythquo gif I leid:
His gudschir thryse hes left this land in deid,
Hary at midnycht murdreist in this toun:
His Cousing last, and zit thay clame the Crown,
Blynd Jok may ges, gif thir be godly deidis,
Brunt be zone Bischop in quhome this barret breidis.

Cut of that Papist Prothogall of partis,
That with his lesingis all the laif peruertis,
Syne Joyne zour forces to the feildis but feir,
Because ze tak zour stoutnes all in startis:
To Hammiltoun in haist quhill ze haif hartis,
Deuyse sum way to pay zour men of weir,
Fra he be gane ze neid nocht gather geir:
Fecht weill, and war yame, and wyn the ryches yair
And gif ze de, in deid ze neid na mair.

Curst be ze baith, bischop and bothwell hauch,
For this foule deid, zour seid man rak ane sauch,
Gif ze twa want the widdie, now thay wrang zow:
Lythquo lament, zour burges may luke bauch,
In beir seid tyme zour burrow rudis by fauch,

Cause of this murther laitly maid amang zow,
Or gif I trowit it helpit ocht to hang zow,
Sa suld ze die: and syne zour towne in fyre,
Sum part for sythment to asswage our Ire.

Ouer thir twa housis, for thair deids inding,
The hand of God dois ouer thair heidis hing
Thame to distroy, I dout not in our dayis,
Hepburnis will wraik, for wyrrying of the King,
Bot Hammiltounis fy, this was ane foular thing:
Is this zour ferme Religioun? zais? zais?
Sic tyme sall cum I trow as Thomas sayis:
Hirdmen sall hunt zow vpthrow Garranis gyll
Castand thair Patlis and lat the pleuch stand still.

Apperandly thir plaigis are powrit out,
To wraik this warld, and wait ze quhair about?
Because we want na vice vnder the heuin:
Sen double murther markis to reule the rout,
With Niniueitis lat vs ga cry and schout,
For to retreit zone sentence Justly geuin,
Zit thow gude Lord that Judgis all thingis euin,
Seand the perrell that ouer the pepill standis,
Lat nocht thair blude be socht at saikles handis.

Now Lordis & Lairdis assemblit in this place,
Ouer lang we talk of Tragedeis allace,
Away with cair, with confort now conclude:
As gude in paper as speik it in zour face,
Gif murtherars for geir get ony grace,
Ze will be schent, think on I say for gude
Sen art and part, ar gyltie of his blude;
Quhy suld ze feir, or fauour thame for fleiching?
Ze hard zour self, quhat Knox spak at the preiching.

First on the feildis mak schortly to lat se,
We want bot ane, and quhat the war ar we?
Sen God wes pleist to pas him out of pyne,

All men on mold ar markit for to de,
With tyme and placc appointit, sa wes he:
Lat nocht in cair zour curages declyne,
For want of ane I wald nocht all suld tyne,
Gar reid at Roxburgh quhen the King was slane,
And zit ane woman wan the hous agane.

Sen than be wemen douchtie deidis wer done,
Barronis be blyith, and hald zour hartis abone,
And lat vs heir quhairfoir ze hapnit hidder:
Thay are na partie, and ze speid zow sone
Albeit that boyd be daylie in Denone,
Lang or Argyle be gadderit in togidder,
Quhen all is done, the counsall may considder,
Quhat is the maist zone murtheraris may do,
Suppois that Huntlie wald cum help thame to.

Had we ane heid wald stoutly vndertakit,
The Barronis sayis thay suld be bauldly bakit,
Mycht thay for tyritnes trauell of thir tounis:
Quhy stand ze aw of Tratouriris twyse detractit?
Think ze not schame to heir zour Lordschipis lakit?
Sum feiris zair flesche, sum grenis to gadder cronnis,
Sum happis thair heids, sum belttis zame vp in gounis,
Luke gif zour partie prydis thame in thair spurring,
Keipand the feildis and fryis not in thair furring.

Wa worth the wyfis that fostred zow and fed,
Ze dow not ly vnles ze haif ane bed,
Keip zow fra cauld, haif claith within zour scho:
I think greit ferly how ze can be red,
Or fray at thame, that last befoir zow fled,
Wantand thair Quene, syne God agane thame to
Quhy ly ze heir with lytill thing ado?
The Barronis biddis zow schortly byde or gang,
Curage decayis fra Scottis men tarie lang.

Haue Lyounnis lukis, and than mak me ane lear,

Be Hanniballis, and heis zour hartis sum hear,
Bot keip not capua, quhil zone Knaifis incluse zow
He neidis not work that hes ane gude ouersear,
Nane neid ze fetch, swa that zour hartis war frear,
Bot be my saule my self culd neuer ruse zow :
I knaw weill for this cryme, Christ sall accuse zow,
For spairing Agag, Saull was puneist sair :
Swa sall he zow, I dar nocht say na mair.

The Lord of Hostes that heuin & eirth commandis,
To keip our King from all vnhappy handis,
The Quene of Ingland and hir Counsall to :
Ze feir the Frenchemen suld ouerlay thir landis,
Bot I heir say be sum that vnderstandis,
The Doctouris doutis bot thay haif mair ado :
Our Quene is keipit straitly, thair stands scho :
Ingland will help zow, and ze help zour sellis,
And be the contrair, craif thame na thing ellis.

This fair ze weill, I flait not to offend zow,
In sempill veirs this Schedull that I send zow.
Beseikand zow to schort it gif ze may.
Steill ze away, the wyfis will vilipend zow
And gif ze byde, the burrowis will commend zow
Best wer I think mycht we preuene zone day
Thair Semblie beis on Sonday I heir say
In Glasgow towne, thinkand to fecht or fle :
It lukis weill thair, ze get na mair of me.

Finis.

The Tragedeis Lenuop.

As men recordis, in deid my Lordis,
I schrink not for to schaw :
Suppois ze crak, ze ly abak,
And lybellis be the Law.

Ze mak not to, as men suld do,
I trow ze stand sum aw:
Suppois ze hecht, to se zow fecht,
That day will neuer daw.

Is na remeid, fra he be deid,
Na man to seik ane mendis:
Or quha is heir, dar brek ane speir,
Upon zone lymmeris lendis?
Ze dar not mum, quhill Saidlar cum,
To sa quhat Ingland sendis:
Thinkand to sayit, and ay delayit,
And swa the mater endis.

With sychis and sobbis, and beltit robbis,
Ze counterfite the dule:
Quhat douchtie deidis, to weir sic weidis,
Except it wer ane fule.
Mak of the towne, and cow thame downe,
Now or zour curage cule:
For Maddie sayis, byde ze aucht dayis,
Ze be not thair quhill Zule.

Is this the thing, quha gydis the King?
Ze can not all aggre:
Now fy for schame, feche Leuenox hame,
Ze haif nane narer nor he.
Gif he want grace, to gyde that place,
Cheis outher twa or thre:
Than war I fane, bot all in vane,
To wis and will nocht be.

And sum thair bene, waittis on the Quene,
Bot gaip ay quhill thay get hir:
And war scho heir, I tak na feir,
The Feynd aby we set hir.
For we are now, als stark I trow,
As farnzer quhen we met hir:

Quhen all is done, thay start ouer sone,
To boist and not the better.

1 think it best, ze tak na rest,
Gif ze durst vndertak it
And we be trew, we ar anew,
Ze salbe bauldly bakit.
Bot sen I se, it will not be,
That meter will not mak it:
The Feynd mak cair, I say na mair,
I rew that euer I spak it.

Finis.

Quod Robert Sempill.

Imprentit at Edinburgh be Robert Lekpreuik.
Auno Do. 1570.

XIIII.—The Exhortatioun to all plesand thingis quhairin man can haif delyte to withdraw thair plesure from mankynde, and to deploir the Cruell Murther of vmquhile my Lord Regentis Grace.

[STATE PAPER OFFICE. Scotish Series, Volume 17, (*February*) Number 18.—LIBRARY OF THE SOCIETY OF ANTIQUARIES OF LONDON.]

ZE Montaines murne, ze valayis vepe,
Ze clouds and Firmament,
Ze fluids dry vp, ze seyis so depe
Deploir our lait Regent.
Ze greinis grow gray ze gowanis dune
Ze hard rocks ryue for sorrow;

Ze Mariguildis forbid the sune
   To oppen zow euerie morrow.

Thow Lauand lurk, thow time be tint
   Thow Margelene swaif,
Thow Camomylde, ze balme and Mint
   Zour fragrant odouris laif.
Ze Baselik and Jonet flouris,
   Ze Gerofleis so sweit:
And Violatis hap zow with schouris
   Of hailstaines snaw and sleit.

☞ Thow grene Roismary hyde thy heid,
   Schaw not thy fair blew blumis:
In syne of dule lat na grene blaid
   On Lawraine grow or broomis.
Ze friutfull treis produce na frute:
   And ze fair Rois treis widder:
In earth ze sweit flouris tak na rute
   But wallow altogidder.

Cum Nettillis, thornie breiris & rew,
   With all foull filthie weid,
Now plant zow quhair thir sweit flouris grew,
   And place zow in thair steid,
Ze plesant byrdis lat be zour sang
   Zour mirth in murning turne,
And tak the Turtill zow amang
   To leirne zow how to murne.

☞ Thow luifsum Lark, & gay Goldspink
   Thow mirthfull Nychtingaill
Lat be zour heuinly noitis and think
   Hes deith for to bewaill,
Ze plesand Paun and Papingaw
   Cast of zour blyithlyke cullour,
And tak the feddrum of the Craw
   In syne of wo and dolour,

Now burne thy self O Phenix fair
    Not to reuive againe,
That we may him to the compair,
    Quhais lyke dois not remaine.
Thow Pelican prepair thy beik
    And grind it scharpe and lang,
To peirs our breistis that we may seik
    How to reuenge this wrang.

All birdis and beistis, all hillis and holtis
    All greinis and plesand treis,
All Lambis & Kiddis, all Caluis & Colts,
    Absent zow from mens eyis.
Ze gleds and howlets, rauins and rukis
    Ze Crawis and Corbeis blak,
Thair gutts mot be among zour cluikis
    That did this bludy fact.

☞ Ze Instruments of euerie sort,
    That gaif to mankynde plesure,
Now turne zour melodie and sport
    In murning and displesure.
Ye Sone and Mone, and Planetis seuin
    Ze glystryng starris bricht,
All ze Celestiall hoste of heuin
    Absconce zow from mens sicht.

Ye zeiris and monethis, dayis & houris,
    Zour naturall course withdraw
In Somer tyme be wynter schouris,
    Sleit, hailstaines, frost and snaw.
For why sum men dois trauell now,
    To turne all vpsyde downe,
And als to seik the maner how
    To reif the King his Crowne.

We had ane Prince of gude Renoun,
    That Justice did desyre,

Aganis quhome the Hammiltoun
  Did traterously conspyre.
Quha schot him of the Bischoppis stair
  In Lithgow thair Londoun,
To bruik this byworde euer mair
  Fy Tratour Hammiltoun.

Sen Christ hes tane him to his fader,
  This is the best remeid,
That ze trew Lordis togidder gadder
  For to reuenge his deid.
Sen thay haue wrocht sic thing agane vs
  Traist weill thay cair not neist
To kill the King, for quhy Cardanus
  The Feind pat in the Preist.

France hes na rest, yat is na bourdis,
  Thocht sum seis not ane styme.
How France dois feide thame with fair wordis
  For to dryue of the tyme.
The Frenche men sayis adueis le fein,
  Quhilk is as muche to say
Quhen euer thay bring hame the Quene,
  Thay sall repent that day.

Ye Lords that now this draucht hes drawin
  Suppois ze haue left Rome,
Zit wald ze that zour Names war knawin
  Athort all Cristindome,
Sa Nero did, bot not for gude,
  Quha brunt Rome to considder
Quhat fyre it was, syne sched the bludo
  Of his Maister and mother.

Sa was he spokin of for sic thing
  Me think as ze wald be,
That sweir oft to manteine the King
  And his authoritie.

Ze did him also King proclame
    And haldis of him offices,
Pensionis ze hald als in Name,
    With teinds and benifices,

Now wald ze change and chaisson yat
    And bring on deidly feidis,
Ze worke maist lyke ze wat not quhat
    With zour Politick heidis.
Now wyselie wirke, be not dissauid,
    For and scho get hir will,
Scho will Reuenge the deith of Dauid,
    Carbarrie and Langsyde hill.

Ze Lordis that now sa faine wald haif
    Up hir authoritie,
Can not yow clenge mair nor the laif
    Of Sum pointis of thir thre.
Heirfoir gif ye sa faine wald haue hir
    To fulfil zour affeckis,
Gif ye may get hir than ressaif hir
    With raipis about your neckis.

☞ Byde ye in Burgh quhill Michaelmes
    Your money will growe skant,
Heirfoir my counsell is expres
    That to your wyfis ye hant.
For quhy it is ane wyfis quarrell
    Ye wald sa faine set furth,
As now ye may heir Maddie tell
    It is bot lytil gude worth.

As ye haif browne now drink ye that
    Ye se how all is cum.
For had I witten that I wait
    Allace is Scotts wisdume.
Now best it war to leif sic thing,
    Lest strangers cum and wrang vs,

Ane God, ane faith, ane Law, ane King,
   Let vs obserue amang vs.

☞ And to conclude I mak ane end
    Praying our God of micht,
To saif our King and him defend
    In his vndoutit richt.
With all trew Subiectis in thir partis
    Of his authoritie :
Beseiking God to ioyne the heartis
    Of our Nobilitie.

Finis.

☞   Imprentit at Edinburgh be Robert Lekpreuik.
       Anno Do. 1570

XIV.—¶ The Cruikit leidis the blinde.

[STATE PAPER OFFICE.   Scotish Series, Volume 17 (*April*)
   Number 71.—BRITISH MUSEUM.—Roxburghe Ballads,
   Volume 3.]

THIS warld it waggis I wat not how,
    And na man may ane vther trow :
    And euerie man dois pluke and pow,
      And that the pure may finde,
    Our Court it is decayit now
      The cruikit leidis the blinde.

Althocht the warldlie wise be cruikit,
This commoun weill he hes miscuikit,

6

Our Lords ar blinde and dois ouerluikit
 He gydes thame as he list
Tak thay not tent he will not huikit
 To gyde thame in the mist.

☞ He halds our Lords at variance,
 He garris the tane put esperancè
Thay will get daylie help of France,
 This he garris thame confide
Sayis Ingland will bring mony Lance
 Unto the vther side.

Our Lords ar now delt in twa sydis,
And euerie faction in him confydis:
Ze will heir tell how he thame gydis,
 And ze leit zeiris few
Sen he hes maid sa mony slydis
 Trow ze he can be trew.

☞ Fra he in Court in credite grew,
 He did ay change the Court anew:
The Quene his doingis sair did rew,
 And richt sa did hir Mother,
The counsall kennis gif he was trew
 To him that was hir Brother.

In Edinburgh quhen they conuene,
Our Lords to him they gang bedene:
As he war outher King or Quene,
 He hes thame at his bidding
His craftie counsall will be sene,
 Quhen Doggs barkis on ye midding.

☞ Albeit he haif the Feuer quartane,
 He suld be made Knycht of the Gartane,
He rewlis Edinburgh and Dumbartane,
 As Maddie dois me tell:

Gif he war Pape I am richt certane
He wald reule heuin and hell.

Gif he gar Atholl do sic schame,
As to consent to bring hir hame :
And gif the gyding to Madame,
   They will put downe the King
The Crowne will alter fra that Name,
Than murderars may sing.

☞ He hes gart Hume begin to tyre,
Althocht that he gat his desyre :
Bot he will leid him in the myre
   Thocht he hecht to defend him,
And Ingland set his lands in fyre
   I wat not quha will mend him.

Als he gat Setoun out of hands,
From forfalting he sauit his lands :
Thocht he be lyand vnder bands
   He will not knaw the King :
Sen ze ken how the mater stands,
   Suld he haif leif to fling ?

☞ Our richt Regent quha was our targe
Laid sindrie things vnto his charge,
The quhilk in deid war verray large
   As is kend with anew,
Ze haif geuin him ane plane discharge
   And sayis it was not trew.

I wat ze saw neuer ane styme,
And wantit baith ressoun and ryme,
Quhen ze forgaif him all his cryme :
   And maid his oddis euin,
Thocht he be fristit at this tyme
   He will not be forgeuin.

☞ I pray zow Lordis on ather syde,
　That ze his sawis do not confyde,
　For I will sweir zow be Sanct Bryde
　　He susseis not thre strais,
　Quha suld be rewlar nor our gyde
　　May he bruke that he hais.

All thir maters he dois bot mock,
He hes deuysit mony sic block:
He can begyle ane Landwart Jock,
　Except he ken him weill:
Thay say he can baith quhissill and cloik;
　And his mouth full of meill.

☞ My Lordis quhat is this that ze mene
　I thinke the holkis ouergangis zour ene,
　I wald sum man wald scheir zow clene
　　That ze micht ze thir faultis,
　And be not blinde as ze haif bene
　　Nor led with thame that haultis.

Finis.

☞ Imprintit at Edinburgh be Robert Lekpreuik.
　Anno Do. 1570.

●❀❀❀❀●

XV.—¶ The Poysonit Schot.

[BRITISH MUSEUM.—Roxburghe Ballads.　Volume 3.—LIB-
RARY OF THE SOCIETY OF ANTIQUARIES OF LONDON.]

　　　　IF wicked vice first sen the warld began
　　　　Had age be age, but punishment Increst?
　　　　In eirth langsyne yair had been nothing than,
　　　　Saif only vice and malice manifest.
　　　　Bot to thir dayis sic meanis God ay drest,

Aganis vice that vertew ay hes streuin :
Thoche āther uther be tyme hes [   ] opprest
Last Justice Judge bure ay the ballance euin.

¶ Sa of hes plesure it plesit him prouyde
Us to exerce as ship vnder the saill :
Sum tyme in storme, sum tyme in temperate tyde
To let vs knaw this warld is but fraill
Betuix gude and euill markand our trauaill
In euills flude not menand our nawfrage :
Princes be Justice he ordanit in this vaill,
Us to conduct as Pilats dois their Barge.

☞ And sa we se in Storeis as we reid,
Ay to their dayis sum Magistrates did ring ;
Sum gude some euill, be tyme as did succeid
At quhais plesure vertew did fade or spring.
The gude did vertew, the wicked vice vpbring
Quhat plesis them the same the pepill suittis
And sa we se the maners of the King
Is ay the mark quhairat his subiectis shuittis

¶ This part to preif be yair particular liues
It war to lang in vulgare veirs expres it,
At lenth the same sen Cronickles discriues
And als experience will cause vs to confesit.
And last of all, how wicked vice Incres it
Amang ourselues throw Mareis negligence,
And how the same began to be suppressit ;
Be Murrayis meane we haif experience.

¶ Quhat vice rais vp reuolue into zour minds
Quhat sin, quhat shame, in hir last dayis did reil
That prudent Prince gif yat he tuik sum pynis
That mys to mend I hope ze haif ane feill.
Gif ocht he socht except ane commoun weill,
The gloir of God and Kingis obedience :
And in that cause maid Justice ay his sheild,
I seik na Judge bot zour awin conscience.

☞ His awin estate he cairit ay to knaw,
For pompe nor pryde can na man say he preist,
Societie he socht, and keipit curage law,
Think and alwayis that mesure was ane feist.
His peple luifit and cairit for the leist,
For profite panst not, nor his commoditie ;
In trouble trauellit : his cūmer neuer ceist
Ay to his wraik, and our vtilitie.

¶ Thus be his prudence vertew was erectit
In him the pure oppressed had releif;
Throw him Idolatrie and vice was eiectit,
Throw him God's Kirk and peple fand releif.
Throw him wes vinqueist the veildars of yis greif
Throw him yis realme fand sū stabilitie
Throw him was baneist thift, murther, & reif,
Piracie puneist and deuillishe sorcerie.

Sa vertew sprang and vice began to faide,
Oppressioun fled, and Justice tuik the place,
His godly lyfe all godly men may aide :
Be his exemple vertew to imbrace.
And als his lyfe may in ane other cace,
All Princes warne heirefter to succeid :
Thair foes to flatter that hes ane double face
And to be war to clap ane traytours heid.

Euen as the man the quhilk be musik playis
Mistonit stringis castis not away we se,
But peice and peice be sundrie wrestis & layis
Ilk ane with vther be tyme causis agre.
Euen so that Prince thocht be humilitie
His peple wyn, and concord to contrake
Bot as sum stringis will rather brek nor be,
Euin so the wickit be mercy will not make.

☞ His mercy wan : bot mair his mercy tint
Not he, bot we, his mercy now may rew

His mercy loist, we wan the swordis dint,
His mercy saifit be murther that him slew.
Suppose his mercy this bergane to vs brew
Zit mene I not bot men suld mercy vse
To penitents, quha myndis not vice renew,
Bot nane to sic continewis in abuse.

¶ His mercy saifit, quha mercy not deseruit,
His mercy did preserue the arrogant :
His mercy sum amangis us hes preseruit,
Thocht thay seme holy in deid yat ar na sanct.
His mercy saifit, we wer the better want,
Thair serpents seid to tyrans wald vs thral
Because sic peple in tyme he did not dant,
But warldly mercy Christ sufferit him to fall.

☞ For mortall malice, and curst couetice,
With wickit Inuy commonit all in Ire :
And prydefull arrogance the mother of all vice
Aganis that Prince did cruelly conspire,
His fais hartis Inflamit all in fyre,
His blude to seik Inuyfull of his gloir ;
Saikles to shuit him ane harlet feit for hyre,
Hangman to Hary, that traitouris wes befoir.

¶ O bludy bouchour bastard of Balials blude
Quha to this Realme had nother lufe nor zeill
O tressonable tratour be tresson yat thocht gude
Murdreis the Prince preseruer of this weill.
O sorrowfull shot, thy poyuson did doun steill,
Not only him, quhom wofully thow woundit :
Bot pure & riche, thy vennoume hes gart feill,
Of his deir deith the stoundis him confoundit.

☞ That shot allace yis realme hes shot in tway
That shot to vice the portis hes oppinit plane,
That shot hes Justice and vertew shot away,
That shot Idolatrie is shuitand vp agane.

Sic shottis vnpuneist gif lāg time yat remane
Vice sall be vertew, and vertew sall be vice:
Wrang sall be richt and richt salbe thocht vane
Ilk ane vnpuneist sall pleis thair awin deuice.

That shot hes sinderit quhilk was togidder knit
That shot hes cuillit our curage as ye leid
That shot hes feiblit our manly force and wit,
That shot our sichts hes blindit all in deid.
We se and spyis not our sorrowis to succeid,
We meint & meinis not this wickitness correck
We wald and will not hank yame be ye heid
Quha hes preparit the swordis for our nek.

¶ Vagabounds we wander in miserie & wo
As ship but Ruther, sa ga we now but gyde:
Weskan we scatter we wait not quhair we go
Spyis not the rock quhairō we rashe our syde
We haif na grace nor power to prouyde,
Aganis this rage and crueltie: remeid
Bot willingly allace throw arrogance & pryde
Offers this Realme as Sacrifice to deid.

In place of peace now murther weir uprasis
In place of lufe Inuy amangis vs springis
In place of Faith his friend falset betrasis
In place of rest Rebellioun with us raigis.
In place of ane, we haue so mony Kingis
The Crownit King gettis na obedience
Sū France for aide, and sum Ingland inbringis,
The ane for wrak the tother for defence.

And so this Realme quhilk enemeis oft sayit
With cruell weir and sturdie stormis fell,
Quhilk feirful force of Ingland neuer frayit,
Of France the feir, nor Spaine in iust quarrel
Quhilk to thir dayis vnuenqueist buir ye bell
Sall now allace be fatell destinie:

As Aiax wes, be vanquer of the sell
On proper knyfe constraynit for to die.

¶ Quhat wald allace our Kings & elders say,
Gif in thir dayis from heuin yat now discendit
To se this Realme so dulefully decay,
In quhats defence yair lusty lyuis thay endit.
Thay wald I trust repent yair time sa spendit
Thay wald I wait yair labouris loist forthink
To se yair Babes ye blude quhilk yai defendit
Aganis nature sa cruelly vpdrink.

¶ Justlie yis plague I dout not we deseruit
Seikand the menis of our awin mischeif :
Bakwart from God because we haif sueruit
Thairfoir we taist his punischment in greif.
Zit in his mercy haifand ay beleif
Still sall I pray his deuine Maiestie
Aganis this rage to send his releif,
Our King to saif and his Nobilitie.

Lenuoye.

Go bony bill deploir
    Of deith the dolent stound,
Quhilk did our Prince deuoir
    James Regent of Renoun.
I pray the go, declair the wo
    Sen syne that dois abound,
I gif command, throw burgh and land,
    The same zow gar resound.

¶ Our cair may moue the stonis
    And hauie rockis to rair :
Swa mony stormes at onis,
    Struke neuer land sa sair.
The cause of that, the heuins wat,
    Not I, I zow declair,

Except it be, to let vs se
How kingdomes ar bot cair.

¶ Zit lat vs not dispair
Into thir walis of wo,
God may conuert our cair
In plesure and in Jo.
He may discord, turne in accord,
And mak him freind was fo :
He may I trest, set vs at rest,
Thocht all the warld say no.

¶ It sulde releue our greif,
To se our King bening :
In him I hope releif
Of zeiris thocht he be zing.
His future age, sum great presage,
Presentis vs in his Ring :
Quha our defence, in his nascence,
Tuik haill in gouerning.

☞ FINIS.

☞ Imprentit at Edinburgh be Robert Lekpreuik.
Anno Do. 1570.

◦❯❯❯❯❯❯❯❯◦

XVI.—¶ The Admonitioun to the Lordis.

[BRITISH MUSEUM—Roxburghe Ballads, Volume 3.—LIBRARY
OF THE SOCIETY OF ANTIQUARIES OF LONDON.]

FOR lois thow Lythquo may miserably lamēt
Thy fait Infortunat, and duilfull destanie,
That precious peirle James our Regent
In the was slane, dissauit duilfullie.
O cursit hour, o deid of fellonie

O waryit hand, o wappin violent,
That spairit not his greit Nobilitie
Sa vndeseruit suddandly to be schent.

¶ In wickit hour he saift the from the Gallous
Or schew his grace to sic ane graceles grume,
Had thow bene hangit Tratour and thy Fallowis
This cōmoun weill had borne the Laurell blume
Better Justice was not from hence to Rome,
Mair quyet peace befoir neuer King heir held,
Allace that sic ane Tratour suld consume
His dayis before our King had bene of eild.

¶ Dowglas & Hume addres zow now anone,
His tressonabill dolent deith for to Reuenge :
With Atholl, Erskyn, and Stewartis everieone
Grame, and Lyndsay remember on this change.
Schaw now he lufit the manly Laird of Grange
Glenkarne, and Sempil, conuene with ane accord
Throw out this Realme lyke Ratches se ze range,
And seik thair blude that hes his body borde.

¶ All vther Erlis and Barrounis of renoun,
Conuene zour selfis with hart and haill Intent,
All partakeris to put to confusioun :
With him that slew that Abell Innocent.
And in zour harts perfytlie do it prent,
Gif one of zow siclyke had loist his breith
How day and nycht he wald be diligent
Zour cause and quarrell Reuenge vnto the deith.

¶ Edinburgh Dundie & vther Burrowtounis,
Remember how the Regent lufit zow weill
Heill nor conceill, reset nane of thay lownis,
Nother art nor part, that did his body keill.
Sen he was keipar of zour commoun weill,
Cleik on his quarrell, and schortly zow dispone
Lat neuer yat Ruffians within zour townis reill
Bot kyith now kyndenes quhen that his grace is gone.

☞ Zoung tender King now behind dois abyde
Thy seruand schot was only for thy saik,
Had he not tane thy Gouernance and gyde
Lang mycht he leuit with Lady An his maik,
Na tratour Hāmiltoun had geuin yat mortal straik
War not in hope to mak thy Grace forlorne
Thay thocht his deith wald mak thy power waik
And than obtene thay socht sa lang beforne.

¶ Bot God that hes thy Maiestie in cure,
Will fruster all thair fulische Interprysis
As war thay Bouchers thy Father did combure
Quha flemit at for thair deuillische deuysis.
Thair fact and act, all Scotland now disprysis,
Thair awin misdeidis hes sa vndone thair weill
Thay dar neuer enter in Jugement nor assysis,
Nor clame thair lands, that did thy Father keill.

¶ Quhat trow ze ·Tygers, that God omnipotēt
Will wynk unsene sic wickitnes and wrang
Ze may be sure his bow is reddy bent
Zow to ruit out, luke ford and think not lang.
Hammiltoū and Hepburne ze will sing baith ane sang
Shrewit is that seruice ze haif schawin to zour King,
Wald poysonit him self, his Father wyrreit strang,
Now slane his Regent to mak your selfis to ring.

☞ Wo worth unlefull meinis manifest,
That ze haif socht to bruik Authoritie.
Zit vn obtenit, quhill that our King may lest
Quhome Christ conserue in his Minoritie.
That tender plant our Superioritie
Suld haif, quha is our kyndely King of nature,
The King of Kingis of his Maioritie,
Mak neuer ane King ouer Scotland of a Tratoure.

¶ Wo to the scheddars of his saikles blude,
Wo cause of wo, sa mony did commend

Wo to thay Gylouris of godlynes denude,
Wo to thay Pelouris, sic Interprysis pretend.
Wo thame Inuolue, now quhen his wo hes end,
Wo and eik wrak, mot fall that bludy band
Wo will thay cry, and rew that they him kend,
For wo quhen that thay lois baith lyfe and land.

☞ Schamt is that sort, with schame yey wilbe schēt
Schamt schameles, schame hes schawin vnto yis natioū
Schamt ar yai tratouris, sic tressoun did inuēt
Schame sorrowles will be thair Castigatioun.
For schame thay dar neuer clame now dominatioun,
To purches place did sa his deith preuent,
Place haif thay loist, and fund thair desolatioun,
That socht sic place, till God had bene content.

And God thair pryde will puneis presentlie,
That dois pretend be murther manifest
To Royall roume, and heich Authoritie,
Huiking na harme sa thay may be possest.
In warldlie welth quhilk wisdome suld detest,
Quhen it proceidis of falset and Inuy :
Vain gloir, dissait, or ocht that may molest
Gude governance throw teinful Tratory.

¶ Wyse Nobill Lords my schedull now cōsidder
And gif the wysest Lord the Gouernance,
Sinder not now that ar assemblit togidder
Quhill ane be chosin the commoun weill to auance.
Sic as will puneis this last vnhappy chance,
And feiris God now sen the roume dois waik
Chosin lyke the tother, ze myster not to pans,
For in all Scotland he hes not left his maik.

☞ Now is he weill and ze in wo God wait,
Zour wickitnes and warkis hes the wyte,
Zour Inobedience hes purchessit Goddis hait :
Zour gredynes to eik zour Rentis greit.,

94   THE SEMPILL BALLATES.

In vaine ze reid the Scripture as ane ryte,
And of the pure hes na Compassioun
Thir ar the causis, that ze of him ar quyte
That rewlit zow, and wald maid Reformatioun.

¶ F I N I S.

☞ Imprentit at Edinburgh be Robert Lekpreuik.
Anno. Do. LXX.

☞)(✠)(☜

XVII.—✠ Maddeis Lamentatioun.

[BRITISH MUSEUM.—Roxburghe Ballads.   Volume 3.]

UHEN bludy Mars with his vndantit rage
With Saturne maid yis cruel cōspiratioun
And curst Juno with birnand feirs curage
Amangis Planettis had greitest dominatioun.
I hard ane voice with drerie lamentatioun
Sayand O Lord help now with thy rycht hand,
Gone is the Joy, and gyde of this Natioun
I mene be James Regent of Scotland.

¶ Quhen Lachesis hir threid had drawin to lēth
Prolonging furth this Princes lyfe in gloir,
Than Atropus extending furth hir strenth,
This fatell threid, allace for to deuoir,
Now Justice (oh) quha sal thy sword decoir?
This cōmoun weil quhat wicht sal now warrād
Sen he is gone, that Gouernd vs befoir
That vpricht Prince James Regent of Scotlād

☞ His gude beginning quha yat culd richt report
Quhen this Regioun of reule was destitude,
In plane Parliament our Nobillis did exhort,
That Innocent to tak the fortitude.
Of this fals Ile, of Justice than denude,
And with thair aithis promysit with him to stād
Justice to keip in mynde he did conclude,
Sa lang as he was Regent in Scotland.

¶ Sen Fergus dayis, his lyke was neuer none,
In equall Justice, and deidis Martiall,
Thir Realmes twa he knat vp baith in one,
Quhilk neuer Prince befoir culd do at all.
The Souage daillis he dantonit and maid thrall
To serue thair King, he gart thame gif thair bād
With fyre and sword for grace he gart thame call
That prudēt Prince James Regent of Scotlād.

☞ This commoun weill, he lufit ouer all thing,
In trew Religioun na Prince mycht be his peir
Idolatrie but reuth he did doun thring,
All sorsarars he puneist far and neir,
Na homiceid, nor theif that durst appeir,
Within his sycht for dreid of dint of brand,
Just men he maid his fallow and his feir,
This humane Prince James Regēt of Scotlād.

The devill seand this godly Prince sa bent,
Throw auld malice he gaif to rage throw feid,
His Spreit Inferne he send Incontinent,
Amangis tratours for to conspire his deid.
And cruelly but mercy or remeid,
With schot of gunne yai murdreist him fra hand,
Schort ouer twa yeiris quhē he had rung in deid
This Innocent Prince James Regent of Scotland.

☞ Ze vertuous men lament his cairfull chance,
Sen he is gone that suid zow fortifie,

All ze that wald the trew Gospell auance :
Beuaill, beuaill, for that sweit Josue.
Zour secund Moyses, that led zow throw ye se.
Had he indurit zour Canane land had stand,
Dispair not zit.   Christ will zour Capitane be,
Sen he is gone James Regent of Scotland.   ·

¶ Ze pure cōmounis that lang hes bene opprest
And ze Burrowis murne and Regrait his fall :
Gif he had leifit, na man durst zow molest
For quhy he was ane watcheman on zour wall
Now sen na Prince may leif uprycht at all,
In this fals Realme on slane in Burgh and land
Adew now Mirrour of Justice Principall,
Maist godly Prince James Regent of Scotland.

¶ This commoun weil he luifit sa tenderlie.
Quhilk to mantene na thing maid him agast
His lufe to it he schew maist faithfullie,
And with his blude he seillit it up at last.
Had he mantenit all Tratours that trespast,
His godly lyfe in Joyis zit had stand,
That wald he not, and sa this Prince is past,
That Innocent James Regent of Scotland.

¶ Now ze his followeris of his Interpryse,
Think on the murther of that Innocent,
Extend zour strenthis and all togidder ryse,
Pasendlang Clyde but reuth incontinent
Meg Lochis get, that did the mys Inuent
That Apostat that Feyndis awin Seriand
Seis not quhill he, and his curst Kin Repent,
The slauchter of our Regent of Scotland.

☞ That infant Babe, that ze haif taine in cuir
Saif him from skaith and stif togidder byde,
Remember quhat ze haif in hand be sure,
Zour fais will lauch quhen thay ze zow deuyde ;

Lat na vaine gloir covetice, nor pryde.
Expell freindschip to wrak zow and this land,
Keip the last wordis of our Just Joy and gyde,
Quhen he deceissit James Regent of Scotland.

¶ Hudge is zour fais within this fals Regioun
With Ithand trystis cōtractand vp new bandis
To bring zow to schame and confusioun,
Gaird zow zow lufe, sen ze wait how it standis.
Zour Prince and strenth, keip weill in faithful hādis
For gif zour fais tryūphis ouer zou to stād
Schaip zow for deid, or dwell in vther landis,
Sen he is gone James Regent of Scotland.

Zour cause is Just, gif ze wald all persew
Bot quhair deuisioun lurkis it is ane pyne;
Christ hes it sed, and doutles it is trew
That Kingdome sall come to greit ruyne,
Quhen that deuisioun hes his sait and tryne,
Thairfoir be war, counsall is na command:
For gif ze perische, zour cause & freindis sall tyne
For now thay want James Regent of Scotland.

¶ Greit is the danger ze stand in now but dout.
And ze haif schame fra zour purpois to fle,
Spair not for geir, bot with bauld hartis be stout
Mantene Gods cause, to commoun weill haif Es
And he that is of maist Magnificie,
Zour baner sall display with his awin hand,
To the confusioun of zour Enemie
Sen he is gone James Regent of Scotland.

O thow that art Omnipotent conding,
Thre persounis Ringand in ane Trinitie,
Help yis pure Realme, & preserue our zoung King,
Fra Schame and deid, and feid of Enemie.
Amangis our Nobillis plant peace & vnitie,
Fra mercyles Strangers saif vs with thy rycht hād

7

Our sinnis is greit, zit mercy restis with the,
Adew for ay James Regent of Scotland.

FINIS.

Imprentit at Edinburgh be Robert Lekpreuik.
Anno. Do. 1570.

XVHII.—Maddeis Proclamatioun.

[BRITISH MUSEUM.—Roxburghe Ballads.   Volume 3.]

N loftie veiris I did reheirs,
 My drerie lamentatioun
 And now allace, maist cairfull cace
 I mak my proclamatioun.
Desyring all, baith greit and small,
That heiris me be Narratioun,
Not for to wyte my rude Indyte:
Sen maid is Intimatioun.

 ¶ I do Intend, nane to offend,
That feiris God arycht,
Thocht murtherars, & blud scheddars,
Wald haif me out of sycht.
Thair malice vane, I do disdane,
And curse thair subtell flycht.
My name is knawin, yair bruit is blawin
Abrode baith day and nycht.

 ☞ For I a wyfe with sempill lyfe,
Dois wyn my meit ilk day,
For small auaill, ay selling caill,
The best fassoun I may.
Besyde the Throne, I wait vpone,
My mercat but delay:

Gif men thair walk, I heir thair talk
And beiris it weill away.

¶ In felloun feir, at me thay speir,
Quhat tythands in this land?
Quhy sit I dum, and dar not mum?
Oft tymes thay do demand.
To thame agane, I answer plane,
Quhair thay beside me stand:
Na thing is heir, bot mortall weir,
Wrocht be ane bailful hand.

☞ Awickit race of grumis but grace
Of Kedzochis curst clan,
Be tressoun vile, quha dois defyle,
Thame self both wyfe and man.
As lait is sene, with weiping Ene,
Thairfoir I sall thame ban:
Caus our Regent maist Innocent
That cursit seid ouer ran.

¶ Quhat cruelteis thay Enemeis,
Hes wrocht be tymes past,
I lat ouer slyde, I may not byde,
Sa fair I am agast
Thair anterous actis, yair furious factis,
Auld bukis quha will ouer cast,
And men on liue, can zit descriue
Thair doings first and last.

Thairfoir my lords, as best accords
Sen se are hapnit hidder,
This I will say tuix sport and play
My wordis weill considder.
And pōder yame for zour awin schame
To mark thame be not lidder:
Lat na mans feid, throw feirfull dreid,
Zour hartis mak to swidder.

¶ For I heir say, thay will display
Thair baners on the feild:
Think and but dout, to ruit zow out,
Or cause zow seik sum b . . . . . . } *
At thame, rycht fane, or . . . . ane, }
That ganzell will thay zeild,
Stand not abak (oh) febill pak,
Bot swordis leir to weild.

☞ Defend zour richt in Goddis sicht
Quhome of do ze stand aw?
Rycht few I trow, will zow allow,
Gif ze zour selfis misknaw.
Stand to thairfoir, fyle not the scoir,
But all togidder draw,
Not in Cat harrowis, lyke cankrit marrowis
For feir of efter flaw.

¶ Do ze not se that mad menez,
How thay ar warin crous?
To wirk zow tene, yai mak ye Quene,
Thair strenth and strang blokhous.
The murther fy, thay do deny,
And countis zow not ane sous
Thair proude pretence throw negligēce
Will be maist dangerous.

To Lythquo toun, thay ar all boun
Quhair thay the murther wrocht,
And thinkis to de, or fortifie,
Thair fellony forethocht,
And trewlie I, can not espy
Quhat vther thing thay socht,
Bot King put doun, & clame the Croun
Be bludy murther bocht.

¶ I pans and muse, how thay excuse
This murther perpetrate,

* Obliterated in the original.

Or with quhat grace haldis vp yair face
Quhair it is nominate.
Gif (as I trow) thay it allow,
Like Wolfis Insatiate;
Quha can repent, that thay be schent,
With blude commaculate ?

☞ Fall to thairfoir I zow Imploir,
My Lords with ane assent,
And think it lang, ay quhil ze fang,
The feiris that did Inuent
This crueltie, be tyrannie,
To sla our rycht Regent,
For thay maist sure, dois still Indure
With hartis Impenitent.

¶ That man in deid, is worth sū meid
His fault that dois confes
Bot quhat rewarde suld be preparde,
For him that dois transgres.
And will not graunt, bot rather vaunt
In his unhappynes
Maist sure the gallous, with all his fallous,
For thair vnthankfulnes.

For gif self lufe, was from abufe
Deiectit out of heuin,
Quhen Lucifer, wald be ane bar,
To God and think him euin.
Quhat sall we wene of tratours kene,
That Ithandly hes streuin
For to deface the Nobill race,
Of Stewarts od and euin.

¶ Considder weill, thair cākrit zeill
Hes thristit mony day,
For to posses but godlynes,
The Crowne withouttin stay,

As now of lait, thair curst consait,
With murther thay display:
Quhen thay thocht gude, to drink this blude
Be that vngodly way.

☞ Bot Sathan sure, dois thame allure
With wordis fals and vane:
Ay promysing, thame to be King,
Quhairof thay ar full fane.
In Paradice he did Intice,
Be subtell craft and trane,
The man first maid, sa God hes said
In Sacrede Scripture plane.

¶ He said that he, suld equall be,
To God Omnipotent,
The Appill sweit, gif he wald eit,
Quhairof was made restraint.
With small defence, he gaif credence
Bot did he not repent?
Quhen efterwart, he felt the smart,
And God aganis him bent.

☞ Sa sall all thay, yat dois yis day
With mischant mynde maling,
Aganis the treuth but ony reuth
And Crowning of our King.
And this thay muse for thair behufe,
To place thair awin ofspring,
But thay repent, thay will be schent,
And hell at thair ending.

¶ Authoritie gif Just he be,
Quhy do thay this Ill will him?
His graitfull gide, throw peuische pride
Allace quhy did thay kill him?
Thair heid supreme in to this Realme
Admit gif thay not will him

Than ze my Lords, cut of with cords
Thame will be troublous till him.

¶ Reuenge this wrang, lat tratourz hang
Gods Lawis dois sa requyre,
Lat Caleb eik, and Josue seik,
The promysit Impyre.
Thocht murmurars, and murtherars
Wald all zour deith conspyre :
In wyldernes with cursitnes,
At lenth thay will all tyre.

¶ That Campion of Babilon,
That bludy beildar vp ;
With Mytrid heid, ane homyceid,
That saikles blude dois sup.
Gar cow his Crowne, or put him doun
That he may taist the Cup
Quhair with oft tymes, for saikles crymes
Mennis lyues he Interup.

☞ And se that neuer, ze do disseuer
From first contractit band,
Quhen ze our King of zeiris zing,
Maid Rewlar of this land.
Lat not Inuy, cause sum ly by,
Bot all togidder stand :
Than God the Lord, misericord,
Will be zour sure warrand.

¶ From Cail mercat, quhair as I sat
Thir wordis I did Indyte,
The wyfis amāg, that thocht greit lang
To se my awin hand wryte.
Gif ony be, that will judge me,
To speik bot in dispyte,
Gar mend the mis, committit is,
And I na mair sall flyte.

              F I N I S.   Quod Maddie.

XXX.— 🐚 The Spur to the Lordis.

QUHAT menis thir mischant murtherars ?
    In muifing mair mischeif,
    Thir Ruggars, Reifars, Romeraikars,
    Waitting of na releif.
The mark that God gaif in his greif
To Cains cursit Kin,
Sall brod thir Burriois in the beif
For thair maist schamefull Sin.

    ¶ Bot breifly for to breif in bill,
Thay seme to be ouerluikit:
Seing our Lordis sa lang ly still,
Men meinis thay will miscuikit.
Zour siluer beis na langer huikit
Gar pay zour men of weir,
Zone bludy Boucheours or thay bruikit,
Fordwart zour selfis but feir.

    ☞ Thay Renigats, thay Rubiatouris
Hes stollin our Regentis lyfe,
Thay treuthles Tygars, thay trinfauld Tratours
Hes steirit vp this stryfe.
Of thame sall nouther man, bairne, nor wyfe
Eschew mischeuous chance:
Thay Ruffyis be thay neuer sa ryfe,
Thay get na helpe of France.

    ¶ That dolorous deid had bene to done
Had concord knit togidder,
The Lordis and Counsall of this Rome,
Of lait that war growin lidder,

That gart our Enemeis considder,
His deith for to conspyre:
Clyde banks thairfoir thay sall find slidder;
Quhen kindlit is Gods Ire.

☞ Fra he was gane, thay thocht that nane
Thair fences micht ganestand,
For why say thay thair is not ane
Dar tak the deid on hand,
That ar not knit all in a band,
We may the Crowne attane,
Zour Counsall we sall contramand,
And Crowne zow Kingis of baine.

¶ Frome lyfe to deith, gif siclyke change,
Had happinit ony of zow,
And he zit leuing to Reuenge
It had not bene till now.
Reuenge ze not his deid I trow,
Gods vengeance is decreittit:
For giltles blude ze knaw not how
Denuncit to retreittit.

☞ Argyle and Boyde sall to zow cum
To gar feche hame the Quene:
My Lords I pray zow all and sum
To mark weill quhat I mene.
It suld zow mufe all to be tene
Quhen ze the message heir,
Sen hautie wordis bot spokin bene
To gar zow tak sum feir.

¶ Ze haif deposit hir as in deid,
Not worthie for to ring,
God was zour ground, weill did ze speid
And haif set vp the King.
Gif ze depois him of his Ring,
Ze grant the former wrang:

And syne the Quene agane inbring,
Na dout scho will zow hang.

☞ Be war thairfoir or ze conclude,
That scho in Scotland cum :
For be my trouth gif that ze dude,
It semis zour glas is rune.
Better it war that ze war dum,
Nor speik zour awin mischeif,
And lippin for na gude to cum
Gif ze wirk hir releif.

¶ Argyle and Boyde befoir war with zow,
And promysit to byde,
And now thay tak on hand to gre zow
With all the tother syde.
Bot I pray God zour hartis to gyde,
For quhen thay find zow rype :
Thay sall not meiknes mix with pryde.
And playis on Dysartis pype.

☞ Fordwart thairfoir with fyre and swords,
For to reuenge this cryme,
And lippin lytill in leing words :
For thocht I speik in ryme.
Treuth it was only to dryue tyme,
That thay war hidder sent :
And had thay force or it war pryme
Ze wald se thair Intent.

¶ Zour Counsalls or thay be concludit,
The Borderis will be brokin,
Than will thay, gif ze vnderstuidit,
On pure trew men be wrokin.
With speiris (in sport) thocht it be spoken,
This murther sone Reuenge :
Thir haistie heitis sa sall ze slokin,
Thocht it seme neuer sa strange.

¶ Not on that reuthles rageing Rebell,
And his vnhappy band,
With creuell causers craifing hell,
Gods bludy curs dois stand
Bot on the countrie of Scotland,
Till that misdeid be mendit:
Thair is na mendis bot sweir in land,
With speid till thay be spendit.

¶ This Rakles Robert did report,
In raggit Ruffyis ryme
Sen Sempill solace to this sort
Auaillis maist in this tyme.
With hardy hart, Reuenge this cryme,
I say na mair Amen,
Ga speik of Eger and Schir Gryme,
And lat the Lordis alaine

¶ FINIS.

☞ Imprentit.   Anno Do.
                1570.

XX.—The Bird in the Cage.

[STATE PAPER OFFICE.—Scotish Series.   Volume 17. (*April*)
    Number 72.]

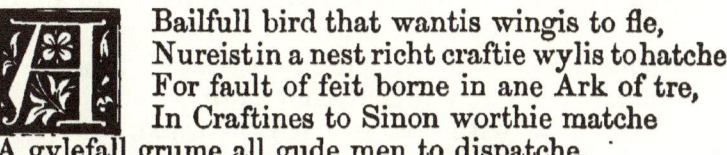

Bailfull bird that wantis wingis to fle,
Nureist in a nest richt craftie wylis to hatche:
For fault of feit borne in ane Ark of tre,
In Craftines to Sinon worthie matche
A gylefall grume all gude men to dispatche.
And be a gyde to blind men in a rank:
Zit for sic seruice seruis bot lytill thank.

¶ A Scuruie Schollar of Machiauellus lair,
Inuenting wylis anoyntit Kingis to thrall.
To heis on hicht pure Pesantis full of cair
From base estait, to Throne Imperiall.
And mychtie men lyke wretchit Irus fall,
And ly alaw lyke Loytring lubbers leud:
For feir of storme fall fane thair saillis to schreud.

☞ And Doegis craft richt cunningly Imprent
Quha can in hart pure Dauids Regne to stay:
Achitophell misordour to Inuent.
A proud Haman the faithfull to betray.
Sobney the Scribe fals tressoun to display.
Uproris to rais ane Atheist Abiron,
To Stalwart Knichtis ane gylefull Ganzelon,

¶ Ane flattring face, with outwart schaw serene
Sour Aloes with bitter gall commixt.
Ane luiring bait fond fischis to wirk tene,
Not spying deith till thay on lyne be fixt:
Quhan tyme is tynt, than find yai trew this text:
Ouir lait it is the stabill dure to steik,
Quhen sturdie steid is stollin and far to seik.

☞ To Ciuill weir, and Intestine discord,
This bird can blaw the Trumpet craftelie,
Quhais strenth and force consistis in pratting word
With Serpentis sting, vnder simplicitie.
A wylie wicht to practeis palzardrie.
With warldly wit weill furnissit at will,
Quhais Deuillische dryftis puttis all in poynt to spill.

¶ This birdis counsall confoundit hes yis land
Turnd vp syde doun of richt and equitie:
Displacit peace with discordis feirfull wand,
That mouit hes thift, reif, and crueltie,
Murther but mercy, bludie terrannie,
Wandreth wanrest, feirfull ambitioun:
Aspyring vp with pryde to heich renoun.

☞ This bailfull bird richt beinly can vpbeild
In Castellis strang hir noysum nest to byde,
The feildis plane can not fra schame hir scheild.
Quha heichest clymmis the soner may thay slyde :
In warldly wit (by God) quha dois confyde,
Will be bet doun be duilfull destanie :
And end thair lyfe with wretchet miserie.

¶ O monstrous bird God nor ye gleddis ze get
Or Rauinnis the rug with bludie beik in bittis,
The Pyet pyke thy ene on gallous set,
As Haman hangit hie on hicht with tittis.
The forkit Clauer besyde the Croce that sittis,
Mot be thy beir at thy last funerall,
Quhen Dustifit to dance sall furth the call.

☞ I traist in God, that anis sall cum the day,
Pluk at the Craw quhen barnis sall with yis bird :
Or blind Hary with hir to sport and play,
With fauldit neif and tak hir mony gird.
Keip weill thy taill gude Phillip, I am hird
The to award, from buffettis heir me by,
The bony boy with sounding voice sall cry.

☞ Dirtin bedreidis the Prouerb sayis of auld,
Ane scabbit hors will feill quhair he is sair :
Quha giltie bene of vicis lastly tauld,
Will deme of thame all men speikis lait and air :
Quhairby thair lyfe is ay bot lasting cair,
Fretting with feir in Inward conscience
As hoiplost wichtis without all patience.

¶ Euin so sum man that menis not in his mynd
Bot monstrously for to mantene misordour,
Achitophellis air, ane Ganzelon of strynd :
Falser than theuis that leuis on the bordour.
Quha craftelie his awin affairis to furdour,
Will think I speik of him in this my ryme
Johne Gukstounis Eye to bleir quhen he thinkis tyme.

¶ The Lenuoy.

¶ Jak in the bokis, for all thy mokis
  A vengeance mot the fall:
Thy subteltie, and palzardrie
  Our fredome bringis in thrall.
Thy fair fals toung, dois still Impung
  Our Crown Imperiall.
Lyke wauering thane, thy proces vane,
  Will brew the bitter gall.

☞ Thy feddrum fair, will wirk the cair
  For all thy Syren sangis,
Ane futles gyde, that mon abyde,
  To pay for all our wrangis.
With wallaway, thoull curs the day,
  Quhen Justice falset fangis,
With helteris hie, to ty on tre
  Thy poysonit Edder stangis.

Remord in mynd thy greit madnes,
Recant thy cairfall cowardnes,
Leid not our Lordis with wilfulnes,
  Lyke blind men in the myre.
Sen thow hes wrocht sic wickitnes,
Be thy auise and craftines,
Or thow depart to hell furnes,
  Repent and haue thy hyre.

¶ This bill Maddie the sendis,
And biddis to end it reid,
It schawis hir dew commendis,
But fauour or zit feid.
God send thame euil to speid:
Our King that vilipendis,
Or zit dois seik thair deid,
That dewly him defendis.

¶ Amen say ane and all,
Of faithfull in this land
And for trew concord call :
As God dois vs command.
Strang is the Lordis hand,
To keip all his from thrall :
And with his threitning wand,
Will mak his fais to fall.

Finis.

☞ Quod Maddie Priores of the Caill mercat.

¶ Imprentit at Edinburgh be Robert Lekpreuik.
Anno. Do. M. D. LXX.

XXX.—The Hailsome Admonitioun.

[STATE PAPER OFFICE.—Scotish Series. Volume 17 *(April)*
Number 73.]

Lamp of licht, and peirles Peirll of pryse,
O kenely Knicht in martiall deidis most ding
O worthy wicht most vailzeant war & wyse,
O Capitane ay constant to the King.
O Lustie Lord, that will na wayis maling,
O Barroun bauld, of Cheualry the floure
O perfyte Prouest, but maik into this Ring
O gudely Grange, but spot vnto this houre,

¶ I the beseik to call to memorie,
The worthie deids done be that Prince sinceir
King James the fyft, quha restis in heuin so hie,
To the quha was his tender seruand deir.
How in the day he vsit the as his peir,
And luifit the so as man culd lufe ane vther

At nicht in bed his fellow and his feir
Esteming the as thow had bene his brother.

☞ And how his Sone our Regent of Renoun
That restis with God, quha did thir thingis persaif,
Thocht he be gone, and with his fais put doun
Zit in his lyfe he luift the by the laif,
Ay geuing the quhat thing that thow wald haif,
Denying nocht that lay into his handis
For thy seruice thy fie was not to craif,
Bot recompancit with gold, with geir and landis.

¶ And quhen the Duke put the to banischment,
And from the held thy landis mony zeir
Thow knawis thy self gif he was diligent
To get thy pear, and slaik the of that weir.
And to the get thy lands thy guds and geir,
Thocht thair was sum that tuik thy rowmis in few
Zit he to the gat thame as is maist cleir,
To preif he was to the ane Maister trew.

¶ Fra tyme the Lord did call him to that cure,
Into this Realme that he suld ring allone
He the estemit of steidfast faith most sure
Thairfoir that hauld, and worthie hous of stone.
He gaif to the with Jowallis mony one,
As vnto him that he luiffit by the rest
The quhilk in deid he wald haue done to none,
Of all his brether that he luiffit best.

☞ Seytoun, Schir James, bot & the Schiref of Air
Efter the feild he gaif thame in thy cure
The Duke him self, and Hereis thow had thair,
For in thy handis he thocht thame ay most sure.
Sum said to him thairin he did Iniure
To put sa mony greit men in thy bandis
His answer was, quhill that he micht Indure,
His lyfe and all, he wald put in thy handis.

¶ Hauing this hauld, as I haue done declair,
In Counsall hous the Toun with ane consent
Cheissit the to be thair Prouest and thair Mair
As man thairto meit and conuenient,
Quhilk office is, in deid richt ancient,
Under the King this Burgh to reull and steir
During thy office, culd thow stand content,
Thow micht to Lordis be perigall and peir.

☞ Thir officis the farther did promote,
It neidis na preif, thy self will testifie
Amang the Lordis thow gat baith place and vote
At Secreit Counsall in materis most hie
Lyke as thame selfis sa thay estemit the,
Into thair caus baith bent Just and vpricht
Quhen tyme requyris, it suld Reuengit be,
Think on his deith, that brocht the to sic hicht.

¶ In humbill wyse heirfoir I the Exhort,
With tentyue eir vnto my taill attend
I the desyre thre thingis in termis schort
First in Gods caus be constant to the end.
Syne nixt our King, with all thy micht defend
Himself, his lawis, his libertie and Croun,
Thirdly vnto the warld thow mak it kend
He was thy Maister Bothwell hauch put doun.

¶ Into Religioun thow was richt feruent,
God gif the grace thairin to perseueir
That tyme at Leith thair was na man mair bent
During that Seige I saw the prick fall neir.
Of lyfe nor landis that tyme thow tuik na feir,
Ay venturand quhair greitest war the dangeris
For to set furth the word of God most cleir
And for to freith thy Natiue Realme fra strangeris.

☞ And now thow seis, how mony dois maling,
Baith tyme and tyde schawand thair force & micht,

8

To that Intent that Jesabell sulk Ring
Quha wald suppres the word of God most bricht,
And from our King (allace) wald reif his richt,
Quhome to thay swore thay suld be alwayis trew
Als dois defend with force baith day and nicht
Thay Tratouris strang, our Royall Regent slew,

¶ The word of God, for euer sall preuaill,
And als his kirk sall haue the ouer hand
Pharo and his, he brocht in mekill baill
Quhen he led Israell saif throw se and sand.
And als the Kingis Authoritie sall stand
As Dauids did thocht Saull did him molest
Sa sall our King at lenth posses this land
As vtheris hes in quyetness and rest.

☞ This godly caus did euer prosper still
Sen he was King, our Gouernour and gyde
Baith at Carbarry and the Langsyde hill
The michtie God was euer on his syde.
Now in the North his fais thay durst nocht byde
Quhair throw that pak did lois thair men of weir
And quhen thay war the last tyme vpon Clyde
Thair durst na fa into thair sicht appeir.

¶ Murther thow knawis will not vnpuneist be,
Nor neuer was sen Cayn Abell slew
The Scripture plane the same dois testifie
That murtherars Gods wraith sall not eschew.
Sall thay eschaip murdreist our Regent trew?
Of vertewis well, of euerie vice denude
Thocht thair war nane his deith that wald persew
The michtie God he wald Reuenge his blude.

☞ Dois thow not se ye hand of God agane yame
Wirking thair wrak, for breking his command
Thocht Lethingtoun with tratling he do trane thame
Garring thame trow the Frenche men is at hand.

And Duke De Alb ay reddy for to land
With mony Hulk on hicht of Arthure sait
Quhill that tyme cum we sall lay on the wand
And gar our fais gif clene ouir all debait.

¶ Quhat neids ye skar, thocht Ingland do support vs,
To puneis sic as proudly dois Rebell
That tyme at Leith thow knawis thay did comfort vs
And maid vs fre quhen strangers did vs quell.
And neuer socht na proffite to thame sell
Thow neids not feir, that hous thay neuer craifit,
The Regent sayis sa far as I heir tell
Wald thow be trew, thair can na better haif it.

☞ Thocht at this tyme, thow haif that warlyke craig,
And is in hart curagious and bald
God will nocht mys to scurge the with a plaig
Gif in his caus thow lat thy curage cald.
As thow may se thick scurgis monyfald,
Lich upon thame that proudly dois disdane
Except the Lord be watche man of the hald
Quha walkis the same, thair laubour is in vane.

Thow hes bene ane, sen first this caus began,
And als hes sene, how God gart it proceid
Heirfoir I pray zit do the thing thow can
Into Gods caus, and to Reuenge his deid.
And gif thow swerue, richt sair in hart I dreid,
That sindrie sall thy doingis discommend
Auise heiron sen now is tyme of neid
Mark weill I pray this Schedull that I send.

¶ Imprentit at Edinburgh be Robert Lekpreuik.
Anno. Do. M. D. LXX.

XXII.—The Tressoun of Dunbartane.

[STATE PAPER OFFICE.—Scotish Series. Volume 18 *(May)*
Numbers 23 and 24.—A Lennox Garland. Edited by
Joseph Irving, Dumbarton 1860.]

IN Mayis moneth mening na dispyte,
Quhen luiffaris dois thair daylie obseruance
To Venus Quene the Goddes of delyte,
The fiftene day befell the samin chance.
The Generall raid with mony Demylance,
Downe to Dunbartaine doand na man Ill,
Quhair furious Fleming schot his Ordinance
Willing to wraik him, wantit na gude will.

Mair I lament the great Ingratitude
Of cruell Catiues kankirt and vnkynde,
Quhat gart zow schute to slay zone men of gude ?
Lunatyke Monsters mad and by zour mynde.
Degenerat Stewartis of ane Hieland strynde,
As mix me balme and poysone put into it,
Rycht as the tre is nureist be the rynde :
Cardanus counsell causit the to do it.

That Bastard Bischop bred ane greiter blok
Laitly expremit, I neid not speik it heir,
Thocht thow be cummin of ane Royall stok,
The Kings hous and als his Consing deir.
Gif naturall kyndness coulde in the appeir,
Thow hes na cause to keip him in thy hous
For airt and pairt ressetting him I feir,
Of thy auld Lordschip beis not left ane sous.

Mycht thow not licence Inglis men to ryde
Throw all this Realme vpon thair awin expensis
Bot thow vaine bable bouistrit vp in pryde ;
Crabit but cause, and caryit by thy sensis.

Throw Sorcerie and vther vain pretensis,
Doist thow beleif the wichtnes of thy wawis
May keip zone knaif that slew our saikles Prencis
Na weill I wait God will reuenge that cause.

Gif that was foule, now foular may be spokin
Without respect to honour lyfe or landis,
Bot not the first tyme that thy faith was brokin
Thankit be God he chaipit of thy handis.
Haifand thy traist as all men vnderstands ;
Dissaitfully thow schot but ryme or ressoun
Bot had not bene ane slack was in the sands
Weill had he payit zow tratouris for zour tressoun.

Ganzelons gettis relict of Synoins seid,
Tratouris to God, and mainsworne to the King
Deir sall ze by zone foule unduchtie deid,
Betraissand strangers vnderstude na thing.
I put na doubt, man for thy deidis Inding,
To se vs shortly in thy place possest
At euerie port a spald of the to hing
As tratouris sould for schuitting vnder trest.

Makcloid, Makclaine, nor he that slew Oneill
Or zit quhat micht Johne Moydirnoch do mair ?
Ane Turk, ane Jow, or than the mekle Deill,
To thy foule tressoun trewly na compair :
Weill hes thow leird it at the Bischoppis lair,
Becum his prentise broderit in his band
Gif thow denyis, thair was ane dosane thair
Better nor thow, dar fecht it hand for hand.

Praise be to God he chaipit of that chance
Ze plaid the knaiffis, and he the Nobill knicht
I hope in God or ze get helpe of France
Of better freinds to se ane blyither sicht.
Our cause is Just, the King hes kyndly richt,
Groundit on God and the foundatioun laid :

Thocht men throw murther mene to mount on licht
Law sall he lycht downe as the Lord hes said.

Ze sawe zourselfis the Inglis men raid neir
For all zour craking caigit within ane Cro,
It is na Fables furth of France thay feir
Cum fra the Paip and the grand Pryore to.
Thay haif zour Quene in keping (quhair is scho ?)
Lang may ze luke or sche releif zour weiris
Ze will not wit quhat Inglismen can do,
Quhill Drureis bells be roung about zour eiris.

Than sall ze cry *cor mundum* on zour kneis,
Murnand for mercy, and able for to mys it :
Quhen ze luke downe to Wallace Toure and seis
Sogeouris of Berwik brekand vp zour kist.
Thair sall ze se zour bastard Bischop blist,
Out of his hoill weill houndit lyke ane tod
That bludy Bouchour euer deit of thrist
Soukand the soules furth of the Sanctis of God.

For saikles blude and murther maid sensyne,
Gone is his grace, ze haif ane godly part of him
Trewly my Lord, and I war in zour lyne
The Deill a bit sulde byde within the zet of him.
Wald ze ga seik ane Secreit place weil set of him
Cardanus pyn weill closand in ane Spreit,
Pull me out that, thair is na mair to get of him,
Bot as ane bledder blawin fra heid to feit.

In waryit tyme that Bischop hes bene borne
Mars hes bene maister at that Balials byrth,
Throw him his freinds ar houndit to the horne
Baneist and slaine, vncertane of ane gyrth
Gone is thair game, and murning is thair myrth,
Thair cattell caryit, thair Granges set in fyre,
The worlde may se thair wisdome was na worth
Murther left ay his Maister in the myre.

Now fair weill Fleming, bot foule ar thy deids
The Generall this Schedul at schort to the sends
Thow sall heir ma nouells as farder proceids,
Bot not to thy sythment as sum men Intends.
The actioun is not honest thow defends,
Gif thow be angrie with ocht that I reheirs
The narrest gait thow can gang seik amends.
Is mend thy maners, and I sall mend the veirs.

Finis.

Imprentit at Edinburgh be Robert Lekpreuik.
Anno Do. M. D. LXX.

XXIIII.—Ane Ballate of the Captane of the Castell.

[RICHARD BANNATYNE'S MEMORIALES OF TRANSACTIONS IN
SCOTLAND 1569-1573. 4to, (Bannatyne Club) 1836.—
Scotish Poems of the Sixteenth Century. Collected by
John Graham Dalyell, Edinburgh, 1801.]

AT the castle of Edinburch,
Vpoun the bank baith greine and rouch,
As myne alone I lay,
With paper, pen, and inke in hand,
Musing, as I could vnderstand,
Off the suddan decay
That vnto this puir natioune
Apeirandly dois come :
I fand our Congregatione
Was caus of all, and some
Whois aucthoris, instructoris,
Hes blindit thame so long,

That, blameles and schameles,
Both riche and poure they wrong.

These wicked, vaine veneniaris,
Proud poysoned Pharisianes,
        With thair blind guydis but grace,
Hes caused the puire cuntrie
Assist vnto thair traitorie,
        Thair Prince for to displace :
For teine I can not testifie
    How wrangouslie they wrocht,
When thai thair Prince so pitiouslie
    In prisone strong had brocht ;
Abused hir, accused hir,
With serpent wordis fell,
Of schavelis and rebellis,
Lyk hiddeous houndis of hell.

These dispaired birdis of Beliall,
Thocht nocht but to advance thaim sell,
        Fra thai had hir down throwin ;
With errore and hypocrisie,
To committ open traitorie,
        As cleirlie now is knowin :
But the grit God omnipotent,
    That secreitis thochtis dois serche
Releivit hes that innocent
    Out of thair rage so fearce ;
Provydet and guyded
Hir to vncouth land,
Whair wander and sclander
With enemeis none sho fand !

Sen tyme of which ejectione,
This cuntrie is come in subjectione
        And daylie seruitud.
With men of weir in garisone,
To the commones oppressione,

By slicht, and suddrone bloud ;
Whose craft, ingyne, and polycie
   Full reddy bent is euer,
Be treasone vnder amitie
   Our nobles to disseaver :
Some rubbing, some budding,
Thair studie thai employ,
That slichtlie, vnrichtlie,
They may this realme enjoy.

This guyding gart grit greif aryse
In me, wha nawayis culd devyis
     To mend this grit mischance ;
And als I argoued all the cais,
I hard ane say, within this place,
     " With help of God and France
I sall, within ane litill space,
   Thy dolouris all to drese !
With help of Christ thow sall, or Pasche,
   Thy kyndlie Prince posses ;
Detrusaris, refuisaris,
   Of hir authoritie ;
Nane cairand or spairand,
Shall outher die or flie.

" Thought God, of his just jugment,
Thole thaim to be ane punishment
     To hir, thair supreme heid ;
Zit sen thay war participant
With hir, and sho now penitent,
     Rycht suirly they may dreid ;
As wicked scourges hes bene seine
   Get for the scurgene hyre,
When synneris repentis from the splene,
   The scourge cast in the fyre :
Swa Mortone, be fortone,
May get this same reward ;
His boasting, nor posting,
I doe it not reguard.

"Bayth him and all thair cumpany,
Thocht England wald thaim fortifie
  I cair thaim nocht a leike;
"For all thair grit munitione,
I am in suire tuitione,
  This hauld it sall me keip.
My realme and Princes libertie
 Thairin I sall defend,
When traitouris salbe hangit hic,
 Or make some schamfull end.
Assuire thame, I cuire them,
Ewin as thei do deserve;
Thair tressone, this cessone,
It sall not make me suerve:

"For I haue men and meit aneugh,
They know I am ane tuilzeour teoch,
  And wilbe rycht sone greved;
When thei haue tint als mony teith
As thei did at the seige of Leith,
  They wilbe faine to leive it.
Then quha, I pray you, salbe boun
 Thar tinsall to advance,
Or gif sic compositione
 As thei gat then of France?
This sylit, begylit,
They will bot get the glaikis;
Cum thai heir, thir tuo yeir,
They sall not misse thair paikis.

"As for my nychtbouris, Edinburch toun,
What salbe thair part, vp or downe,
  I can not yit declair;
Bot one thing I make manifest,
Gif thei me ony thing molest
  Thair buithis salbe made bair.
Gif fyre may thair buildingis sacke,
 Or bullat beat thaim downe,

They sall nocht faill that end to mak
  The staires made in this toun.
Swa use thaim, and chuse thaim,
What pairt thei will ensew;
Forsake me, or take me,
They sall drink as thei brew!"

He bade me rise and muse na mair,
But pray to God both lait and aire,
    To saue this noble ludge,
Which is, in all prosperitie,
And lykwayis in aduersitie,
      Our Princes plane refuge.
Thairfoir, all trew men I exhort,
  That ze with me accord,
  That we all, baith in ernest and sport,
    Aske at the leving Lord.
That hanged, or manged,
Mot ilk man mak his end,
Wha dewlie and trewlie
Wald nocht this house defend!

Finis.

XXIV.—The Exhortatioun to the Lordis.

[LIBRARY OF THE SOCIETY OF ANTIQUARIES OF LONDON.]

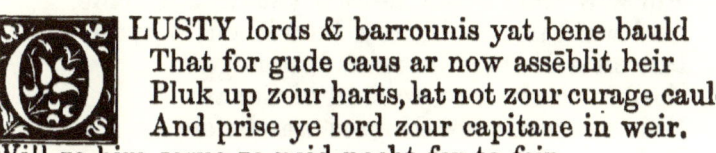 LUSTY lords & barrounis yat bene bauld
  That for gude caus ar now assēblit heir
  Pluk up zour harts, lat not zour curage cauld
  And prise ye lord zour capitane in weir.
Will ze him serue ze neid nocht for to feir,
The craft, the wit, nor policie of man

For quhy the Lord will zit zour Baner beir
As he hes done sen first this caus began.

   ☞ Haue ze forzet how that he did vs luif
That time at leith quhē strangers did persew
Our enemeis harts ze saw that he did muif
To cum ouir Tweid vs to help and reskew,
Quhair we and thay our enemeis ouirthrew
Making vs fre that lang in thrall had bene
Syne in this Realme plant.. his gospel trew
but scheding blud, quhilk hes not oft bene sene

Fra ze began from blude to purge this land
Thay murtherars thay neuer durst zow bide
He gaif hir anis, and put her in zour hand
But ony blude, vpon Carbarrie syde.
Syne efter that, quhen lymmers loust y^r bryde
He faucht for zow vpon the Langsyde hill
Zour fais wist not in what hoil yame to hyde
Sū chaist, sum slane, sum tane into zour will.

   ¶ He send Moyses to gouerne zow and gyde
Zour commoun weill to reule and als redres
quhair throw yis realme but rest did rin & ryde
To bring the same, to rest and quyetnes.
His diligence my toung can not expres
Planting Justice baith in Burgh and land
Dāting rebels, quhilk proudly did transgres
His malk rāg not, gif yat his dayis had stand.

   ☞ Richt prudently the Lord he did prouyde
For zow from tyme, he saw yat he was slane,
And wald not thoill, zow be without a gyde
But efter Moyses he raist Josua agane.
Zow to conduct to ye land of Canan
Mair Fortunat nor Moyses was befoir
In faitis of weir ane worthy Capitane
The Gentiles lands to zow for to restoir

Thair Parliament of Linlithgow he did stay
Syne Breichen gat it, bade him not ane blast
Down was geuin ouir, for feir of weir assay
Paslay he wan, and now Dunbartane last
His Capitanis maid all his fais agast
Sum tane, sum slane, sum chaist into the se
Thir deids suld not, with silence be ouir past,
Bot worthie ar Eternall Memorie.

Zour godly caus hes now tane gude succes
In Ingland lait, I neid it not declair,
Quhair my lord Chancelar tuik greit besines
With your gude freind the Clerk of Registrair
Thair trauell, wit, nor gudis yai did not spair
For to vphald the Kings Authoritie,
In presence of thay strangers that wer thair
Working for him in his Minoritie.

☞ Ze do tryumph, albeit that ze be few
Zour enemeis thay dar zow not ganestand
Quhat ye do schaip, ye Lord himself dois sew
Quhat ye duyse, he wirkis it with his hand,
Thairfoir mak haist, lat nane be in this land,
To leif lyke Lords, syne proudly to rebell
Gar thame baith sweit and subscriue ye band
Or failzeand this, do with thair leuings mell,

And gif ze dreid, yat sum will ait his ouirhaill,
And will not keip, nor zit obserue thair bands
For startling hald the kow fast be the taill
Appoint nane sic but pledgis in zour hands,
And keip thame sure, sen ze se as it stands
For cum that tyme that all yat sort desyris,
That wil but dout send zow in vncouth lāds
To seirche and seik, zour meit into the myris

Sen thair Intent to zow was neuer gude
As be thair deids richt cleirly may be sene

Gif thame na leif to play with yow buk heid,
As thay haif done, ay waitand on yair quene.
Bot puneis all the quhilk ye knaw vnclene
Of outher blude, & quyte yame for yair meids
And spair all sic will serue his grace serenc,
And had na wyte of nouther of thair deids.

I wald ye did sum mair at this Canuentioun
Nor did your fais at thairs thay held at Pace
Quhat yai did yair, I neid not to mak mētioun
Bot weill I wait, sū of yame rewis yat race.
Zit top of wit was borne vp throw ye streit,
This commoun weill had stand in better cace
Had it fallin in his toung fell in his feit.

Sen God hes put the sword into your hand
Justice to do alyke to riche and pure.
Tak heid yairfoir and na wise brek command
Be circumspect of this your charge and cure
Gif ye neglect, than God I yow assure
Will frō yat rowme thoill you to be detrusit
Planting vthers into that charge ye bure
And gif yat sword to yame can rychtly vsit.

Be bent yairfoir, and byde not this in blūder,
Baith the word of God & comoun weil auāce
Ze neid na ma bot Gedronis thre hunder
To quhip your fais or yai get help of France
Mak to lyke mē sen ye haif ordinance,
Ding draffen doū yat hald quhairin yai pryde yame
Bring in ye north with būvart bow & Lance,
Gif thay rebell with fyre and sword ouir ryde yame

How & what way ye suld appost your bordour
Maddeis counsall is verray excellent
Scho did prescriue ane gude & godly ordour
That to performe, had ye bene diligent :
Hard ye the pure, I wait ye wald lament
Sa cruelly thay Tyranis dois oppres thame,

Slaying yame selfis, yair gudis reit and rent
For feir of God, I pray yow to redres thame.

Quhat mā did hoip of grāge now dois appeir
His cloikit craft of malice dois outspring,
As in his Proclamatiouns ye may heir
He dois Rebell and will not serue the King,
Traitours yai ar agane yow to maling,
He being Crownit in lauchfull Parliament,
Quha dances fastest with him into yat Ring,
To his Crowning baith sweir & gaif consent.

Quhen the Regent gaif him that hauld ye saw
He was the Kingis, & sweir theirfoir to stand,
Albeit yat now, his grace he will nocht knaw,
Nor zit Lennox for Regent of this land.
Zit Robert Hepburne being in his hand
And saifly enterit within that place,
He said he was reset by his command
And send Robert to my Lord Regents grace.

Quhill yat he gat yat hauld and hous in hand,
Into this caus he was baith bent and bauld
Bot fra thyne furth than he gaif ouir yat band
And in this caus he leit his curage cauld.
This is the treuth as trew men to me tauld,
That samin tyme his maister was on lyue
He wald not lat him enter in that hauld
With na seruands bot outher four or fyue.

☞ He hes not onlie sueruit fra our actioun
Bot dowbill murther he dois fortifie
Desyring bargane of ony of our factioun
Of his degre, estait, and qualitie.
We haue nane sic, ye knaw in cumpanie,
Hirn for to match quhilk playit ye dowbil knaif
For first he slew ane Maister cruellie,
And syne betraist the last ye may persaif.

☞ Bot zit I knaw yair is ane hundreth heir

Of gentill men, and cum of Royall Race
On hors or fute, with quhinger sword or speir,
Dar weill him matche, & meit him face for face
And preif him fals and Tratour in this cace
He dar not fecht for this is his refuge,
He wald compeir at euery tyme and place
Gif that he had ane unspectit Judge.

¶ And als ye se, he planely dois accuse,
The Regents grace of cruell Tyrannie
Aganis his fais quhilk he dois schaw ane vse
In casting doun baith place and policie,
Sen thay misknaw thair Just Authoritie,
And will not serue, nor zit obey cpmmands
Ze may be Law subuert thair places hie
Syne tak fra thame yair lyuis geir and lands.

I knaw thir letters ye fand into Dunbartane
Quhilk dois declair his dowbil deids Inding
Is only caus, I am baith sure and certane
Quhilk garris him mak yis boist & manassing.
☞ Bot zit ye knaw it is ane commoun thing
For weill I wait ye hauc sene mony sic,
Tuiche anis the gaw, & yan the hors wil fling.
Fra tyme ye spur and hit him on the quik.

¶ It is your hous that maks him be sa bauld,
Agane baith God and King for to disdane
Except the Lord be watchman of the hauld,
The Psalmist sayis thair watching is in vane
As ye haue sene within thir monethis twane,
Ane greiter strenth ye gat as I record,
Swa will ye zone, to God gif ye be bane
And swa commits your wisdomis to the Lord.

¶ FINIS.

Imprentit at Striuiling be Robert Lckpreuik.
Anno. Do. 1571.

XXV.—Ane Admonitioun to my Lord Regentis grace.

[STATE PAPER OFFICE.—Scotish Series, Volume 21 (*November*),
Number 100.—It is there marked "1571, November.
A ballad against the bringing in of English forces into
Scotland." Another copy of the same is marked "Decem-
ber," 103-1, and Indorsed by Lord Burghley, "A ballet
to yᵉ Regent agaynst coming in of Englishmen."—Sir
Richard Maitland of Lethingtoun'sManuscript Collection
of Poems 1555-1586, in the Pepysian Library, Magdalene
College, Cambridge.—Ancient Scotish Poems, never be-
fore in print. But now published from the MS. Collections
of Sir Richard Maitland. Edited [and mutilated] by
John Pinkerton, London, 1786. — The Poems of Sir
Richard Maitland, of Lethingtoun, Knight. With an
Appendix of Selections from the Poems of Sir John
Maitland Lord Thirlestane, and of Thomas Maitland.
Edited from the Drummond MS. in the Library of the
University of Edinburgh. 4to, (Maitland Club), Glasgow
1830.—The Authorship of this Ballate is doubted, while
not unlike those of Sempill, it is supposed to be by Lord
Thirlestane. As it, however, evidently forms one of
the series, it has been judged right to reprint it here.]

MAIST loyal lord, ay for yi lawtie lowitt,
   Now be not lakkit for deloyaltie!
   Thocht to ye princis place thow be promowit,
   Be not abusit be authoritie.
Bot schaw thi treuth, and thy integritie.
Sene we sa far ourselfis hes submittit,
And king and contray Lawes and libertie
Unto thy cair, and cradit, haue committit

Thy hous hes ay bene trustie, and inteir;
Defamit nocht with fraud, and fickilnes.
Bot schaw thyself bayth scharp, sage, and sinceir;
Indewit with vertew, wit, and worthines,
Ingyne, jugement, justice, and gentilnes;
Craft, conduct, cair, and knawlege to command:

9

Heroik hart, honor, and hardines :
Or in this storme thy stait will neuer stand.

We haive the chosin to ye cheifest charge,
Oure tossit galay to governe, and to gyde.
Bewar with bobbis ! scho is a brukill barge,
And may na bitter blastis weill abyde.
Thow may hir tyne, in turning of a tyde,
Cast weill thy cours ; yow hes ane kittil cure.
Off perrellis pance ; and for sum port provyde ;
And anker sicker, quhar thow may be sure.

All Boreas' bitter blastis ar nocht blawne :
I feir sum boide, and bobbis be behinde.
Be tyde and tempest thow may be ovirthrawne ;
And mony fairlie fortouns thow may find :
As channellis, cragis, bedds, and bankis blind ;
Lekand wanluks, quhairby thow may be loist.
Bewar, thairfoir, with weddir, waw, and wynd,
With uncouth coursis, and unkawin coist.

Be war w^t strangears in thy sterne to steire
Thocht on ane course we can nocht condescend
Suppois sum present perrell now appeir
And sum hes wyritt and will no^t with us wend
Be meitar meanes thow mon that make mend
Noe dangeris be ye double to divert
Thairfor I pray the prudenthe spend
And put nocht all in perrell for a pairt.

Thow will put all intill appeirand perrell,
Gif Inglis forcis in yis realme repair.
Sic ar nocht meit for to decyde oure querrell ;
Thocht farlandis fules seme to have fedderis fair.
Be thay acquentit, thai will creip inner mair ;
And wilbe noysum nychbours, and Enorme :
And schortlie will sit till our sydes as sair,
As now the rebells, quhome thay suld reforme.

That freindschip is ay fecfullest afar;
And langest will indure with lytle daile.
I feir with ws and tyme it wirk to war,
Fra thai aganes oure partie anes prevaile.
Quha wait bot syne thai will ourselfis assaill;
Auld fayis ar sindill faythful freindis found :
First helpe the halfe, and syne o^r harrill the haill,
Wilbe a woful weilfair of oure wound.

Oure brethren may remember zit in France
The fay^t and freindschip yat thai w^t thame fand
And how thay did the word of God avance
Fra the new heavin they gat into yair hand
And how thay never pairtit w^t that pand
Quhill bayth ye syddes yame forcit to reteir
Even at Leith gif yat yow lat thame land
The samyn practis plainlie will appeir.

Be thair exempill learne experience,
Ane foreyne mache, or maister, to admitt.
Reid, fra the Saxons gat preeminence,
How sone thai socht as souueraignes to sitt.
Reid quhow thay forcit the Britoun folks to flitt;
And zit posseids that peipils propertie.
Bewar! We may be weltred or we witt :
And lykeways lose oure land, and liberty.

Ane thousand sic exemples I could schaw;
And mony nobill natiouns may name,
Quha lost at lenth thair libertie, and law,
And sufferit hes great sorrow, sy^t and schame ;
That for to helpe thair hermes, and hurte at hame,
Feycsit forayne forcis in to thair support,
Quha fuilzeit syne thair fredome, force, and fame ;
And thame subdewit in the samyn sort.

Fleand Charibe bewar in styll to fall;
And sa eschew cruill dissentioun,

That oure estait to strangers be not thrall,
The canker of our auld contentioun
Will keip na coūnand nor conventioun.
Bot gif yow gif thame credit to correct us,
Be craftie way, will, and conventioun,
And subtell slycht, thai will seik to subject us.

This realme w^t eis the rebellis may repres
We neid na forene forces for sa few
Thair landis thay loup that reagne is les and les
Sa suit not sic as seiks us to subdew
Qlk gif thow do quhat euer may ensew
To fergus blude we rather will obey
Nor in o^r tyme be trators toyitt vntrew
And gif o^r realme to Ingland as a pray.

Scotland came never zit in servitude,
Sen Fergus first; bot ever hes bene frie.
And hes bene alwais bruikit be ane blude;
And kin of kings descendit gre be gre.
Gif that it be in bondage brocht be the,
Thay wareit weir thy weirdis and wanhaip!
Thairfoir thir forene fechis sa force,
That catcheit we be nocht with ye eftir-claip.

Markand mynt at the honour, laude, and prais,
The vertew, worde, worschip, and vassallage,
Off sic as doichtelie did in thair dayis
To keip this realme from thraldome and bondage:
Mark als the vyle vituper, and the wage
Of untreuth, tresoune and of tyrannie:
And how sum hes honour, and heretage,
And Lyfes, losrt, for thair deloyaltie.

Sa for thy factis thow may be suir to find
The lyke rewaird of vertew or of vyce
Thairfoir be not sylit as a bellie blind;
Nor lett thyself be led upone the yce,
Nor, to content thy marrow's covatyce,

Put not thyself in perrell for to perish.
Nor beir the blame, quhair vthers takis the pryce.
Nor beitt the buish, that vthers eit the bereis.

The throne of tryall, and theatre trew,
Is for to regne, and rewle above the rest.
Who hes the woyne him all the world dois vew;
And magistrat the man dois manifest.
Sen thow art in the princes place possest,
Louk to be prasit as thow plays thi pairt.
And, as thow levis, so luvit be and lest;
And always delt with eftir thi desert.

Finis Amen.

Supposit be Lord Thirlstane.

XXVI.—The Bischoppis lyfe and testament.

CALLING to mynde the mutabiliteis
    Of this Inconstant warld sa variabill,
    Lyke to ane Schip that saillis on the seis
    Tost with winds & wallis Innauigabill.
Bot sen I se na plesure permanabill
Bot as the weid it widderis sone away,
Lat vs go seik the gloir Inestimabill
Quhair we man pas perpetually for ay.

☞ With spreit opprest this plungit in to cair,
Remembring me quhat mater to compyle
Endlang ane Park I past without repair

Be Snawdoun syde the seuint day of Apryle,
And as I walkit wandering not ane myle
Ane pieteous spreit appeirit to my thocht,
Sayand, allace, and waryit be the quhyle
That I was borne, or in this warld upbrocht.

☞ Can I nocht tell gif be Illutioun
Or gif be feir sic fantaseis we tak,
Bot this be said in schort conclusioun
Deplorit ane plaint, and planelie to me spak
Poetis of me hes mater for to mak
In tragedie quhat tyme I heir remanit
And with that word I went sum thing abak,
And bad say on, and with God saif me sanit.

¶ I was (said he) ane Lord leuand on lyfe,
Ane bastard barne that can I not deny
My Father was ane Erle and had ane wyfe
Thocht he abusit his body and lay by.
In Goddis Ire begottin sa was I
My mother was a Dame in Dundaf mure
Bot quhidder it was in feild keipand the Ky
Or fischand Lochis Lin I am not sure.

☞ As for my surname seik my mothers aith
Quhylis Cuninghame yai callit me heir & yair
bot gude John Cowane gaif me meit and claith
Quhill I was seuin yeir auld and sū thing mair
the Prouest of Hammiltoun cūmand by for cair
Fand me with Ky ane kyndlie occupatioun,
And Hammiltoun he me huif I sow declair
Ane sorie Surname for my awin saluatioun.

To preif myspreit and say my scharo ꞇngyne
With John of Cliddisdail yai .. usit* t˺e to striue
Be worsting first in faith the feild wa⸴ myne,
I brak his heid to haue prerogatiue.

* Obliterated in the Original.

Quhat sall I wryte zow in my wittis fiue?
I was coequall with Achitophall,
Or subtill Sinone knaifrie to discriue
And all my deidis mair Diabolicall.

☞ In leirning letters lang tyme at ye Scule
My pregnant spreit surpassit all the laif,
Quhill I was cowit and cled up lyke ane Fule
In Stemming Rokket riches to ressaif.
Than twa yeiris Noueis notit for ane knaif
Zond in Kiluinning my prentischip I past
Bella fortuna to me sic giftis gaif
To want na graith and ay the Gallous last.

¶ Thā my Lord Arrane from Albany ye Duke,
Obtenit the gift of Murray be ane myance
Quhen Abbotschaw sic hauie haitrent tuik
At the haill hous of Lennox and thair alliance.
Quhaitfoir he coist and left thame at defyance,
Than I fund Jok was into Paslay plaist
Smart in my schuitting & singular in my sciēce
And sum men sayis the bybill I Imbraist.

☞ For feir of that, thay gart me fle to France
In waryit tyme I trow I went of towne,
Quhair I begonth with guthorne for to dance,
To loup on Lassis lait and play the Lowne.
My Stēming Sark, & Rokket was laid doun,
Fra tyme that I hard tell the King was deid
Than I began haill Tutour to the Crowne
To steir my tyme the temporall lawis to leid

☞ The first that euer vaikit was Dunkell
And I was gaipand lyke ane gredie gled,
The Cardinall deit, and than Sanctandres fell
My power haill unto the Paip I sped
Quhen whan they had rypelie all my b . wes* red,

* Obliterated in the Original.

Aganis thair Cannoun Law thay gaif decreit
For I was bastard borne of vnlawfull bed
Zit furtherit I becaus thay fand me meit.

☞ Without respect to God or feir of faith,
Plumand but pietie I did oppres the pure
Be fenzeit causis I confiscat graith
Men criminall to accuse I tuke na cure,
Quhen it was gottin I gaif it to my hure
Quhome I possest in speciall Stanehous wyfe
Of all the barnis my Lady Jeltoun bure
Scho me constranit to mak Ilk ane a lyfe.

Rowpand for riches quhill all my barnis wer staikit
As houngrie Lyoū lousit out of a band,
Sum benefice I bocht or euer it vaikit
And sum I wardit waitand on thair land.
Kilburnie haldis Drumry behind the hand
Raith and Bernbowgall & mony honest man
Na wrangous conqueis Christ wil thoil to stād
Euill was it wairit, and weill war I it wand

☞ Be iustice airis I pledgit all the pepill
Than spairit nane, thocht thay wer Innocent,
To Magnifie my name I maid ane Stepill
Of euerie pleuch I tuik fyue pund of Stent,
Swa of this lyfe the Lord was miscontent
Seand my faith not foundit on ane Roik
As babell fell sa Paslay may repent
That I the maid of Malesounis of foik.

☞ Than was I Legat licent be the Paip,
With dispensatiounis, sawis for euerie sair
To eik my pois I leit thame pas gude chaip
By quha sa wald, I wantit na sic wair.
For holynes thay heipit on me mair
Greit Metrapolitane of the Kirk of God,
Quhen I was Hird the scheip was in anesnair
Lyke till ane flok of hennis befoir ane Tod

¶ Quha landit than, bot Lennox out of France
To battel boun with him was bernis bauld,
Sair I in dreid, quhill I deuysit that dance
Of Glasgow Castell gat it bocht and sauld,
Greit was the riches fund within that hauld,
Plairrer .... or pois we neuer left ..... plak*
Coistlie apparell that can not weill be tauld
We left him bair till all was on his bak.

☞ Efter the feild we followit him sa fast,
Spuilzeit his places, & tuik baith gudis & geir,
Quhill all the land he left us at the last
Quhair Lawrence Neisbit chaipit verray neir.
Contrair my conscience, and the actis of weir
Murdreist his men that micht me nocht resist
That saikles blude rang fer and twentie zeir,
Quhill Palmsoneuin that same day I deceist.

☞ Bot to my taill heir I returne agane,
Quhen ze began in goolynes to gloir
I tuik my womit wickitlis in vane,
Contrair my conscience I profest befoir
My mynd was than the Messes to restoir,
Bot now to lait, I lat that Law allane
Had I fund graith my honour to decoir
I caird not by, quhat way the warld had gane.

¶ At Haryis Mariage I bure hid Inuy
Feirand he procreat children with the Quene
His putting doun I publictly deny,
Zit botis & hūmis declairis zow quhat I mene
And scho wer wrakit, all the warld may wene
Than sould the Duke but dout ressaif ye croun
This was my purpois planely to obtene
Under sum craft to cow the Stewartis doun.

☞ Than was scho caryit captiue as thay tell
And quha nor I was fainer of that fact ?

* This Line is much obliterated in the Original.

Except the countrie come not with our sell
Quhilk was the only caus we bure abak.
For feir of Murray sic myance gart I mak
Be fraud and gyle we gat hir of Lochleuin,
Seikand our gloir we gat baith schame and lak
Our fals intent was sa tryit out in heuin.

¶ Zit cuttit I away their wardly strenth
James Erll of Murray Regent of Renoun,
As I sall schaw zow schortly at mair lenth
I being captiue tane to Striuiling Toun
Dunbartane Castell Deuill mot ding the doun
Quha wald beleif but thow was wicht aneuch
Bot zit the Lord is Maister of Mahoun
Inspyrit thair spreitis, & gart thame speill that heuch

☞ Bot quha may leif, fra tyme his glas be run
As I haue schawin heir schortly to conclude,
Sone was I helterit fra the hous was wun
To Snawdoun syne, accusit with men of gude,
Of pointis four, bot stifly I withstude,
Except the Regentis deith I nocht denyit,
I was the only man gart spill his blude
And mekle mair gif all the treuth wer tryit.

☞ Gude pepill heir to haue zow not abusit,
Just ordour led I lat zow vnderstand
In Parliament I was forfalt and accusit,
Quhair I was baith connict of lyfe and land.
Denuncit Rebell, and fugitiue fra hand
Quhairfoir I knew my deid gif I wer gottin,
Thay socht na Law, bot thay befoir yame fand
And will be vsit quhill we be deid and rottin.

☞ And quhair ze speik of auld perticular
Without auise of thair Nobilitie,
The Erll of Angous and my Lord of Mar
Glencarne, Ruthuen, Cathcart, and Duchiltrie

Methuen, Lochleuin, with Lairds aboñdantlie
The Justice Clerk my dittay red perqueir
Than fra I saw I was condampnit to die
This was my haill Confessioun ze sall heir.

¶ Sequitur Confessio.

✠ Gude pepill all, I pray zow to pray for me,
Quhat may my rent of riches now decoir me ?
This far I speik in presence of zow all
Complenand heir with pietie I deploir me
Quha is the Lord to lyfe may now restoir me
Heirfoir go mark this in Memoriall
Twyse being bischop with sic beriall,
Hard to beleif sum tyme to se me hing
Gif I had seruit my God, and syne my King.

Quhair ze accuse me of the Kingis v ... *
Gif I it knew, God nor I want my heid
Exceptand quhen I hard the hous was fyrit
I feirit myself and dred sum deidly feid.
Than I persauit that he was past remeid
I knew sum Tratouris had his deith conspyrit
Thocht Johne my seruand said as he desyrit
Under Confessioun speikand to ane Preist
Mair beist was he that bure it not in his breist

My former faith I can not weill Recant
Nane I accuse I come not heir to Sant
Gif to reueild, may help me heir I dout
As to the Regentis deith in deid I grant,
I weill awow it, becaus he leit me want,
That ze may tell till all that standis about
My voce is waik, I may not weill speik out,
And of my Manus tuas I haue sic haist
With ite missa est said I gaif the Gaist.

¶ This being said, the cludis obscurit the sky
And I was feirit and hamewart did me hy,

* Obliterated in the Original.

Maid to the Towne and steppit vp the streit
And as I past the Potence I espy
Quhair the annoyntit Bischop hang to dry.
I was Sanct Thomas quhill I tuichit his feit
On Palmsoneuin this paper I compleit,
Euin word be word, as to the treuth belang
And gif I lie, God nor the liers be hangit

¶ Finis.

☞ Quod Sempill.

¶ Imprinted at Striuiling be Robert Lekpreuik.
Anno. Do. M.D. L.X.X.I.

XXVII.—A Lewd Ballet, 1571,

Taken wt ye L. Setons writings.

[State Paper Office.—Scotish Series.   Volume 21 (*December*) Number 107.]

FIRST quhen the newes begonthe to ryse gretly
they maid me wondre.
Quhow that so grett a gospellar so fellounly
could fondre
Bott seing quhow all erdly thingis wor subiect to imitatioun
Than said I, it no grett mervall albeit the congregatioun
Wor no les than ye puir Papistis Inclynit to fornicatioun.

Now is the cours Platoman completit haillely ;
The sone, the mone, and sevin sterris reuoluitt in ye sky,
That makis the worlde tourne top o taill, & will resson
to ryde
The plewche befoir the oxin go, the best the wan to gyde
And all things to misrewlit be owte of all tyme and tyde.

The subiect now commandis the Prince, and Knox is
    grown a King
Quhat he willis obeyit is, that maid the Bisshop hing
The soutar is the grett prechor; the gray freir moks ye
    shone
Quhat mervall than thochte chaist forett prouosit be ye
    mone
Hichit on ye hure so opinly, sen all is owtte of tone

Quhat mervell thochte on ye fryday wy^t silks he did
    him dek
And on sonday his garment wes of ane harne sek
Quhat mervall tho^t ye cerimouy and claith of penitence
Is vsit, and ye oy^r clay^t of diuine reuerence
And ministration yat Aron woure is putt in negligence

Zitt I beleiff els mony myndis thochte, ha loury, ha, ha,
Quhen Dauid vnder ye sek did loure, as toungs did coy
    or say
Quhen ye puir preist to scaffald went ye auld bisshop
    befoir
In Aronis weid, for quhay wald not lauche q^{ll} his hart
    grew soir
To se forett ye holy frere his fakking so deploire

Bott quhat, I think, thochte Dauid quhen he wes to
    lowpe the lowne
Or quhow did he his conscience so sincere cloik or gowne?
Evin as meffan his scuill maistre, yai se, schew him ye
    way
Quha ney^r wy^t oy^r mannis wyffe nor maid, bot wy^t his
    awin los lay
Than lat us sing, O fak and flok zour deid is not lyk zo^r say.

The preist, I grant, his concubine wald hyde in hall or
    boire
And quhylis quhen he tyrit of ane, wold gett in oy^r in
    stoire

The Ministre far todlyar * his hure in houshold chereis
Bott quhen he listis he schaks hir of be diuorce, or hir
　　wirreis.
Sum for ye hure garris heid yameself, and is not yᵗ a
　　mareis ?

Quhat mervall than thoᵗ chaist forett monit be luyf &
　　zeill
Qlk he beris so feruently vnto ye Common Weill
That quhen he not promouis ye sonne he—il scantly
　　dit ye day
To stoir ye wordle lay on ye lass, sen it dois plainly say
Cresite, my dowis, et multip litanniay.

The Duvill, yatt man kynd he may trūmpe, tokis forme
　　of Angell bryte
Bott at ye last ye grace of God his trumpry bringis to
　　lychte
Sa, lolarts, yoʳ hypocrisy yat se fane ze wald hyde
Ze se wyᵗ tyme in spyte of zow dois peice & peice owt
　　slyde
Schawing quhow wolfs in lam skynis ye puire scheip
　　ze misgyde.

XXVIII.—¶ My Lord Methwenis tragedie.

[LIBRARY OF THE SOCIETY OF ANTIQUARIES OF LONDON.]

HOW emptie pen pas but experience
　　with dull indyre and do thy diligence
　　This pure Cōplaint with pietie to deploir
　　Of Muses vane I ask na Eloquence
Bot only God of his greit Excellence
Him to ressaif in Euerlasting gloir
Quhome dolent deith hes laitly done deuoir

* " Todlyar may cum fra tod, as godlyar fray God."—*Note on the margin of
th original.*

Unlukellie allace, gif man micht mend it
Slane with ane schot, sa is the gude Lord endit.

Methwen may murne, and all the bounds about
For Hary Stewart, that was bauld and stout
Constant and kynd with qualiteis conding
In smallest danger nane beleuand dout
Invyous Fortoun swa did waill him out
Lyke as at Roxburgh raid scho slew our King
Ane greit foirtakin of ane weill war thing
To se the saikles puneist sa with roddis
The scharper scurge is cūmand for the Toddis.

Sic is thair craft in clymming to the Crowne
The pure King Hary pieteously put downe
Nocht be thair force, bot fyring of ane trane
The Erle of Murray murdreist with ane lowne
And Lennox last ze saw in Striuiling Towne.
Gude George Ruthuen with thay rebalds slane,
Garleis, Dundas, quhilk wer baith trew & plane
Dowglas of Lyntoun, & gude westiraw was last
with lytill meaning fra the men be past.

¶ Bot to my taill and Tragedie returne
The gude Lord Methuen makis me to murne
That all my senses suddānly doun fais
Quha hes the breist nor it in baill wald burne?
To se zone tratoures do sa foule ane turne,
Gif that our Lords wald craib for ony cais
wa worth the tyme he went about zone wais
wa worth the Towne, the Castell and the craig
Sic tyme sall cum, that God sall pour his plaig.

wa worth his weirds (gif ony weirds can be)
Parcas, Lacheses, Atrapus all thre
Fy on the Fortoun with thy fenzeit smyle
war deid substantiall maid of stane or tre
I suld not rest bot me reuenge on the.

Micht thow not spair yat Lord to liue a quhyle?
Ane of the best was borne in all this Ile
Gif it wald rute, to reckin out sic taillis
Gude to be war, quhen wickitnes preuaillis.

☞ Of twentie zeiris, zing and sa discreit
Meik of his maners, mansuetude and sweit,
Lord lyke allace, he had ouir lytill feir
Aganis his fais, ay formest on his feit
With lāmis vult, and with ane Lyouns spreit
Quha had mair grace to gouerne men of weir
And gif I spak, of Culuering, bow, and speir
He was not borne was better of sic playis
(war he not Lord) nor lyke him of his dayis.

¶ Zing, lusty, lufesum, liberall and large
Ane greit defender of our chosin Barge
In trublous time yow micht haif steirt ye ruther
Few better heir bene Chiftane to haue charge
Aganis Lord Greid to beir the goldin Targe
In all this land thow left not sic ane vther
The sācts of God may say thay want ane brother
Sic as at na tyme can thay get for graith
Sa frak, sa fordwart to defend thair faith.

☞ In the was wit, wisdome, and worthynes,
In the was grace, groundit with godlynes,
In the was meiknes and humilitie,
In the was fredome, force and ferynes,
In the was manly mowis and marynes,
with mercy, science, and ciuilitie
To the Dame nature gaue abilitie
Pringnant of wit, of policie but peir,
Rype of ingyne, with iudgement perqueir.

¶ In honest pastyme was thy haill delyte
Thow bure the toung that neuer spak dispyte
Walkryse in weirs, and watcheman to the rest

For na offence culd thow be forsit to flyte
Aganis thy seruandis, thocht thay wer to wyte,
But with thy wysdome weyit it at the best
Thy houshald trim, and treit weill thay confest
Quhairfoir thay mys the mair nor all the laif
Quhen thay remember on the giftis thow gaif.

Had Stewarts stoutnes, as the mater stands
Thay wald not faill to fecht it with thair hands
To se yame murdreist doun yat dois belāg yame
Bot sum ar feirit for fyring of thair lands
And sum ar lyand obleist under bands
That dar not steir, suppois the tother hang yame
Blist be the barne yat is not borne amang thame
Thay beand beistis, that hes bene men befoir
Cōpairit with Gedds, that dois thair fry deuoir.

¶ Fy on the Atholl, quhat dois thow requyre?
May not thir murthers mufe thy hart to Ire
Gif thow had mettall man to bring the to
Thy dowbill faith may not abyde the fyre
Swa misbeleif fall leif the in the myre.
Or hes thy wyfe the wyte of it, quhair is scho?
Defend the caus man quhill the King cum to
Gif naturall kyndnes kindillis vp thy breist
We beand doun, na dout thow salbe neist.

¶ God saue King James, thow may say allace,
Exceptand only God mon gyde thy grace
For temporall Lords thay leif the few on lyue,
Thy Father murdreist in ane mischant place
Syne baith thy Regents of ane Royall race
with sindrie vther Nobilis four or fyue
And last of all, I laith wer to discryue
The manly Methwen mischantly put downe
Slane for thy saik, for sauing of thy Crowne.

¶ For the mantenance of thy lyfe and law
I note bot few, or nane with sic ouirthraw

10

As only Ruthwen, this my ressoun quhy
His Father first, gif I the suith suld schaw
Deit in exyle for honest caus ze knaw
His douchtie brothers deith can nane deny
Now Methwen last, beleuand sorrow by,
Quhilk hes mair barrat to his breist inbrocht
Nor all the laif gif he culd leif his thocht.

☞ Thocht we be subiect to mortalitie
Zit God Indewis vs with sic qualitie
That natural kyndnes causis vs to cair
Bot let na Carnall Corporalitie
Conplane on Christ for partialitie
To tak his awin men outher lait or air
Lat deid to deid and die not in dispair
Ryse and reuenge the Ruthwen on zone rout
Quhat will it mend to murne thy senses out.

☞ As to the Lords that hes begun this actiou
I feir thair tyme be turnand to detractioun
Gif thay repent not this I spak befoir
Exame thair conscience of particular pactioun
Gif thay be fauourers of the tother factioun
(And gif swa be) thair mys mon be the moir
God will not be abusit with sic vane gloir,
The storme approches quhen ye Poills ar fairest
The langer spairit, the plaigue is ay the sairest

¶ The day is neir, as I dar weill deplane zow
The wraith of God is lyke to gang aganis zow,
For spairing men of Macheuillis Scuillis
How may ze saue zone smaiks yat wald haif slane zow
And ze wer in yair hāds yai wald not hane zow
Thay play the men, & ze the febill fuillis
Quhat is the caus, let se zour curage cuillis ?
Particular proffeit durst I speik it out
Zit thay ar daylie murdreist doun thay dout.

¶ To mak sic change, ze wair zour wit in vane
As thairs for ouris, and ouris for thairs agane
Thair mō ze grant yair groūd als gude as zours
Bot quhair ze gat thame, wald ze flour the grane
That beand done, na dout thay wald be fane
For to renounce thair Law and cum to ours,
Do ze not sa, ze sall thoill scharper schours
Sic vane excambion can I not considder
As marrow tratours and the trew togidder.

¶ I dar be bauld to say sen this began
Had we bot vsit the victorie we wan
With gloir to God that gaif them in our hands
we nedit not or now to want ane man.
Bot quhen we tak thame solistatioun than
Dois clap thair heid, the counsall sa commandis
Quhairfoir I feir, that God sal burne ye wandis
As for exempill I can let zow seit
For spairing sinfull how the saikles deit

☞ As Quheit is strukin for the stra besyde
And siluer fyne mon to the Furnes glyde
To get the dros deuydit as we se
Thocht King Josias did in Christ confyde
Befoir the plaigue come God will sa prouyde,
He will not thoill the just with thame to die
Bot quhair he takis away sic men as he
The riche, the wyse, the Capitane, or the gyde
Thair sall the pepill punischment abyde.

¶ Quhat nedit Noy for sin to suffer wrak ?
Nor faithfull Lot, bot for the wickits saik,
Caleb and Josua in cūming to the land
For Ophny and Phines that the Battell straik
The Innocent Ely all his banis braik,
The Ark of God was caryit of thair hand
And zit thair fais micht better haue lattin it stand
Suppois the saikles slane was for offences
Zit did the Phelistims faill of thair pretences.

☞ And gredy Acan for the geir he hid
Twa goldin braislettis lytill thing he did
Zit was the pepill puneist for sic playis
Haue we sic wrangous geir ? na God forbeid
As Crowats, Sensours, or ane Challeis leid
Quhilk will be found na fault now heir a dayis
For spairing Agag as the Scripture sayis
The hous of Saule was puneist and his seid
Not spairing Jonathan for his douchtie deid.

¶ Siclyke King Dauid thoillit pane and greif
His wickit barnetyme brocht him to mischeif
His Capitane Joab Absolone forbure
Bot far ma Joabs heir for thair releif
with solistatioun quhen we tak ane theif
Suppois ze wist he wrocht zour self iniure
Swa sum beleuis haue baith the sydes sa sure
And zit I hope thay sall not want thair hyre
As Absolone set Joabs corne in fyre.

☞ The King Roboam raschely did ouirluik
The auld wyse counsall, and the fulische tuik
Quhairfoir he tynt his kyndlie Trybes ten
And Jeroboam in that samin buik
Set vp new Idols and his God forsuik,
Quhill Abiah slew fyue hundreth thousand men
Swa Bennadab was Captiue as ze ken,
Bot quhair the iust dois ioyne thame with forsakin
Be war thay get not wickit Acabs takin.

☞ Quhat dois it proffeit Poetrie prophane ?
Sen trew Preicheours speikis it to zow plane
Zit neuer mercy in zour mynd remordis
As fruteles seid it neuer growis a grane
Bot to my taill heir I returne agane
This Tragedie may staik to tell the Lordis
Ane thousand fyue hundreth Sempill sa recordis

Thre scoir and twelf suppois the veirse be vane
The thrid of marche was worthy Methwē slane.

¶ Finis   with the Dytone
☞ Quod Sempill

☞ The Lord to delyuer the laif of this blude
And send vs ane sythmēt of yis suddane slauchter
The King & his counsall inspyre yame with gude
And mak vs not an futestuil to our fais lauchter.

Imprentit at Sanctandrois be Robert Lekpreuik.
Anno. Do.   1572.

⚬•═══•⚬

XXIX.—Ane premonitioun to the barnis of Leith.

ANE Cūning Clerk Experience
And Maister of Intelligence,
New landit in Inchekeith;
This lytill Sedull schortly sends
To all that the gude caus defends
That is the barnis of Leith.

☞ Becaus I hard of ane Conuction
Now to be maid for this dissentioun
That is into this land.
That anis thair may be finall pace:
How sone I vnderstude the cace,
I maid me to frahand.

¶ To send this Sedull in a gayth
That nane of zow kep ony skayth

For laik of Premonitioun :
For ofttymes into treating trewis
Cūis tydingis yat richt mony rewis
Be Tratorie and Seditioun.

☞ As for exempillis gif I list
I haue anew wald I insist
Baith Forane and at hame
Bot to my purpois to proceid
Of peace and concord thair is neid
In pure Scotland be name.

¶ Quhilk neuer in sic perrill stude
Sen that our Lord deit on the Rude
Foull fall thame hes the wyte :
For it is ouirgane with a flude,
Of murther and of saikles blude :
Allace for leif to flyte.

Scotland this blude hes first begun,
And lang in bludschedding hes run,
Ane Patrone of mischeif :
The rest at it beginnis to leir
Allace that pietie is to heir
I pray God send releif

☞ For innocēts ar murtherit downe
without remors in land and towne,
Quhat leid may leif on lyfe :
And thay hald gait I trow frahand
Sir murther salbe in all land
Of Children man an wyfe.

That seis als greit as Moyis stude
Sall drowne ye warld of māis blude
Quhat mischeif do thay mene :
Zone cursit battell as I trow
Quhilk thay at Trent did all auow
Thay think now to sustene.

For murtherars dois all considder
Thay and ye Papists rynis togidder
Thay ar ane blyssit pak.
And thair wer not a God abone
I wald be fleit I tell zow, sone
That all suld gang to wrak.

Bot sa lang as our God dois Ring
Quhilk salbe ay without ending
We neid not for to feir.
Thocht yai suld all rin by yair mynd
Our God to vs salbe sa kynd
Thay sall vs neuer deir.

Bot zit sen baith in France and heir
Thay haue one butt as dois appeir
That is to cut all doun,
That Justice lufis and haitis vice
Thairfoir my ladds of Leith be wice
Ze ken zour warisoun.

☞ I pray zow all be circumspect
Zour enemeis dois not neglect
Occasiounis to ouirsyle zow,
And gif thay may, thay will not spair
Outher be foull play or be fair,
Agane zit to begyle zow.

Ze haue mair neid thame now to feir
Nor quhen thay come in feir of weir
Downe to the Gallow Ley:
For than ze knew thay wer zour fais
Bot now thay cum in freinds clais
Quhilk is ane sairer sey.

☞ I speik not this that ze suld stay
From zour Cōuentioū and zour day
Or ony wayis dissaue thame:

Bot that ze may prouyde befoir
To haue ane pyn for euery boir,
And to be richt war with thame.

☞ Ze knaw thair faith in tymes past
Thairfoir luke that ze festin fast,
And tak gude tent about zow :
For trewly and ze be not wyse
Ze sall not mys to se ane gyse
That sall not weill content zow.

And zit I rid yame leaue yair tressoū
And euin be weill content of ressoun,
Sen Fortoun with a Reill
Hes wrocht thame ane vnabill charr
And blawin thame blind or thay wer warr
With turnin of hir Quheill.

☞ For quhy befoir thay did pretend,
The Quenis authoritie to defend,
To gar men trow thay ludehir :
Howbeit yai wald haif wist hir swou mād
Intil a bait vpō Lochlowmōd
But boddum air or Ruther.

Thairfoir hir caus thay did procure
Becaus yai thocht yat scho was sure
And keipit to thair hand :
Bot zit sic farleis hes bene sene
That Frāce wil haif hir brocht hame Quene
And fred out of Ingland.

☞ And gif that be I wald thay wist,
That sū of thame mon flit thair Kist,
For all this brawling beir :
Bot sillie saulis thay ar sa daft
Thay ken nathing I trow, bot craft :
Thay ar bot zit to leir.

¶ It wer ane pitie to begyle thame
I wald blind Jamie wald gang wile thame
The moyane for till find :
How that yai micht eschew ye quene
And that thay micht (the parrel sene)
Go saill ane vther wynd.

Zea thocht sum leuch and sum did dāce,
Quhen thir blak tydingis come fra France
Blind Jamie tauld me ells.
That quyetly yai news did fyk yame
And sum of thame dois euin mislyke thame
Als mekle as zoursells.

Thairfoir I trow and thay be wyse,
Thay sall leaue of thair Interpryse
And rather gre with zow :
Nor with the hous of Guyis to mell
Quha is als godles as thair sell
And kens thair gymps I trow.

for get yat hous yair hād abone yame
I wed my heid yat yai sal tone yame
And trym yame for thair triks :
Ze thay can think on auld done deids
For brint barne the fyre ay dreids,
Thay will not thole sic prikis.

I wald fane warne zow of al dāgers
I coūsal zow be war with strangers
That halds zow baith in hand,
I dreid ze ly lang be the eiris,
Or thay think time to end the weiris
And troubill in this land.

¶ It wer gude gif ze culd aggre
Amang zour selfis and let thame be
Ze may wit quhat I mene :

for quhē yat strāgers reuls zour roist
It wilbe sure on Scotlands coist
As hes bene hard and sene.

¶ And wer ze weill aggreit I tell
Than Scotland micht do for the sell,
And set als lytill by thame
As they do it for all thair power
thay wald be fane to seik zour fauour
And to zow als apply thame,

☞ Bot till aggre and ze delay
Than Scotland will be bot ane pray
As will be schortly sene:
Till gredie gormondis waitand on
Quhen thay may se occasion
To rute zow all out clene.

For sword and derth hes zow opprest
And also ze haue felt the Pest
Bot zit few dois amend:
Than desolatioun is the last,
Of Gods plagues quhē thir ar past,
Quhilk doutles he will send.

Zea I foirspeik ceis not thir weiris,
The tyme sall cum within few zeiris
That nane of Scottis blude:
In Scotland dar him self auow,
Mair nor in Jurie dois the Jow
For feir of Natiounis rude.

☞ Thau sall zour pure posteritie
In wandering wyde fra this coūtrie
Amang all vther Natiounis
Cry out and murne with woful cheir
That pitie salbe for till heir,
Thir kynd of exclamatiounis.

¶ Allace that euer thay wer borne,
That dwelt in Scotland vs beforne
And loist vs sic ane land,
quhilk our forbears ans thocht ours
with plesãd castells townis & towrs
And all things at command.

Sum Lords sum Lairds sũ les degre
Thair commoun welth and policie
As ony Natioun had,
And now na Scottisman dar be thair
Allace quhat hart will not be sair
To see Scottismen sa sad.

☞ Than sall thay warie curse & ban
The murtherars yat yir weiris begã
Quhen Chronickles thay reid,
Thã Edinburgh that Castell strang
Sall wareit be that stude sa lang
Sic murther for to feid.

Thairfor yir plaigs wald yai eschew
I counsall thame in tyme to rew
And thair mischeif repent:
Quhilk gif thay do ze may aggre
Bot otherwise na pace salbe
Thocht ze thairto consent.

For thocht that Saul wil Agag spair
Zit God will haue his will but mair
Fulfillit or he sace:
Gif this ze do not vnderstand
Speir at John Durie or John Brãd
Thay will expone the place.

thocht murtherars says yat yai thrist blude
Zit let na nobill mẽ of gude
Be craft that was brocht on it

And rewis yat yai haif tane sic part,
Repenting trewly from thair hart
Feir, thocht Johne Knox expone it

Bot gif yat thay grow proud & heich,
And skar at zow as thay wer skeich,
And on na wayis will bow thame
Let yame pas on to thair defensis
It salbe on thair awin expensis
Or all be done I vow thame

Than quhidder ze conuene or nocht.
Keip thir premissis in zour thocht
Ze that of Leith ar barnis :
The abstinence drawis neir ane end,
Thairfoir I pray zow now attend,
Think on Experience warnis,

¶ F I N I S.

☞ Imprentit at Sanctandrois be Robert Lekpreuik.
1572.

XXX.—The lamentatiō of the Cōmounis of Scotland.

QUHAT thift, quhat reif, quhat murther, and
oppressioū ?
Quhat saikless slauchter, quhat mortal me-
serie ?
Quhat pouertie, quhat derth and Tribulatioun ?
Dois Ring be Grange all leidis on lyfe may se
The schame is thyne, thocht we the sorrow dric
Curst Nemrod richt of Babilone the cheif,
We Commounis all lowd vengeance cryis on the
Blaming thy tressoun the caus of all our greif.

¶ We sillie pure anis quhair we wer wont to gang
With Coillis and Cokillis with Fische and sicklyke wair,
Upon our bakis als mekill as we micht fang
With mirrie sang all tripping into pairis.
To wyn our leuing in mercat at sic Fairis
Now we allace but reuth ar reft with theif,
Haue we ane lyart na baid bot all is thairis
    Blaming thy tressoun the caus of all our reif.

¶ Na vther lyfe we pure men bade of better
Nor with our Naiggis to gane to Edigburgh sone,
With Peittis, with Curuis and mony turfe of Hedder.
Ay gat gude saill syne lap quhen we had done.
For mirrynes and with the licht of Mone
We wald ga hame but outher fray or chace
Quhair now in sorrow fra dure to dure we clune,
    Blaming thy tressoun of all our cair allace.

We Coilzearis, Cadgearis, and Carteris in ane rout
Be bludie Wolfis that grange hes maid to steir,
Our hors is reft, our selfis ar doung but dout
Quhair we did trauell we dar not now appeir.
Out of our Ludge we tak of thame sic feir
Thocht it wald vs ten thousand Crownis auance
With morning Prayer we curse thame maid this we..
    Blaming thy tressoun the caus of our mischance.

Allace we Chapmen may with Creilmen murne
Thay sillie men that brocht thair butter and egges
To Edinburgh Croce and did na vther turne,
And we agane wald by ane Fraer of Fegges
Baith prenis and nedillis and sell to landwart megges
Than micht we trauell quhair we dar not this day
Bot lyis at hame, but meit, na drink bot dregges
    Blaming thy tressoun the caus of all our fray.

¶ Quhat wicht on lyfe will not vs pure pietie ?
That wont to bring the woll, the skin, and hyde

To Edinburgh Towne in peice and Cheritie,
Fra Selkirk, Hawik, and the partis of Clyde.
Quhair now allace in hoill and boir we byde
As wratches werie the Corenothe we carpe
Dar not keik out for Rebellis that dois ryde
    Blaming thy tressoun of this our sorrow scharpe.

We Tinklaris, Tailzeouris, we craftismen out of nūber
That be our craft had ay ane honest lyfe,
We wait of nocht bot mekill cair and cummer
Our Joy is turnit in wo and mortall stryfe.
All our gay garmentis of sindric fassounis ryfe
We thame wedset our bodyis to sustene
Na work ado bot beg baith barne and wyfe
    Blaming thy tressoun that causis vs complene

We Merchandis all that with our Merchand pakkis
Did trauell ay, fra Towne to Towne, to Fairis
Thow hes vs baneist. thow hes vs fleit fra crakkis
We sit at hame na saill is to our wairis.
Thocht we wald trauell thy reiffaris sa vs clairis
With reif but reuth, but pietie with extortioun
But mirth in meserie thay horribill houndis vs tairis
    Blaming thy tressoun the caus of our oppressioun.

We commounis all with cair we may lament
That had sic peice sic rest and vnitie
And now allace ar rugit, reuin and rent
Our steidis are flowne, our cattell reft trewlie
With weiping wallaway nane may we wyte bot the
Thow Feind Infernall thow garris vs walk our so
Quhair we afoir did sleip richt quyetlie
    Blaming thy tressoun the caus of all our wo.

Bot sen with sith ze Cammounis do complene
With sob full sair richt trewly sall I tell
I James Dalzell Indwellar in the Dene,
Be Grange smaikis I wait send be himsell

Hes schot my wyfe throw birsket lyre and fell
Scho greit with barne syne gaif the gaist with plane
Than cryit my bairnis with mony zout and zell
    Blaming thy tressoun that had thair Mother slane

¶ Thay reuthles Ruffeis but reuth with crueltie
Did slay my husband but caus into my sicht
Downie Ros be Name ane Cuitlar of craft trewlie
With gūnis him gord but mercy on the nicht
I and my bairnis sall craif Goddis plaigues ful richt
To fall the grange thow cruell Cokadraill
With fourtie ina nor did on Pharo licht
    Blaming thy tressoun that causis vs bewaill

Sen not but caus we wyte the of this wa
With panefull pech, with mony grank and grane,
The curse, the wareis, but blys fra top to ta
Lat neuer thy freind se oucht of the bot schame.
With cursit deith that mony man the blame
Lucifer was heich, bot Lord thow threw him downe
Sa will he the, thow graceles Grange be Name
    Blaming thy tressoun with sorrow but Renowne.

☞ O tenefull Tyrane, O Gyant mekill but micht,
Of vitious deidis thow art the only Fontane
Quhairfra all vice but vertew springis full richt
As dois the watter out of the Rok or Montane
We pure sall cry with erie hartis fast dontane
To the O God, to scurge this wickit wicht,
In Just exempill to all the warld maist certane
    Blaming thy tressoun the caus of all our plicht.

☞ Had thow bene trew but tressoun to our Roy
And to his Regent, gaif the that hauld to keip,
As thow did sweir, we had not had this noy   ·
We micht had peice, quhair now in weir we weip,
In wo but weill, but plesure in pane sa deip
Be the O Tratour, that Rebellis did ressaif

Into that hauld with the thairin to creip
   Ha tressoun vntrew will gar ane widdie waif.

¶ Now lat us all with hart and mynde vs dres
Baith euin and morne, richt law downe on our kne,
With hyddeous schout all we baith mair and les
For vengeance Just, with tene to fall on the.
O thow O Lord, and God in persoun thre
Consume this wratche with Brintstane fyre and thūder
That persecuitis thy Sanctis with crueltie
   Ha tressoun vntrew ane tow will schaik in schunder.

¶ Preserue with micht fra slicht of fais defend
Our King gude Lord, and als his Regent eik :
Lat neuer thair micht, but richt, with hand ay bend
Haue strenth or power thame for to hurt or wreik.
We thy pure liegis sall pray and als beseik
To send the grace, lang space in weilfair wend
That we may se the puneis vice but meik
   Ind tressoun all sessoun with this we mak ane end.

FINIS.

¶ Imprentit at Sanctandrois be Robert Lekpreuik.

ANNO. DO. M.D. LXXII

XXXI.—The Lamentatiou of Lady Scotland, compylit be hir self, speiking in maner of ane Epistle, in the Moneth of Marche, the zeir of God 1572.

[LIBRARY OF THE FACULTY OF ADVOCATES, EDINBURGH.—Scotish Poems of the Sixteenth Century, collected by John Graham Dalyell, Edinburgh 1801.—I now find that there is also in the Library of the Faculty of Advocates, Edinburgh a copy of No. X. (*page* 50) "Ane Tragedie, in the forme of ane Diallog betuix Honour, Gude fame," &c.]

¶ To the Richt Honourabill and godly Leirnit Gentilman, the Laird of Dune, (John Areskine,) Minister of Goddis Word, and Superintendent of his kirk in Angous, Mernis, &c., P. R. his humbill Seruant. S.

O quhome suld I my Rurall veirse direct,
Bot vnto him that can thame weill correct
Befoir quhome suld this mater ga to licht,
Bot to ane faithfull Godly Christin Knicht
To quhome can I this lytill throuch propyne,
Bot vnto ane of Excellent Ingyne
Not for the termes, nor for the worthynes
Of ony thing that I do heir expres :
Bot for becaus I aucht, of bound dewtie
To dedicat to him sum Noueltie.

Go, bill, than, to the Laird of Dune I send the ;
Beseiking him to tak his pen and mend the.
Mend the, (alaik) quhy suld he tak that pane ?
To sicht the ones, it will bot vex his brane.
For as, in sum Schyre, thair is bot ane myre,
Quhilk is ouir all, that man and beist dois tyre ;
Sa into the, he sall bot ane fault find,
Quhilk is ouir all, befoir, and als behind.
Zit not the les I knaw him sa discreit,
Gif he mend not thy veirse and haulting feit,
Zit at the leist sa surely he will byde the,
That Poets nane sall se the to diryde the.

11

Pas on, than, bauldly, and to him deploir
This present stait fair weill : I say no moir.

¶ The Lamentatioun of Lady Scotland, &c.

ZE vapurs wak, and watters in the air
Ze Seyis sa deid ze fludis and fontanis fair
Heir my complaint ; to zow my cace I mene.
That ze may wellis gif to my febill Ene,
To testifie with teiris my wofull cace,
And with zour murning weid absconse my face.
    ¶ My husband, deir gude Johne, the Comounweill,
To quhome I did all my affairis reueill,
As he to me did in our faithfull dayis,
But fraude, or gyle, or tressoun ony wayis :
Than, lusty, gay, and flurisching wer we,
Trew faithfull Children he begat on me.
Sic lufe and faith to vther thay did beir,
That thay knew not quhat beist was Ciuile weir.
My heid wald not disdane my leggis and feit,
My Eine foirsaw all perrallis micht me meit.
My hands and armes, ay reddy to defend me,
To snib my children gif thay did offend me.
My body was weill cled with Policie,
My Hat was of Justice and Equitie.
My Coller, of trew Nichtbour lufe it was,
Weill prenit on with Kyndnes and solas.
My Gluiffis wer of fre Liberalitie,
My Sleiffis wer of to borrow and len glaidlie ;
My Lais and Mailzeis of trew parmanence,
My Stomak maid was of clene Conscience ;
My waist was gyrdit with Sobrietie,
My Leggs and feit schod with Simplicitie ;
My hart was haill, my stomach weill disposit ;
Of peice and rest my Bowellis wer composit.
Quhat wald ze moir Schir commoun-weill and I
Held hous lang tyme ; bot Sathan had Inuy

To se vs so; than callit he Seditioun,
With pryde his Sone, to quhome he gaif cōmissioun,
To tak with thame discord, and Nichtbour feid,
(Efter, I mene, that our gude bairnis wer deid,)
To poysoun me with thair Infectit cryme,
With sum of my awin children of this tyme,
Of quhilks I pray the Lord God mak me fre:
Ambitioun will not lat thame aggre.
Thir mony zeiris thay haue me disconfortit,
I trauell zit as I had thame aduortit:
The malice greit that ilk to vther beiris,
Dois ryfe my bowells with thair Ciuile weiris:
Sair boistit thay my husband commounweill,
And maid thair vowis and aithis him for to Keill.
In ony part quhair thay him with me fand:
Quhairfoir, for feir, he fled from me Scotland.
Away, sum sayis, to Veneis is he gone,
Or to the Swisches, as thay do suppone,
Quhair he is saif from danger, hurt, or skaith:
Heir wald he deit of cauld and hounger baith.
Thus am I left as wedow in distres,
For commounweill; my bairnis left Fatherles.
¶ Children I had, in all vertewis perfyte,
To peice and Justice was thair haill delyte.
Sum of displesure deit for wo, and cair;
Sum wyrreit was, and blawin in the air;
And sum in Stirling schot was to the deid,
That mair was geuin to peice nor Ciuile feid.
Bot ane was slane, vnto my skaith and schame,
Becaus he socht to fetche my husband hame:
He was my deir and best belouit Sone;
All that he did, for my weilfair was done.
Lyke ane gude Medciner, or gude Syruge,
Of euill humouris, he did my body purge.
Quhat wald ze moir sen James in Falkland deit,
Nane for my weill sa weill with me aggreit,
Nor zit sa weill did lufe Schir Commounweill,
Nor vnto me bure sic ane feruent zeill.

Murdreist he was in Lythgow tratrouslie;
The murtherars vnto my heid did fle,
Quhair thay tuik hald, and zit dois hald thame fast,
And ay sensyne my heid hes bene agast.
For quhy throw falset and Subtillitie,
Thay chaist away Justice, and Equitie;
For laik of quhilks, my heid dois wark and zaik,
And all my body trymbill dois and schaik:
For quhen the heid is seik, the Prouerb is,
That all the members be the worse, I wis.
    ¶ My claiths ar reuin, that pietie is to se;
Particular weill hes spuilzeit policie.
My Coller rent is be Dame Fremitnes,
The Prenis thairof ar reft be sad Nysenes;
Dame Nigartnes my Gluifis hes hint away,
Tak for himself my Sleifis dois reist and stay.
My Lace and Mailzeis tane be variance,
My Stomak worne is be dissimulance;
My belt is cuttit of pure Gluttonie,
My leggs and feit now schod with Pouertie;
My hart is seik, my stomach keipis na meit,
My bowells Rumbills, as thay wald vther eit.
Now, for to couer all this vilannie,
Ane Cloik thay gif me of authoritie.
Authoritie (alaik) na les thay mene,
For thay desyre neuer to se thair Quene;
Bot that thay may in hir Name bruik offices,
With power to cleik vp the benefices.
Nane I excuse on ather syde; for quhy
Ilk ane his awin hous seikis to edify,
And nane dois cair for Commounweill ane prene.
    ¶ I grant I had ane Douchter was ane Quene,
Baith gude and fair, gentill and Liberall,
Dotit with vertewis and wit Naturall;
Prignant in Spreit, in all things honourabill,
Lusty, gude lyke, to all men fauourabill.
Schamefull to euill, baith honest, meik, and law:
Thir vertewis all, scho had quhyls scho stude aw

Of God Eterne, as of hir Gouernour,
And quhen scho did regaird hir hie Honour.
Bot at the last throw filthy speiche and counsell,
That scho did heir of sum curst Kittie vnsell,
Fra scho gaif eir to sic vyle bawderie,
God, Schame, and honour, scho forzet all thre.
It wer to lang the vices to reheirse,
Quhairin from thyne scho did hir self exerce.
The Reider wald thame think maist Insolent,
Bot I thame leif, becaus thay ar Recent:
For quhilks scho was thocht vnworthy to Ring,
Ane Crowne to bruik, or ony Royall thing.
Sa all my Children, with hir awin consent,
Deposit hir in oppin Parliament.
Than wald scho that thay suld hir awin sone crowne,
Quhilk thing thay did sa Syce vp and Sink downe:
God saue his grace: for quhy the same is he
In me that hes the trew authoritie.
Praisit be God, I haue fre at command,
That fair zoung Prince in Stirling, my richt hand.
Wer not in hope I leif to se that day,
That he sall purge thir foull humouris away,
And me restoir agane vnto my helth,
Zea, caus my Children flurische in all welth.
Wer not he is brocht vp in all gude thing
Affeiring to ane Godly Prince and King,
Be gude Lord Deddy my trew faithfull freind,
Cum of ane race of men to me maist kynd.
For Lady Minnie, I dar tak in hand,
Happy is he hes sic ane Gouernand.
Wer not thir things that maks me leif in hope
At libertie to se this Lyoun scope
One day to Rore, and Ramp vpon his fois,
To bring thame law, that now sa proudly gois;
Wer not thir thingis, I say, and vtheris mo,
I wald dispair, and die for pane and wo.
To zow Vapouris, and watters in the air,
And seyis sa deip, I downe my plaint declair

Ze seyis, I say, gif passage, and ze can,
Till sum faithfull to bring hame my gudeman.
   ¶ And ze, my Kirk, my Faithfull Mother deir,
That purgit art of Channoun, Monk, and Freir,
Of Papist Priest, Papist and Papistrie,
Bot not, allace, clene of Hypocrasie,
Of auarice, pryde, and ambitioun,
Thocht ze haue left all Superstitioun.
I grant the word of God is trewlie Preichit,
And in the schuills Exercise trewlie teichit ;
Zit, sayis the Commounis, ze do not zour office,
For upaland thay haue not dew seruice.
The rowmis appointit pepill to confidder
To heir Gods word, quhair thay suld pray togidder,
Ar now conuertit in scheip Coits and Fauldis,
Or ells ar fallin, becaus nane thame vphauldis.
The Parische Kirks, I mene, thay say misgyde,
That nane for wynd and rane thairin may byde.
Thairfoir na plesure tak thay of the tempill,
Nor zit to cum, quhair nocht is to contempill,
Bot Crawis and Dowis cryand and makand beir,
That nane throuchly the Minister may heir :
Baith Fedders, Fylth, and Doung, dois ly abrod,
Quhair folk suld sit to heir the word of God ;
Quhilk is occasioun to the aduersaryes,
To mok and scorne sic things befoir zour eyes.
Thus to disdane the hous of Orisoun,
Dois mak folk cauld to thair Deuotioun ;
And als thay do disdane to heir Gods word,
Thinking the same to be ane Jesting bourd,
Thay go to labour, drinking, or to play,
And not to zow vpon the Sabboth day :
So thay prouoke the wraith of God, allace,
Quhilk hes maid me to fall in this distres.
Zit suld I not blame zow, that sic dois perische,
Bot Lords and Lairds, & Cōmouns of ilk Parische,
The quhilk wer wont for to caus euerie pleuch,
In vphalding the Kirk, to pay aneuch.

To do the same, ze suld thame zit exhort,
Togidder that thay suld the pure support.
The Prouerb is, of Palice, Kirk, and brig,
Better in tyme to beit, nor efter to big.
Ze Collegis and Uniuersitie,
That to all vthers suld exempill be,
I se zour tempills cassin downe and reuin,
The maist part are bot theikit with the heuin.
This quhilk to zow I do sa plancly wryte,
The Commounis speiks of zow, and dois bakbyte.
Amend sic things, I humblie zow beseik,
And dit the mouths of thame that sa dois speik.
Making zour lyfis and Conuersatiouns
To preiche and teiche lyke vnto zour persouns.
It suld be ze, Mother, suld me Instruct;
It suld be ze, to Christ suld me conduct.
It suld be ze, suld schaw me the richt way,
How I suld serue my God baith nicht and day;
It suld be ze, that suld do diligence
For to aggre this Ciuile difference.
It suld be ze, throw Preiching, suld me mufe
To Cheritie and freindly Nichtbour lufe.
It suld be ze, that suld gif gude exempill
Of lyfe and warks to thame dois zow contempill.
It suld be ze, that suld be at all tyme
Clene without spot, and purgit of all cryme.
It suld be ze, Mother, it suld be ze,
To quhome the pepill suld giue eir and Ee;
It suld be ze, schortly, I say no moir,
That to all vertewis suld zow Indeuoir.
¶ And ze, my Barrouns and Nobilitie,
That dois oppres my pure Communitie,
Quhair is zour wit, zour ressoun, sence, and feill,
To fle away my husband Commounweill,
Quhat haue ze wyn sensyne, lat se zour ganis: .
Gar pryse zour proffeit & esteme zour panis.
The panis, I wait, the proffeit will surmont
A greit daill moir nor ze can mak zour compt.

I find, sensyne the Zow hes borne the bell,
Wyfis Maisters bene in geuing haill Counsell.
To Lords and Lairds; I speik generallie,
As may be sene, allace, ouir weill on me.
Hwine, Huntly, Grange, and all ze of that syde,
Behald now how ze do the mater gyde,
To caus my Sisters France & Ingland scorne zow.
That walterars of Courts ze lat suborne zow:
Zit ze and thay did sweir with aithis conding,
And did subscryue to be trew to the King.
In takin quhairof with all ze did aggre,
To Crowne and place him in authoritie.
Gif ze wirk weill, zour deids ane day will schaw,
For raising fyre aganis my actis and law,
In halding towns and strenths zour King aganis,
Putting the rest of zour brether to panis;
Quhome I excuse not, as I said befoir,
For I persaif ambitioun and vane gloir,
And gredynes to reule, dois blind zow baith,
Quhilk dois redound to my greit hurt and skaith.
Zour tennents plenzeis, that thay ar opprest
Be zow and zours, that dois thame soir molest;
Ze hicht yair maills, yair pleuchs ze dowbil on yame;
Thay tyne thair tyme at sic things to opone yame;
For na rest will ze get into zour raggs,
Gif sum sect knaw that thay haue geir or baggs.
Zour Nichtingaills will sing sa in zour eiris,
That ze sall nichtly haue Domestik weiris.
Zone carle, (quod scho), my Joy, dois beinly dwell,
And all prouisioun hes within himsell,
In barne or byre, in hall, Girnell and Seller;
His wyfe weiris weluot on hir Gowne and Coller;
Thay ar sa riche, that thay do vs misknaw;
Than better sone to drug, nor lait to draw.
Sone is his Gersum hichtit, and his Maillis;
Him self growis waik, his geir and houshald faillis:
Quhair sic wer wont to haue Guse, Cok, and Hen,
Breid, drink, and bedding, to treit honest men,

Now drink thay Mylk and Swaits in steid of Aill,
And glaid to get Peis breid and watter Caill:
Quhair sic wer wont to ride furth to the weir,
With Jak and Sword, gude hors, Knapscall & speir:
Quhair sic wer wont brauely to mak thame bowne,
With Lord or Laird to ryde to Burrowis towne;
Quhair sic wer wont at all Games to be reddy,
To schuit or loup, for to exerce thair body:
Now mon thay wirk and labour, pech and pant,
To pay thair Maisters Maillis exhorbitant.
Ryue out the Mures, the bestialls gers intak;
Thay ar sa waik thay dow not beir a Jak,
And gets waik bairns, euill nureist, in distres:
Sa be sic wayis my Commouns dois dicres.
My torment sair constrynis me this to speik;
Na inerwell quhy, for I am wondrous seik.
Beseiking zow my seiknes to remeid,
Quhilk may be done, ceissing zour Ciuile feid.
To follow Christ and his Commandement,
Quha said, befoir his last department,
Ilk one lufe vther with sic freindly lufe,
That ze may be the bairnis of God abufe,
And cleith zow with fair Garments clene & quhyte,
Without malice, coutentioun, or dispyte,
Aganis my cūming, quhilk trewly salbe,
Quhen ze leist wene, in twinkling of an Ee.
Thus said the Lord to zow, and to all men,
That be thir marks thay sall Gods children ken.
Heirfoir, my Nobills, seik peice, do that ze can
To follow Christ, and chais away Sathan,
With his Supposts, and all that taks in hand,
For to diuorse me from my gude husband.
  ¶ Now ze, my Burges, Craftis, & Merchand men,
And ze my Commounis, with my hynd zemen,
To zow I haue sum purpois for to say,   .   ·
How, quhen, and quhy, my husband fled away.
First thair come in lurkand vpon zour gait,
Pryde and Inuy, with falset and dissait.

Thir four socht ludgeing all the towne about,
Quhat suld thay seik, lang tyme thay lay thairout.
Till ane Zule euin, zour wyfes to counsall went;
Than spak ane Lawers wyfe, baith trym and gent:
Cūmers, (qood scho), it is pietie to se
Folk in a towne for cauld and hounger die ;
It is mair schame in Burgh for to se beggers,
Nor is it skaith in Crawmont to want dreggers :
Quhairof dois serue our greit cheir and fair bigging,
Bot for to help the pure that gais a thigging ?
Quhairof dois serue our husbands gold and rent,
Bot to sustene the pure and Indigent ?
Zit lat vs ludge zone twa that gais befoir,
Pryde and Inuy, gif we will do no moir.
And gif our husbands speirs quhy did we so,
Answer we may, we left them vther two.
Now gif ze pleis Cummers, I sall begin
This same cauld nicht to tak ane of thame in.
We knaw thame not, (quod thay) ; bot tak ze ane,
We must not leif the vther bird alane.
Sa thay did skaill ; and scho tuke with hir Pryde ;
And on the morne scho come furth lyke ane bryde,
With hir new Gaist als proud as ane Paycok,
And in hir hart scho did hir Cummers mok ;
Quhilk quhen thay saw, with speid thay ran in hy,
And for dispyte amangs thame ludgit Inuy,
In counterfuting hir in all kin things,
Courche, Coller, Cloik, Belt, Braislets & Rings.
Then wox the Lawers wyfe richt proude in hart ;
Bot zit hir Cummers callit scho apart,
Saying, Cummers, quhat is the caus, and quhy,
That, in dispyte of me, ze treit Inuy ?
Becaus, (quod thay), that ze alone tuik Pryde,
And thocht that we suld not marche zow besyde.
Thairfoir we thocht in that point ze did wrang vs. :
Aggre, (quod scho), and ludge thame baith amang vs.
Quhilk thing thay did, and all did condiscend
To treit and keip thame to the warlds end.

Thus hes zour wyfis thir twa tane to be thairs,
And left the vther twa for zours affairs.
Quhilk seing ze and zour wairs gros and grof,
And with zour wyfis thir two so muche maid of;
Ze gros geir left, and went for wyne and spyces,
Frenche claith and silks for to cleith vp thir vyces;
Quhilks for to out with dowbill met and mesure,
The vther tway ze ludgeit at thair plesure.
Quhat wald ze moir ze wait weill quhat I mene;
Disluge thame now, and chais thame from zow clene.

¶ Ze Hammer men, ze that maks schois & claiths,
Ze treit thir twa with mony manesworne aiths;
And ze lykewise, all Crafts in Generall,
Alaik, I feill zow to thame bound and thrall:
Mairouir, zour drinking Extraordinair
Maks of zour wyfis and biarns euill to fair:
Quhen ze wald drink in hous, ze may be bauld
To do the same at hame with zour houshauld.
All byganis mend: in tyme to cum, luik ze
Begyle na man, bot wirk zour wark trewlie.

¶ To yow, my Commouns, quhat mair can I say?
I pietie yow as far furth as I may;
Now pure ze ar, zit purer wald ze be
For vsing proud pure Prodigalitie.
Thair is na Lord nor Laird in all this land,
Bot ze man counterfait in claiths fra hand,
Fra top to ta, thocht ze suld beg and borrow.
Johne, ga your way, for it will not be for zow;
Ze suld your ground grube with Simplicitie,
And mak your claiths conforme to your degre.
Bot ye, your wyfe and bairns, can tak na rest,
Without ye counterfait the worthyest:
Buft brawlit hois, Coit, Dowblet, sark and scho,
Zour wyfe and bairns conforme mon be thairto.
Leif of, and leirne your bairns to saw and teill;
Sic doings chaist away the Commounweill.
All thir foirfalts that I haue done reheirs,
That Lords, Lairds, Ladys & Lawers dois exerce,

Kirk, Burges, Merchand Cōmouns Crafts and all,
Hes haill the wyte of this my wofull fall.
Amend heirfoir, and call to God for Grace,
Beseiking him to gif vs rest and peace
In our lyfe tyme, that we may trewly knaw
Ane God Eterne, ane Faith, ane King, ane Law;
And at the last to bring vs to his gloir,
To Ring with him in blys for euer moir.   Amen.

The Conclusioun be P. R. to all and Sum.

¶ All that this reids, the mater sad will think;
Sum that this heiris, I wait, will discommend it;
Thocht all and sum heir at partly do schrink,
Zit sory I that thay suld be offendit;
Heirfoir, I wald that this wer blythlie endit.
For to mak all or sum lauch at the last,
Than all and sum sall heir, in tyme bypast,
Quhen Fornicatioun haldin was na cryme,
How that sum Prelats did walk, pray and fast,
And serue in Kirk according to that tyme.

¶ A Prelat ane day in his bed, to sport him,
Did clap his lufe with kissis soft and sweit;
In this meane tyme, thair was, to recomfort him,
Peirtryks and pleuers pyping on the speit.
Than vp he rais, and maid him for thame meit,
With gude quhyte wyne and all the partinence.
Quhen he had tane this on his Conscience,
He gaif ane greit pech, lyke ane weill fed stirk,
Och Lord, (quod he), now gif me patience;
Quhat stres thoill we to serue thy haly Kirk?

FINIS.

¶ Imprentit at Sanctandrois Be Robert Lekpreuik,
1572.

XXXII.—Ane new Ballet set out be ane fugitiue Scottisman that fled out of Paris at this lait Murther.

[GEORGE DANIEL'S Collection, now in the possession of HENRY
HUTH Esq., 30 Princes' Gate, London.—THE PHILO-
BIBLON SOCIETY :—Ancient Ballads and Broadsides, pub-
lished in England in the Sixteenth Century, chiefly in
the earlier years of the reign of Queen Elizabeth. Re-
printed from the Unique Original Copies, mostly in
Black-letter, preserved in the Library of HENRY HUTH,
Esq., London. Printed by Whittingham and Wilkins
1867.—A COLLECTION OF SEVENTY-NINE BLACK-LETTER
BALLADS AND BROADSIDES, printed in the Reign of Queen
Elizabeth, between the years 1559 and 1597. Published
by Joseph Lilly, London 1867.]

NOW Katherine de Medicis hes maid sic a gyis,
    To tary in Paris the papistes ar tykit,
At Bastianes brydell howbeit scho denyis,
    Giue Mary slew Hary, it was not vnlykit;
Zit a man is nane respectand this number,
I dar not say wemen hes wyte of this cummer.

Zone mask the Quene Mother hes maid thame in France,
    Was maikles and saikles, and schamfully slane,
Bot Mary conuoyit and come with ane dance,
    Quhill princes in sences was fyrit with ane trane ;
Baith tressonabill murtheris the ane and the vther,
I go not in masking mair with the Quene Mother.

¶ Italianes ar tyranis, and tressonabill tratoris ;
    For gysours, deuysours, the Guysianis ar gude ;
Bot Frenche men ar trew men, and not of thair natouris;
    Than, Charlie, I farlie thow drank thy awin blude,
I wyte bot thy mother wit, wemen ar vane,
I greis neir to Ganzelon, nor grit Charlie Mane.

¶ Thy style was Treschristien, maist Cristen King,
    Baith hiest and friest, and neist the impyre;
Bot now Prouest Marschell in playing this spring,
    And ressoun for tressoun prouokis God to ire;
Beleuis thow this trumprie sall stablische thy style?
Our God is not deed, zit be doand an quhyle.

¶ Suppois that the Papistes deuysit this at Trent,
    To ding vs and bring vs with mony lowd lauchter,
With sic cruell murther is Christ sa content,
    To take the and make the ane Sanct for our slauchter?
Albeit he correct vs, and scurge vs in ire,
Be war with the wand syne he wapis in the fyre.

¶ For better is pure men nor princes periurit,
    Baith schameles and fameles, we find thame sa fals;
With sangis lyke the seryne our lyfis thow allurit;
    Ouirsylit vs, begylit vs, with baitis in our hals;
Or as the fals fowler, his fang for to get,
Deuoiris the pure volatill he wylis to the net.

¶ In Ilis nor in Orknay, in Ireland Oneill,
    Thay dar not, thay gar not thair lieges be stickit:
Solyman, Tamerlan, nor yit the mekle Deill,
    Proud Pharao, nor Nero, was neuer sa wickit;
Nouther Turk nor Infidell vsis sic thing,
As be their awin burreo, being ane king.

¶ Baith auld men and wemen, with babis on thair breist,
    Not luking nor huking, to hurll thame in Sane,
All beand murdreist downe, quhat do ze neist?
    Processioun, confession, and vp Mes aganc;
Proud King Antiochus was sum tyme als haly,
And yet our God guschit out the guttis of his belly.

Thy syster thou maryit, thy saces was sour,
    Sic cuikrie for luikrie was euill interprisit;
Ze maid vs the Reid Freiris, and rais in an hour,

Abhorring na gorring that micht be deuisit;
Thou playit the fals hypocreit fenzeing the fray,
But inwart ane rageing wolf waitand thy pray.

That France was confidderat with Scotland I grant,
　　Baith actit, contractit and keipit in deid ;
The kyndnes of cutthrottis we cure not to want,
　　Denyis thame, defyis thame, and al thair fals seid ;
It was bot with honest men we maid the band,
And thou hes left leifand bot few in that land.

Our faith is not warldly, we feir not thy braulis,
　　Thocht hangmen ouirgang men, for gaddaring ourgeir;
Ze kill bot the carcase, ze get not our saulis,
　　Not douting our shouting is hard in Goddis eir ;
The same God from Pharo defendit his pepill,
And not zone round Robene that standis in zour stepill.

¶ Now, wyse Quene Elizabeth, luik to yourself,
　　Dispite them, and wryte thame ane bill of defyance ;
The Papistis and Spanzards hes partit zour pelf,
　　As newly and trewly was tald me thir tythance ;
Beleue thay to land heir, and get vs for nocht,
Will ze do as we do, it sal be deir bocht.

Giue pleis God we gre sa, and hald vs togidder,
　　Baith surely and sturely, and stoutly gainstand thame;
They culd not weill conqueis vs, culd ze considder,
　　For our men are dour men, and likis weill to land thame;
Quhen Cesar himself was chaist, haue ze forzet,
And baith the realmes be aggreit, tak that thay get.

¶ For better it is to fecht it, defendant our lyfis,
　　With speir men and weir men, and ventour our sellis,
Nor for to se Frenchemen deflorand our wyfis, ·
　　Displace vs, and chace vs, as thay haue done ellis ;
I meane quhen the Inglismen helpit at Leith,
And gart thame gang hame agane spyte of thair teith.

¶ I cannot trow firmely that Frenchmen ar cummen,
  Persayfand thame haifand thameselfis into parrell;
The Lord saue Elizabeth, thair ane gude woman,
  That cauldly and bauldly debait will our quarrell
With men and with money, baith armour and graith,
As scho hes befoir tyme defendit this Faith.

Thocht France for thair falset be drownit in dangeris,
  For causis and pausis thay plait into Pareis,
Zit we ar in war estait, waitand on strangeris,
  Not gyding, deuyding our awin men from Mareis;
So weid the calf from the corn, calk me thair dures,
And slay or ze be slane, gif sic thing occures.

Bot how can ze traist thame that trumpit zow ellis,
  Decoir thame, do for thame, or foster thair seid;
And thay may anis se thair time, tent to zoursellis,
  Baith haitfull, dissaitfull, ze deill with in deid;
Anis wod and ay the war, wit quhat ze do,
And mak thame fast in the ruit gif thay cum to.

¶ God blis zow, my brether, and biddis zow gud nicht,
  Obey God, go say God, with prayer and fasting,
Christ keip this pure ile of ouris in the auld richt,
  Defend vs and send vs the life euerlasting;
The Lord send vs quyetnes, and keip our zoung king,
The Quene of Inglands Maiestie, and lang mot thai ring.

¶ Finis, quod Simpell.

¶ Imprintit at Sanctandrois, be Robert Lekpriuik.
Anno Do. 1572.

XXXIII.—¶ The Sege of the Castel of Edinburgh.

[BRITISH MUSEUM, LONDON.—A FACSIMILE REPRINT IN BLACK
LETTER with a Prefatory Notice by David Constable, Advocate, Edinburgh. Sm. 4to, (TWENTY-FIVE COPIES PRINTED),
London, 1813.—Scotish Poems of the Sixteenth Century,
Collected by John Graham Dalyell, Edinburgh, 1801.]

USCHMĒT of Beruik mak zow for the gait
To ring zour drūmis & rank zour mē of weir
Addres zour armour boūd zow for debait
With sound of trūpet mak zour steids to steir
Sen ze are freikes that weil dar fecht but feir.
As for exampill we haue sene zow ellis,
Lyk as the last tym that zour Camp come heir
Lend vs ane bourrouīg of zour auld blak bellis.

Zour camp conuoyit but cūmer throw the land
In gude array and rewlit by thair rank.
Reddie to pas as plesit us command,
Throw all our bounds to the west sey bank.
Thocht sum mē say ze serue bot lytill thank
Suppose occatioun cum first of thaine sellis,
As thay haue brouin yᵗ bargane sa thay drank
And rewis yᵉ tyme yᵗ euer thay saw zour bellis.

I will repeit na poleceis put doun,
Sen plesit God that we aggrie to giddir.
Except thay crak thair credence to tho Croū.
Than fair weil thay the find resseue the fidder
God saue hir G. that will our cause considder
And as I dout not will ourdryue thir dangeris
As scho befoir tyme send hir forces hidder
To keip yis coūtrie cline fra forrane strāgeris.

To call to mynd hir mony fauld gude dedis,
First scho reformit the fals Idolatrie,
I am in dout in ony realme quha redis.
Of sa lang tyme with sic tranquillitie,
Sic faithful justice with ciuillitie.
Sic frendschip keipit to hir fais sa lang.

12

Scotland may say for oure utilitie.
That neuer ane bettir prince in Inglãd rang.

That beand done scho did conferme a pace,
And maid thã freindis y^t lãg tyme had bene fois
With stancheĩg bludesched wes not eith to ceice
That men may pas not sperand quhair he gois
Syne at the sege of Leith scho sparit ane pois
And dang the frenchmē quhilk we docht not do
Quhill hame thay past in spyt of all thair nois
With lose of men and left munitioun to.

Quhat toung hes langage to declair at lenth
Thair greit artalzerie nor thair men of weir.
France wes not able to withstand thair strenth
For powder, and bullet, bowis, and uther geir
Quhat chargis wes hir schipis at, may I speir,
Surmonting fiftie hunder thowsand frankis,
And zit for all the graith hir grace send heir,
Ingraitfull people gaue hir lytill thankis.

Our Regent slane syne as I said befoir
Stryfe and contentioun rais in to the land.
Treasoun, inuy, did uertue sa deuoir,
Quhill all wes done as murthour did cõmand.
Wes nan sa stout durst tak the steir on hand
Sa has the cause bene quat wer not for shame.
Quhil we sic frendschip furth of Ingland fand
Thay send ane army heir with Leuenox hame.

Conuoyt with Drurie duchtelie in deid.
And as I hoip mair haist wes neuer done.
To Glasg^w past with mony trapit steid
Thair skalit the sege releuit the castell sone.
Doun to Dunbartane on the morne at none,
He raid bot few not fering thame agane him.
Zit of that parrell I prayse the Lord abone,
He chapit weill fra uillanis wald hauc slane him.

That panefull progres I think ill to tell,
Sen thay ar bowit and bruderit in our band,
Bot at this present tyme exem zour sell,
Quhat comfort hes thair Quene send to this land.
Is not the cannones cum at zour cōmand,
Strecht to distroy the tratouris wald ouir gang us
Commonis may crye lang mot that frendschip stand
And blis hir banis sic blythnes broucht amang us.

At Leith thay landit harmeles in the Heuin,
With powder and bullet gunne and uther geir,
Drest all thair platfurmes into dayis seuin,
Not laiking na thing that belangit to weir.
Sum workmen had we or the camp come heir,
Jacques Gelliam gangand lyke ane besy be.
The gabiounes makand haist the trinschis neir,
Quha mycht do mair but ordinance nor we.

The walis wes heith we culd not weil persew thame
Bot quhen we gat thame doun full deir thay bocht it
Be syde the woll at syndrie tymes we slew thame,
That euer thay saw us some of thame forthocht it
And poysonit woll to drink quhat docht it.
Infekit watter sowlit thame cheik and chin,
Persauing that sorrow mair thay socht it.
Bot keppit standfulis at the sklatis thair in.

The castell segit and all beset about,
With sowseyis wyde inueronit be flycht.
Montanis and myndis leit neuer man luik out,
For ordinance thay dang at day and nycht.
By weirlyk uolyis thocht the walis wes wycht,
Zit dowbell battrie brak thame all in inschis,
Of Daueis toure in all the toune menis sycht,
Thay riggein stanes come tumland ouir the trinschis.

The uehement schot zeid in at ather syde
By threttie Cannonis plasit at partis seuin.

Quhill thay thair in mycht not thair heidis hyde,
For Pot Gun pellettis falland from the heuin,
The Bumbard stanis derectlie fell sa euin.
That in to dykis by dint it deidly dang thame,
Quhil all the houssis in the place was reuin.
The bullatis brak sa in to bladis amang them.

Continewand this ane dosand of dayis or mair,
Quhill tyme apointit neuer man durst steir.
The larum rang the Regent self wes thair,
My Lord Ambassat to stuid uerry neir.
The manlie Generall lyke the god of weir,
Not usit to sleip quhen sic thingis ar a do,
Our Cronall als quha is ane freik bot feir,
With all his Capitanes reddie to ga to.

Schir Harie Leis wes present at that charge,
My Lord Burlayis sone to stuid besyde.
Cottoun and Dyar saw the sowt at large
And Schir George Carie to the knauis he cryde,
Zit Hume and Crafurde to the laue wes gyde,
With certane Soiouris of the garysoun.
Four Capitanis followit at thair bak to byde,
Sempill and Hectour Ramsay and Robesoun.

Bot Hume wes first that ouir the walis wan,
As I heir say I wes not thair my sell.
The Generall sayis he playit the uailzeant man,
With prayssis mo nor I intend to tell.
Thocht Crafurdis ledder wes to schort an ell,
Zit ouir the walis he wan I wat not how.
Dunbartan to quhen sic lyke fortoun fell,
Thir wes the men that wan it I tell zow.

The Generallis band come bauldlie at thair bak,
Schir Frances Russall with ane gudlie grace.
Zarlie and Crintoun nather of thame wes slak,
Twa uther Careis, Knowis, and Capitane Kace.

Than wes persewand at ane uther place,
Breikwell, and Lammy, Mechell & Capitan Game,
Bauld Capitane Reid, that euir held to his face.
Pickman, and Wood, did uailzeantly the same.

Spreill, Spadyn, Traill, Hutsoun, and all the laue,
Bartoun and Stirlie, Capitan Duberie slane.
Thoise at the bak wall wes the brasche thay gaue,
For lake of lederis thair thay wrocht in uane.
The men within maid sic defence agane
Thay schot gude Manfrild in athort the throit.
Quhill force did faill and than I saw thame fane.
To cry *Peccaui* with the waithman noit.

Halyburton Strauchan with thair standarts stuid
Seirburne & Schaftoun hes followit on thame fast.
Aueris and Barrat baith wer men of gude,
Gresseone and Hanis wes laith for to be last,
Crippis and Cantrell to the parrell past.
Auld Capitā Leirmount with ane luik to bang thame
Gude M. Setoun maid thair grumis agast,
He gart the Cannones ga sa thik amang thame.

Out gais the Hergbut in the Cannon glydis,
Brak al in bladdis thay docht not weil abyde thame.
Trottar and fiftie fell and loste the bydis.
The laue sa fleit thay wist not quheir to byde thame
Dismontit cannones slew the men besyde thame.
The Suddartis swarfit and said thay wald not sar
The house wes gude had thay had grace to gyde thame
Quhen all wes done we had not bene the war

Let na man lipin in to warldlie strenth,
Bot Godlie ground thay may na thing induir.
Tratouris and treasone sal be tryit at lenth.
Quhen men wald fanest all thair uices smuir
Sa Grange beleuit the Madin Castelliuir.
Haueand sic forssis to defend his touris.

Bot Mell with Madenis quhen thay play the huir,
Win anis the entrie and than the house is zouris.

The Madene Castell it wes callit long,
With honour ay that nobill style it buir,
With wemenis will ze do thame lytill wrong,
To iaip thame sa I think it na iniuir,
Na mair our Madene Castell playit the huir,
Bot tuik appointmēt quhen thair wes na parel
Smaikis had the wyte I say the hous wes suir,
Had thay bene gratious with ane Godlie quarel.

Thay micht not byde it for the greit munitioun,
Bot drew in factiones quhan the larum rang.
Sum thocht it gude to cum and seik remissioun
And sum said best the Secreter to hang.
To his ilusiones we beleuit ouir lang.
Ane cruikit Ethnik and ane crewall Tod,
Inuentand wichecraft ay deuysand wrang.
Lat nan geue credence to ane drytand God.

Then Grang grew sleyit & wald na mair defēd it
For want of watter with ane poysonit well,
His men wes slane and mekle powder spendit
And wantit force to fill the wallis that fell
Thair febill smaikrie I think ill to tell
With luik lyke Lyouncs and sa lytill done.
Fy drūkin dastartis ze haue schamit zoursell
That said sa weill and syne gaue our sa sone.

Durīg this pointmēt thair wes change of graith
Sū gat ane butiene for thair being thair
Gien wes the credence giuen to suddartis faith
Baith gold and siluer and of Marchand wair
Ane tho . . . . tuik to ane . . . skaith*
Be thair expenssis for thair cuming hidder.

* This Line is much obliterated in the Original.

Than on the morns thay maid the pluk up late
Baith Scottis & Inglis syne all zeid togidder.

Upon that spuilze I will spend na tyme,
Thay socht na tailezours for to bule thair breikis
The suddartis luiffis wes sa ouirlaid w^t lyme
Sum gripit gold and gat the thing he seikis,
Sū stude beside and gat not worth twa leikis,
As I heir say I wes not thair to se.
Sū gat thair handfull of thir halfmark steikis
Will haue na mair within ane zeir nor we.

Thay schot na keyis to brek the coffiris than,
Ane day of blythnes for the men of weir.
Sum stuid besyde ane wondderous forte man
Ane duilfull day for thame that loist thair geir.
First saw it tane and syne thay durst not steir :
Thair wes compleit the prophecie of Knox,
Doun fra that Crage Kircaldy sall reteir,
With schame and sclāder lyke ane hundit fox.

With gild of pepile sa thay brocht thame doun,
As birdis but plumis spulizeit of the nest.
Part cryde quhair is he lat us se the loun,
Go to and staen him lat him tak na rest.
Quhē thay y^t buir him saw thame selfis opprest,
Thay cryit for succour for to saue thair lyuis
The Generallis lugeing thair thay thocht it best
Thay led him in thay war sa red for wyuis.

The Regent then gart mak ane inhibitioun
To leue the spuilze under pane of deid
He carit for thing bot the Kingis munitioun,
As for the leue thair wes bot lytill leid.
To tak the hous thair wes na mair remeid,
With all the faultis mycht follow he wes fane.
Againis ane Haiknay I sall wed my heid
Grange beis not Capitan of that Craig agane.

With this the Generall wes reterit a bak,
Went doun to Leith quhair he had bene befoir,
Speik as ze pleis it wes ane uailzeant ak,
And Drurie deulie did his full deuoir.
God gatand thākis the Quene suld haue ye gloir
We thank hir Majeste as the mater standis
God saue hir grace hes scho not gart restoir
Zone captiue rebellis in the Regentis handis.

By expectatioun of the commoun speiking,
Wes it not thocht that Ingland suld begyle us
And sum allegit it wes the Regents seiking
To sell the King and sa thay wald ouirsyle us.
Creip in our stronthis and suddanelie exyle us
O Rural pepill rusticall and rude.
We ar the men that all the warld dois style us,
Remembring ill and gaue na thankis for gude.

Ingratious pepill ignorant and uane,
Quhy do ze noit zour nychtboris ay with ill.
Wer thay not blyith for to get hame agane,
Thocht sum beleuit thay wald haue tareit still
To do zow plesdir thay haue schauin gude will
Baith spent thair lyues & largelie of thair geir
Alace my Joyis ze had bot lytill skill
That trowit that Inglād wald haue tareit heir.

Quhat danger wes to bring sa greit munitioun,
In forane landis with sic ane force indeid,
The only caus wes to auoyid suspitioun,
That men suld say thay come not heir for greid.
Thocht sum thair be of cankreit Cain seid,
Sawaris of discorde dois na uther thing.
Speik as thay pleis schame fal thair lippis y^t leid
Thay mene na thing bot to mantane the king.

Haif thay not thre tymes in this threttene zeir,
Ay quhen we socht thāe send thair forces hedder

Baitht Schippis & Gūnis & martial mē of weir
To win our kyndnes geue we culd considdir.
And now the last tyme quhen we send to bid her
Hes scho not helpit to holk out zone Tod,
Lang moit thir countreis leue in pace to gidder
And grow in freindschip to the feir of God.

☞ The Lenuoy to the Regent.

O richteous Regent of ane Royall race,
Tratours may trimbill to behald thy face,
Fering thy furie for thair foull offencis, .
Geue gloir to God that hes the geuen sic grace.
Riches with reasoun for to reuill that place.
Thow beand plantit in the sait of Prencis,
Geue thow wald prosper in thy iust pretences,
Beir equall ballancis baith to riche and puir
That beand done lang mot thy dayis induir.

Sen God hes wrocht it I am weill content
To mak of the that onlie instrument.
To caus this countrie for to knaw the king:
It wes the leuing Lord Omnipotent,
That maid the Barrones sa obedient,
And not the force that thow to send may bring.
Did neuer Regent in this Realme sic thing.
Considdering alwayis as the mater stude,
And maid sic greance with sa lytill blude.

To speik of Regentis we haue had sic thre
Sen God wes borne thair na bettir be.
For wisdome, manheid, and for Godlynes,
Quhairfore hes God now laid this charge on the
Bot lat us ken that it is onlie he.
That rewlis the Realme & not thy richteousnes
Remember Ahab for his febilnes.
Quha gart king Benhadab in scherat go,
Quhilk wes his wrak be war ze do not so.

Quhairfor put God the powar in zour hand ?
To puneis lounes that hes ourlaid this land.
By murthour, treasoun, done fra zeir to zeir.
Geue ze obey not brekand that command,
I am in dout geue zour estait sall stand.
But sone be rutit fra this Realme I feir,
Spair neuer Agag for na brybe of geir.
Quhat come of Saull with his face Ocin thair
Ga reid the Bybill it will sone declair.

To seik exempillis of that samin tone,
My Lord of Murray wes degradit sone,
For not fulfiling of the Lordis desyre.
First God promouit him in the place abone
Bot fra he saw that Justice wes not done.
He leit the wickit cast the wand in fyre,
Be war sic materis moue not God to yre.
Geue ze be myndit on this mold remaine,
And plesit God I wald not change agane.

Lanuoy to the Ambassade.

My Lord Ambassade I haue lang forzet,
Quhairfor indeid I haue not done my det.
And be sa cairfull for oure countrie men,
For wit and wisdome worthie to be tret.
In baith the landis thair is bot few to get.
That wrocht sa Godlie in this muse ze ken.
My dull indyte can not direct my pen,
And thocht I culd it wald contene ane buik,
To put in paper all the panis he tuk.

He is not borne of better qualytie,
Of quiet speiche with greit moralytie.
Swering nor bairdrie may he nan abyde
Detestand pryde and prodigalitie.
As equall Juge but persealytie.

For feid or fauour unto ather syde.
Abone all uices subject leist to pryde,
Ferme in his faith and full of Godlynes,
With marciall hart myrrenes,

Weill micht the counsals beir ane gude euend [cōmend ?]
That sic Ambassade into Scotland send.
To speik uprichtlie and the treuth declair,
For na expensis did he spair to spend,
Quhill pece wes brocht into ane finall end.
Quhar as he fand us at the pluckup fair.
With walkryfe labour and expensis sair,
God knawis in Scotland quhat he had ado,
With baith the sydis or he culd bring us to.

In winter weddiris baith in wind and raine,
Sum tyme with seiknes sa ourset with pane.
He raid throw montanes many mose and myre
In frost and snaw quhen all the folkis are fane,
With double bonatris for to hap thair brane.
Then wes he worssand our ane wondie swyre,
Sum tymes at nycht syne not to se ane fyre
Ar we addettit to sa trew ane strangear,
That for our proffeit put him sell in danger.

As Caleb send wes for to se the land,
The gydis that come gart Moyses understand
The land wes feirfull and the pepill strang,
Because he knew it wes the Lordis cōmand.
He wald not stay bot stoutlie tuik on hand,
Richt unabasitlie all that gait to gang.
Ourthrow thair castellis & thair gyantis dang,
Brocht thāe to miserie maid ane mynt to wrãg us
He wes yᵗ Caleb sen he come amang us.

I dar be bald to say this hundreth zeir.
He wes not stangear borne mair welcum heir
Nor plesit the Preichours half se weill as he,

On pure nor riche he neuer sparit his geir,
And geue ane Suddart had bene schot in weir
He somzeit not to ga him self and se.
Quha with this countrie culd sa weill agrie.
To play the wise mā quhen he wes with Lordis
Syne help the puiranis as the cause recordis.

Sou reasoun wald that ze returne a bak
We thank zow hartlie of the Godlie ak.
Ze wrocht amang vs for to saif our blude,
I zow beseik thir sempill wersis tak.
With als gude will as ony man can mak
Because ze knaw my cunning is not gude.
Ze man excuse my rurall rymis rude,
God saif our King and send him lytill a do,
The Quene of Ingland and hir Counsall to.

F I N I S.

Quod Sempill.

¶ Imprintit at Edinburgh be Robert Lekpreuik.

Anno. M.D.LXXIII.

XXXIV.—Ane Complaint vpon Fortoun.

[GEORGE DANIEL'S Collection, now in the possession of HENRY
 HUTH Esq., 30 Princes' Gate, London.—THE PHILO-
 BIBLON SOCIETY :—Ancient Ballads and Broadsides, pub-
 lished in England in the Sixteenth Century, chiefly in
 the earlier years of the reign of Queen Elizabeth. Re-
 printed from the Unique Original Copies, mostly in
 Black-letter, preserved in the Library of HENRY HUTH,
 Esq., London. Printed by Whittingham and Wilkins
 1867.—A COLLECTION OF SEVENTY-NINE BLACK-LETTER
 BALLADS AND BROADSIDES, printed in the Reign of Queen
 Elizabeth, between the years 1559 and 1597. Published
 by Joseph Lilly, London 1867.]

INCONSTANT warld, fragill and friuolus,
    With feinzeit Fortoun, quha confides in the
Sall find his lyfe cairfull and cruellus,
    Led in this vale of wofull miserie;
Quhat potent princes in prosperitie,
    Hes sho deposd from their imperiall places!
Hir craft quotidian we may cleirly se,
    As men in mirrouris may behauld their faces.

The worthie Bocas, in his morall buke,
    The Fall of Princes plainly dois compyle;
Amangs them all quha euer lykes to luke,
    Sall finde Dame Fortounis fauour for a quhyle;
For with the one eye sho can lauch and smyle,
    And with the vther lurke and play the loun;
Sum to promotioun, and some to plaine exile,
    Lyke draw-well bukkets dowkand vp and doun.

¶ That variable witch makis all the warld adó!
    Quhat kingis and countreis hes sho brocht to end!
Assyrians, Persians, Grekes, and Romains to,
    The monarches foure micht not hir force defend.

Bulworkis nor battellis bydis her nocht a bend;
   Quha may withstand her straik, quhan sho list
     stryke?
This nicht aneuch, the morne nathing to spend!
   Imago in **Luna**, and sho lukis baith alyke.

To pen the speciallis it passis mony a hunder,
   And makis the tyme ouer tidious to declare;
Sum sho promouis and sum sho puttis to vnder,
   And sum rewardes with wandring heir and thair;
And sum incastrat captiues in the snair,
   And sum for flatrie dois hir freindship find;
To all estates vntruethfull, quhat sould mair,
   Turnand her volt lyke woddercok in wind?

To paint her out it passis mine ingyne,
   How wonderfully she wirkes in all thir thingis!
Sum fra thair birth brocht vp with doggis and swine,
   Tane fra the pleuch and placit in sait of kingis.
The brutell beist ane barbour wolfe vpbringis
   The first borne **Romain** callit Romulus,
Quhais blude as zit into that regioun ringis,
   By expectatioun of auld Amelius.

Cyrus siclyke was be ane bitche vpbrocht,
   Cround as a king ane cruell man of weir.
Pareis in Troy that all the toun forthocht,
   Preseruit from slauchter be souking of a beir.
And swa was Thylaphus with ane hinde, I heir,
   Medas with imates and maid ane michtie prince;
Plato with beis quha did sic prudence leir,
   That all men meruelled of his eloquence.

Without respect to blude royall or clan,
   Pureanis promouit that na man wald presume;
Torquinius Priscus, a baneist marchant man,
   Chaist out of Corinth and cround a king in Rome.
Siclyke was Seruis from ane shipherd grome,
   And Tullus Hostilius fand her fauour neist;

Is, was, and salbe quhill the day of dome,
   Sic doubill dealing in Dame Fortounis breist!

Quha findis hir freindship of fauour hes aneuch,
   To warldly glore sho gydes them all the gait;
Tuke sho not Gordias from the spaid and pleuch,
   And quickly placit him in a princes sait?
How far may Darius bragge of her debait,
   Tane fra the stabil ouer Persia to ring;
Pure Agathocles from a law estait,
   Ane porteris boy to be ane potent King?

Of Justine the suinehird sho maid ane empriour,
   Ouer Constantinople ane king and cround him thair;
Gyges the gait-hird ane michtie conquerour,
   To Lydia land she maid him lord and aire;
And Wallancianus from his landwart fair,
   Tane fra the pleuch to place imperiall;
Cambyses, Nero, be the contrair clair,
   Was thair awin burreois to thair buriall.

Sa Fortoun mountit neuer man sa hie,
   Fostered with folie, suppose she make them faine;
Bot with ane tit sho turnis the quheill, ze sie,
   Doun gois their heid, vp gois their heillis againe!
Of Alexander to write I war bot vaine,
   Ouer fifty landis he lord was at the leist;
Zit threttie dayis lay efter he was slaine,
   Unbureit in Babell lyke a brutell beist.

Xerxes, quhose armeis maid the riueris dry,
   And schippis subumbragit all the seyis on breid,
Did sho not wait him with sic foule inuy,
   Pray to Pericles, that put him to his speid?
Of Julius Cesar gif thow lykes to reid,
   In his triumphant toun victorious,
Slaine be his Senatis, schamefully in deid,
   By his awin kinsmen Brutus and Cassus

Sum auld exemples heir I man induce,
  To bring my purpose to more speciall ;
Quha was mair worthie gif I wald make ruse,
  More stout, more trew, nor hardy Hanniball?
Dauter of Romaines, to Carthage ane castell wall,
  The onely thing quhairin he maist reioysit ;
Do quhar he docht in deidis marciall,
  By his awin pepill petiously deposed.

Sicklyk was Sipio, saiklesly schot furth,
  That vinqueist Hanniball lyke a warriour wicht,
His vailiant workes was weyit bot litils worth,
  Quhen he was baneist with a bair gude nicht ;
Not lyke a captaine, nor a kindly knicht,
  Bot lyke ane beggar baneist in exile ;
Sa Fortoun montit neuer man on hicht,
  Bot sho can law him within a litill quhyle.

Alchebead of Athenis was Duke,
  Of princely parents and ane royall race,
To keip his toun sic trauell undertuke,
  He maid his fo-men fle befoir his face ;
To his rewarde he gat nane vther grace,
  Ingraitly baneist to their awin grit skaith :
And Tymistocles in that samin place,
  By their awin burgessis thay wer baneist baith.

Experience teiches me not to flyte with Fortoun,
  With auld examples that dois na thing belang vs ;
Marke James of Dowglas present Erle of Morton,
  And of the best that euer was borne amang vs ;
Danter of theuis that dayly dois ouer-gang vs,
  Key of this countrie that kepit vs from skaith ;
I speik na farther in feir thay sould gar 'hang vs,
  Preichouris and poiettis are put to silence baith.

Few things wer done bot Mortoun interprisit them,
  Dumbar and Brichane and mony vthair bloke ;

Speik quhat thay pleis, he wrocht them and deuisit them;
   He and his freindis ay formest in the flocke ;
He faucht zour querrell as kein as ony cok,
   Reuengit zour murthers ma nor twa or thrie ;
Ane nobillman and of ane ancient stoke,
   His valiant deidis demereitis not to die.

¶ Ane of the speciallis did mentene zour croun,
   Zour ferme protectour in zour tender zeiris ;
He maid zow vp and all zour fo-men doun,
   His marciall manheid did mentein zour weiris ;
Gif he did wrang, rewarde him as effeiris.
   Gif he did gud, God wald he sould be tret ;
Bot as the prouerbe speikis, it plaine appeiris,
   Auld men will die and barnes will sone forzet.

Was he not rewler ouer zour realme and rigioun
   Quhill all was pacifeit be his prudent wit?
Stude he not stoutly be the true religioun,
   Ane of the first that maid the freiris to flit ?
Franke on the feildis, and formest at the bit,
   Without respect to baggis or bodie to ;
Zour faithfull subiect, and sua he sal be zit,
   To do gude seruice, as I haue seene him do.

Than at Carbarrie hill he held a day,
   With litill bludeshed Bothwell was put a-bake,
Quha slew zour father and fibilly fled away,
   Syne socht zourselfe to bring this realme to sake.
How mony clawbackes than suppose thay crak,
   Conuenit with Mortoun quhan Bothwel tuk the
      chase ?
Try or ze tine him and trow not all thay spak,
   Lat workes beir witnes, vaine wordes sould have
      na place.

Sone efter that the Counsell crouned zoursell,
   Quhan godly Murray as a regent rang,

13

Zit thair was some that bauldly did rebell,
   That to zour lawis wald nouther ryde nor gang.
Quha thair conuenit for to reuenge zour wrang,
   Albeit zour action was thocht innocent ?
It was the Dowglasses douchtaly them dang,
   And pleit zour proces in that parliament.

Quha could declare our langsum lyfe in Leith.
   Fechtand all day and syne lay in our clais ?
Gif Lindesay lykes, that Lord can tell zow eith,
   Quha was zour friendis or quha zour mortall fais,
Or quha gaid formest breistand vp the braies.
   I dar not pen the speciallis, I do plaine zow;
Bot weill I wait, howeuer the warld now gais,
   Thai find maist freindship was fardest than again
      zow.

Syne at Langsyde feild zour grace may ken,
   Mortoun was thair ane man amang the rest;
In Striuiling toun, out of his dowie den,
   Maist lyke a fox thay fyrit him in his nest.
In Edinburgh Castell quhair thay war possest,
   He them desplaced that purposit to undo zow.
Quhan ze grow auld, I wait ze will confest,
   Mortoun hes bene ane faithfull saruand to zow.

Quhan Regentis deit and all the lytes inlaikit,
   The Counsell did conuene and set ane day ;
Thay cheisit him Regent in that rowme that waikit,
   With sad adwise, for few or nane said nay;
Bot zit I think thay playit zour grace foule play,
   Gif he was knawin than of thir crymes conuict,
Gif he be saikles, surely I dar say,
   Thay haue defamit him with ane fulich trick.

To dant the theuis had he nocht mekill ado,
   Abandoned the borders that na man durst rebell ?
The Armestrangis, Eluottis and the Johnestons to,

With twentie vther clans I can not tell,—
During his dayis thai durst not ryde ane ell;
    The hirdis and hinde men in their labeis lay;
Bot thair estait, as now ze sie zoursell,
    All nicht to walke and fane to wirk all day.

Aganis grit lordis committing small offence,
    With iniust challenge thay aucht na man to chessoun;
Mortoun hes ay bene vpricht with his prince,
    But spot of cryme or ony point of tressoun.
Albeit gude saruice be not tane in seasoun,
    His workes may witnes he neuer sparit for perrell;
Laitly accusit but outher ryme or ressoun,
    As sindrie schawis me for a saikles querrell.

Daft fulis defyis him because thay finde him sage,
    And cowartis contrarious for his hardiment;
Young men for glaikrie can not agrie with age,
    And waisteris inuyis him for his gouernement.
And sacreit counsell can not be content
    To suffer lordshippis in equalitie;
Zit I beseik zour grace of gude intent,
    To play the prince but parcialitie.

Adwise zow weill, sen he hes not offendit;
    To keip sic senattis it sall decore zour land;
Of rasche detreitis cums rew and may not mend it,
    As Scottismens wisdome dois behinde the hand.
Wyse lordis are ill ta make I vnderstand,
    And trewly in kingis is to abhorre;
This sempill counsall, syr, is na command,
    Bot wald to God that na man louit zow war.

FINIS, quod Sempill.

Imprintit at Edinburgh, be Robert Lekprewicke,
dwelling at the Netherbow.

XXXV.—Heir followis the Legend of the Bischop of St Androis Lyfe, callit Mr Patrick Adamsone, *alias* Coustcane.

[Scotish Poems of the Sixteenth Century. Collected by John
Graham Dalyell, Edinburgh 1801.—Dr DAVID IRVING
in his "History of Scotish Poetry, Edinburgh 1861" remarks that "This Poem of Semple is supposed to have
been written so late as the year 1583," and "to have been
printed from a Manuscript; but where the Manuscript is
to be found, the Editor has not thought proper to inform
us."]

The Preface.

ALL fayᵗful brether that on the Lord dependis,
   Mark weill this schedule that I have send
    you heir,
   Pestiferus prelatis, that Papistrie pretendis,
Sic deuils but dout sall in oʳ dayis appeir;
Yit God forwairnis you be the weidis they weir,
To ken the lupus in a lamb skyn to appeir,
Makand thair godis of warldlie gudis and geir,
The flock new foundit, and thay in furringis happit.

   Veneriall pastoris, in vomiting thair fayᵗ,
Lyk to ane tyke returning to it agane,
Filling thair purses with the spirituall grathe,
Plucking the pellottis or ever the scheip be slane:
Goddis true preceptis and preiching to prophane,
Layand thair cuires in warldlie busines.
Thir are the propheitis, I speik it to you plane,
Coverit with coule of clockit holines.

   Lyk to the scrybes, closing the yeattis of heawin,
Sayand the Pope sic power to thame gave;
Hyding the keyis was treuly to thē gewin,
Thinking yᵗ Christianis shall na entres have,
A scabbit scheip wald fane infect the lave,

Causing sedition into the kirk to ryse.
Heirfoir, bewar what sermond ye resave;
In rottin bosses no balme liquor lyes.

To Bischop Balaam brecking the law of God,
They may succeid weill as his sone and air;
Or Coran, Dathan, reving Aarons rod,
With thair vsurpet priesthood playit no mair.
To Amasias I may them weill cōpair,
Sleayand the fay⁺full flock wᵗout offences;
Tane and incarcerat, keipit heir and there,
Beggit and banist, bearing the wraith of princes.

In Maccabeis, wha ever lykis to luike,
By Alchimas and Jason they may leir,
Mensuorne byschopis that Moses law forsuike,
Renūcing God for warldlie gudis and geir,
With Kingis unchristned cūand to the weir,
Contrair thair cōsciēce and their kyndlie friendis.
What dois our bischopis now, may I noᵗ speir,
Servandis to Sathan for his takkis and teindis?

I may cōpair thō to a plunted fyre,
But heit to warme you in the winteris cauld;
Or to a visioun* cled with trym attyre,
Covering a skyn vncomelie to behald.
The pleasan plane-trie will the leavis vnfauld,
With fairest schaddow to save the sone in sȳmer.
Be thir lait bischopis may this teall be tauld,
Bearand no fruite bot barren blockis of tymber.

Vntruethfull teacheris, in thir tymes bypast,
Some hes bene sene from yeir to yeir;
Bot in this latter aige they flock so fast,
That I beleive in deid the day be neir.
Judas Iscariot, for a gleib of geir,
Betrayed his Maister lyk a tratoʳ tod.

* Or, *visorne.*

Annas and Caiphas, gif they both war heir,
Culd do no mair to slea the sanctis of God.

Blind Baals bischopis, provocking God to yire,
Your sinfull leaving hes the scheip ouersyled,
Compared to swyne returnīg to the myre
In thair awin filthes to get thair fames defyled.
Albeit they be now Tulchin bischopis stylit,
Having proude kingis and counsallis to decoir thō,
Auld God, is God, and will not be begylit,
When Plutois palice beis provydit for them.

May Scotland beir sic bischoppis for the gallous,
St Androis, Glasgow, for yᵗ gait anes grantit,
What have ye lost, forloppen, leying fellowes ?
Fraudulent fellowes, that tuyse there fayᵗ recāted.
The spreit of God was anes into thē planted,
Preiching his doctrine, as indeid they did,
But fra they gat the drapping grise they wald [wanted]
Thair clocket knaverie culd na moir be hid.

Vngratious guydis, yᵗ God has never anoynted,
Lyk to our fayᵗfull pastouris past befoir,
But be the devile, I dout not, heir appoyntit,
Godis holie scriptour for to cloik and smoir.
For no rewarde they work but warldlie gloir,
Plaing *placebo* into princes faces,
With leyis and letteris doing thair devoir,
Pynand true preichouris, for to possess there places.

Voratious woulfis, I wish you to rewolk,
Ere in the den of darknes ye most lye ;
Of Godis true mercies, lyk to mercat focke,
Selling for lucre, quha so lykis to by ;
Libidinous drūckardis they dowe not to denye ;
May no man had thē be thair yeis and nayis.
Thir are the propheitis, planelie ze may espye,
The Lord called lyers in the latter dayis.

Thair maister, Pluto, hes there spreitis posses,
Who with his Lord in lyk contritione fell.
Thinkand his wit and beautie by the rest,
Against the word of God he wald rebell.
Through his presūptous pryde he past to hell,
Leaving the heavinlie harbrie whair he satt.
Gif they repent not sone, assure they sall
Receave sic mercie as thair maister gat.

This Adamsone may weill be borne of Eve,
Takand his vices of his wicket mother;
Lykkest to father Adam, I beleive,
Surpassing Cain cursed, or ony vther:
For he slew nothing bot his onlie brother;
And this hes drowned hole dioceis, ye sie.
Wanting the grace, when he shuld gyde the ruther,
He lattis his scheip tak in at luife and lie.

Reforme thair faythis, gif they be found astray
From thair vocatione cleane degenerat;
Preis not to enter be the wrangous way,
As bastard brethren, being reprobat;
With hert cōtreit, and handis elevat,
Seik thair salvatione of the samyn sort;
They will not find the father obstinat,
When synnaris knoxis in casting vp the port.

Heirfore, deir Bretherne, I wish you to bewar;
Sen ye are wairned, I wald not ye were blekkit;
To thair deceatfull doctrine come not nar,
Singand lyk syrens to deceave the elected;
Both art and part of Papistrie suspectit,
As ye may see be thair workis inventit.
To Edinburgh baillies my buike salbe directed,
Desyrand lycence to get live to prent it.

Ground you on God, the rocke and corner stane,
As Paull dois speik to the Corrinthianis.

Swa live thir lyars, and thair lawis allane ;
Packand thair penche lyk Epicurianis,
Contrair to Christ, lyk Antichristianis,
The plane polluters of his holie tēple ;
Lyk to Scrybes and fals Pharisianis,
Bellie god bischopis : Quoth your brother Semple.

A Lenboye.

Now, papir, pass ; and gif they speir who send the,
Tell thame, a true mā bay^t to King and Croun. .
Curious poyetis, I knaw, will vilipend the,
Saying, thou fares but of ane saucie lowne.
Yet with the rascall people up and downe,
Finding our friendis, cōfess to be myne,
From the New Castle cūing to this towne :
Concluding this, we toome a tas of wyne.

**The Legend or Discourse of the Lyfe and Conversatione and Qualiteis of the
Tulchene Bischope of Sanctandrois. Set furth by R. S.**

TO all and sundrie be it sene,
　　Mark weill this mater quhat I meine,
　　The legend of a lymmeris lyfe,
　　Our Metropolitane of Fyffe ;
Ane schismatyke, and gude swyne hogge,
Come of the tryb Gog Magoge ;
Ane elphe, ane elvasche incubus,
Ane lewrand lawrie licherous ;
Ane fals, forloppen, fenyeit freir,
Ane rāungard for greid of geir,
Still daylie drinckand or he dyne,
A wirriare of the gude sweit wyne ;
Ane baxters sone, ane beggar borne,
That twyse his surnaime hes mensuorne
To be called Cōstene he tho^t schame,
He tuke vp Cōstantine to name.

Some to the schoolis this knave cõvoyes;
Beggand his breid amonges the boyes,
He come to letters at the lenth;
Then when he grew to witt and strenth,
He tuike the ministrie on hand,
And servit at *Syres* vp a land;
Bot through presũptious height and pryde,
He layed that office sone asyde;
Manna and quales he tho^t no fude,
The pottis of Egypt was tuyse as gude.
Thinking that poore professione vaine,
He changed his surname over agane;
Now Docto^r Adamsone at last.
Whairthrow he ower to Paris past,
As pedagoge to young M'Gill,
Imploying ay his spreit to ill.
To lerne disceat and subtil sawis,
He studeis long tyme in the lawis;
Ilk day devysing sindrie wylis,
Not ane nor tua that he beguyles:
Thair was no Scotismã dwellane thair,
Bot he deceaved them les or mair:
Maitland, Melwill, and Matchevellous,
Learnet never mair knaifrie in a scholehous;
Which tua resembles, as I suppone,
Architophell, and fals Triphone:
Then finding out ane new fas cast,
Amongis the prentaris is he past,
And promeist to set foorth a buike.
Grit sowmes of money from them he tuike;
Bot Bacchus, and the bordall toe,
Maid him sic busines adoe,
That he my^t gett na buikis cõpyld;
And sua the prentaris were beguyld.
Now Holyglass, returnĩg hame,
To play the sophist, thought no schame:
Through sindrie realmes tho^t he had ranged,
Yit nathing in his maneris changed.

Then, heiring tell how Lowrie landit,
The cōgregatione him cōmandit
To serve a kirk, and keip a cure;
Persaving thair professione pure,
He tho^t it but ane vaine vocatione.
He thristed, ane easiare occupatione,
Amonges the lawers for to lyve;
Bot fra that rang not in his sleyve,
He wald with thame no mair remane,
Bot maid him for the court agane.
The erle of Lennox, levand then
Our regent, and a worthie man,
Vnto his brother him directed,
With secreit earrandis vnsuspectit,
For pois to pay his men of weir;
Bot how, alace, as ye shall heir,
Betrayed thame bay^t with a tryme cōvoy.
Makand his bargand with a boy,
Was ower to Flanders fled and ferreit,
Cryand out, harmesay, he was herreat;
Laméting sair his lose and skaith;
And this gait he beguylit thame bay^t:
Bot yit with tyme his trickis were tryed,
He had nea toung for to denye it.
Than, gif he had not fled for feir,
Gude Matchewell had mist his meir.
To tell how he bestowit his poise,
The faice is weill sene on his noise:
For be his craig ye may weill ken
Gif he be ane of Bacchus men.
Than, whan he had na vther vaine,
He maid him for the kirk againe.
Bot for to tell what test he tuke,
Dysertis Duschet was the buike;
And maid ane sermone, some confydis,
To plesour fock on bayth the sydis.
His mynd was mair on heich promtione,
Groundit on geir, nor gude devotione,

Without respect of true religione,
As we have manie in this regione.
Yet in the pulpet we saw him greit,
Playand the publict hypocreit.
Then men, beholding his cōtritione,
Beleavand he had changit cōditione.
Then through to Paislay he was send,
Lascivous maneris for to amend.
What fruite come of his ganging thair ?
Sic preist, sic pariche ; what suld mair ?
For, neather with preiching nor w^t reiding,
Tuke he that faythless flock in feiding ;
Bot meit in campo did cōmand them,
And left thē some war nor he fand them.
To tell you quhat this cāpo meins,
Thair daylie to the drinck cōveins
The obstinat papistis of the toun ;
This pasto^r with his scheip sat doun,
Bot maid no work, I mak you plane,
To bring the lost scheip bak agane.
To copowt cōplene there he calld thame,
Bot never findis whair he forbade thame
Thair vglie aithis abhominable.
They finding him so favorable,
They thankat God that they had fūd him.
Ecce quā bonū et quā jucundū.
Est habitare fratres in unū.
Freir Johnstoun, and Maquhane about him,
Tua pallartis that the Pope professis,
Rysing at mydnycht to there messis ;
Vidi, scivi, sed non audiebam,
Potum merū cū fletu miscebam ;
Carruse, and hald the cānikin klynclene,
Yit wha were there to sie thair drinking ?
They hald it still vp for a mocke,
How Maister Patrick fedd his flock ;
Then to the Court this craftie lown,
To be a bytescheip maid him boun ;

Becaus St Androis then dependit,
To heich promotione he pretendit.
The kirk began to tak suspitione,
Then knawing weill the knaifis cōditione,
They callit him into thair Assemblie,
Bot not so welcome thair as hamelic.
Greit oethes he sweiris, w^t feinyeit face,
That he suld never inioy that place ;
And bad thame hald him vnsuspect,
He was not gewin to that effect.
Bot bettir packet afternone,
The foullest turne that ever was done,
Ben ower the bar he gave a brocht,
And laid among them sic a locket ;
With *eructavit cor meū*,
He hosted thair a hude full fra him ;
For laike of rowme, that rubiature
Bespewit vp the moderator ;
While the Assemblie thocht grit schame,
Saying he was seik, and send him hame,
And laid him backwardis in a bed,
But not so weill nurtorit as fed.
Sone efter that, incontinēt,
Earle of Mortoun gat the regimēt ;
Then sett he to, with saill and ayre,
To seik some lowiner harbore thayre,
And caist his anckers on the raid,
And long tyme with the Lord abaid.
His towes, I find, hes bene so fyne,
For all the stormes hes bene sensync,
His schip come never on the schalde,
But stack still on the ancker halde.
His office daylie was, indeid,
The chapter to expone and reid.
When he that sermone celebrat,
He had a word accustomat ;
The propheit meinis this, gif ye mark it,
Auld Captane Kirkburne to him harkit ;

Perceaving weill St Androis vaikit,
And syne how sone the knave was staikit,
To all men levand he compleinis,
I watt now what the propheit menis.
This foirsaid bischope beand deid,
Maister Johne Wynramc was maid heid,
For sowmes of silwer that he had lent thē;
Bot he besoght thame to content thē:
He cravit na digniteis prophane,
But his awin silver hame agane.
Fra Holiglass sone hard this thing,
He toned his dussie for a spring,
And held the Regent so in hand,
And maid him weill to vnderstand
That he sould pay the foir said sowme,
Gif he were enterit in the rowme;
And mair, as he wald bid him doe,
To give his servantis pensiones toe.
Sua, with his craft, this carlingis pett,
Hes fangit ane grit fisch in his nett.
Bot fra he was a byschope stylit,
Mr Johne Wyndrome was beguylit,
Had he no^t had a sure probatione,
And cald him on his obligatione.
Bot Docto^r Patrick still replyed,
With trickis and delatouris he denyed,
And maid manifest to men of law,
That he had his discharge to schaw.
Bot how his discharge was gotten,
When Holieglass is deid and rotten;
His smaikrie sall not be forgett,
How Docto^r Patrick payit his debt.
Ane new cōceat this knaif hes tane;
To Willie Vylie he hes gane,
The Regents awin cubicular,
His servant and his secretare,
And him besought to lat him see
Of missive wrytingis tuo or thrie,

Fra Maister Jhone Wydrome to my Lord,
And hecht him crownes for to accord.
This simple boy, suspecting nocht,
Thrie of the wrytingis to him brought.
Ane of thame law subscryvit, ye ken,
As custom is to noble men :
He cuttit off the bill above [abone]
And filled the blank with falset sone,
Discharging him the foirsaid sowmes.
It cūand in the Sessiones thowmes,
To Maister Wyndrome they cōpleanet,
Wha swair that he had nevir sene it,
And tuike in hand for to impryve it.
Thair Matchewell had bene mischevit,
Were not his falsett was cōfessit,
And sic a moyen with him dressit,
Five hūdreth merkis he to him gave,
And tuik in hand to pay the leave.
At certane dayis, thair was na doubt,
Bot fra he fand the tyme ryn out,
He pat him off with mowis and mockis,
And had no will to louse the boxe.
The superintendent saw na better,
Bot raid agane, and raisit a letter,
And gat the harlat to the horne.
Bot Howliglass, lang or the morne,
New falsat forged out for to defend him ;
Ane fair suspentione he hes send him.
The vther to the Sessione pleinyeit,
And said it was both fals and feinyeit,
And socht inspectione for impriving.
The lymmer, feiring lyfe and leving.
He saw na bute, but bagis to louse,
And swoir he maid it but in mowis :
As Maister Andro Wilsoune wrocht it,
And secreitlie said he forthoght it ;
Beseikand him to keip it close,
Or word ran to the cōmon woice.

The vther wald na mair reprive him,
Bot all men he forbade beleive him,
Or ever to trow ane word he spak,
But Holiglass behind thair back.
So in Sanctandrois happened then,
Ane callit Scot, a mareit man,
Nocht verie riche in worldlie guddis :
Save tua pure aikers of borrow ruddis ;
Yit with the glaikis he was owergane,
And in adulterie he was tane ;
Maid to be punisit for his paik ;
But he was stubburne in his talk ;
Iniurit the elders, what suld mair ?
This byschop, beand present thair,
Desyrit him hame, and he suld seay
Gif he culd lerne him to obey ;
For all his crackis, doe what he can
To knaw the law of God and man.
Sua to his castell tuik him hame,
This dubil drunckerd thought na schame ;
Fuorth secreitlie he callis him syne,
And fillit him fow with aill and wyne ;
Persuading him to sell his land,
And gat his letters in his hand.
This beand done, as I have said,
Vpon his duschet vpe he played,
Gevand the man so mony terroris,
That brocht him in a thousand erroris,
That for his lyfe was no remeid,
Gif he abaid the law but deid.
The pure man, being fleid for feir,
Gave him the land, and gat na geir ;
Maid sayle syne to the Easter sees,
And, lyk ane dyver, thair he deis ;
Whairto this bischop tuik reguard,
And enterit sone to Nabothis yaird.
The sillie wedo a quhyle defendit,
But scho grew pure, and so scho endit,

And left hir malisone, cōsider,
To Lowrie, and the land together.
Whether hir malisone tuike effect,
Or gif it was the gude wyne sect,
Or surfeating of sundrie spyces,
Or than a scurge for clockit vyces ;
Bot sic ane seiknes hes he tane,
That all men trowit he had bene gane ;
For leitches my^t mak no remeid,
Thair was na bute to him bot deid.
He, seing weill he wald not mend,
For Phetanissa hes he send,
With sorcerie and incantationes,
Reising the devill with invocationes,
With herbis, stanis, buikis, and bellis,
Menis mēbers, and south runīg wellis ;
Palme croces, and knottis of strease,
The paring of a preistis auld tees ;
And, *in principio*, sought out syne,
That vnder ane alter of stane had lyne,
Sanct Jhones nutt, and the for'e levit claver,
With taill and mayn of a baxter aver.
Had careit hame heather to the oyne.
Cutted off in the cruik of the moone ;
Halie water, and the lāber beidis,
Hyntworthe, and fourtie vther weidis :
Whairthrow the charmīg tuik sic force,
They laid it on his fatt whyte horse.
As all men saw, he sone deceissit :
Thair Saga slew ane saikles beast.
This wald not serve ; he sought ane vther,
Ane devill duelling in Anstruther,
Exceading Circes in cōceattis,
For changene of Wlisses meatis :
Medusa's craftis scho culd declair,
In making eddars of her hair :
Medea's practicques scho had plane,
That could mak auld men young agane.

By Achates, the witches god,
Mercurius, with his charmed rod,
The aunciēt king of Bactria,
That first inventit magica,
Could not so weill of stowen geir tell,
As could this vglie hund of hell.
With this, the word yead through the toun,
How lurcan Lowrie played the lowne:
Heiring how witches wrang abusit him,
The kirkmen calld him and accused him,
And scharplie of theis pointis reproved him,
That he in sorcerie beleavit him,
Whairthrough his saule my^t come to skay^t.
The witche and he cōfessing bayth,
Scho tuike some part of white wyne dreggis,
Wounded rayne, and blak hen eggis,
And maid him droggis that did him gude.
His ansr. being rashe and rude:
Suppoise the devill maid that graith,
The seiknes sua oversett my faith,
At that tyme, to asswage my sair,
I wald have tane it, I tauld thame thair.
Then did the elders him desyre
Vpọn the morne to mak a fyre,
To burne the witches both to deid:
Bot or the morne he fand remeid.
He dred sa sair they suld have schawin
How his knaverie was to thē vnknawin;
Laich in a lyncbus, whair thay lay,
Then Lowrie lowsit thē, long or day,
And had no will they were corrected;
Yit with the people he was suspected,
Trowing the teallis befoir was spocken,
Becaus they saw no presone brocken.
There was his pretticques weill espyed;
But with his ansr: he replyit,
And said, na man, at his cōmand,
Wald tak the presone hous in hand;

14

Into that dūgeon was sic din,
As Beelzebub had bene therin ;
That nevir a man durst stire qll: day :
And sua he neckit thame with may,
And brocht the teale bravelie about,
How Pluto come and pullit thē out.
Yit few or nane this Lourie beleavit,
Becaus they culd not get it previt :
They prayit him to amend his lyfe,
And trow na witchcraft in a wife.
For oght the kirk culd him forbid,
He sped him sone, and gat the thrid ;
Ane carling of the Quene of Phareis,
That ewill win geir to elphyne careis ;
Through all Braid Abane scho hes bene,
On horsbak on Hallow ewin ;
And ay in seiking certayne nyghtis,
As scho sayis, with sur sillie wychtis ;
And names out nytboris sex or sewin,
That we belevit had bene in heawin.
Scho said scho saw thame weill aneugh,
And speciallie gude auld Balcleuch
The secretare, and sundrie vther ;
Ane William Symsone, hir mother brother,
Whom fra scho hes resavit a buike,
For ony herb scho lykis to luike :
It will instruct hir how to tak it ;
In sawis and sillubs how to mak it;
With stones that mekle mair can doe
In leich craft, whair scho layis them toe.
A thowsand maladeis scho hes mēdit.
Now being tane and apprehendit,
Scho being in the bischopis cure,
And kepit in his castell sure,
Without respect of warldlie glamer,
He past into the witchis chalmer,
Closing the dure behind his bak,
And quyetlie to hir he spak,

And said, his work lome was no^t worthe,
Lowsing his poyntis, he laid it furth.
Scho sayned it with hir halie hand;
The pure pith of the pryo^ris wand:
To help that raipfull scho hes rest him,
Whairfore, ye say, my ladie left him.
For scho had sayned it tuyss or thrise,
His rubigo began to ryiss
Then said the bischop to Jhone Bell,
Goe, tak the first seye of hir yor sell.
The witche to him her weschell gave,
The Bischops blessing to resave.
What dayis of pardone then scho wan!
The relicques of that holie man
Micht save her saule from purgatorie.
His wyfe, cōceiving jelowsie,
Cryed out his deid, when it was done,
Ran through the tovn, and tauld it sone.
Ane syiss was socht sone to the wyfe.
Whairas ane aunciēt laird of Fyiffe,
Of gude report, that may be trowit,
Befoir this Bischope weill awowit,
Eather at Semblie or at Sessione,
As he wha hard the wyffis cōfessione,
That this was suirlie thair proceiding.
Whair sic men gettis a flock in feeding,
The sillie scheip wilbe devorit,
And Goddis true doctrine daylie smorit.
This beand done, he thought sic schame,
He my^t not tarie weill at hame,
But ower to Edinburgh he hes past,
Procured a licence, at the last,
To ryde to Londoun with a letter,
Becaus they culd not get a better.
Wist he what his cōmissione bure,
He my^t weill serve for sic a cuire.
Sic lipps, sic lattouce, lordis and lownes,
Auld creased workis payit with crackit crownes.
Bot heir I will no mair remane,

Returnīg to my text agane.
It may no^t be no more forborne,
How he beguylit pure David Horne,
Ane honest man, ane messinger,
And was St Androis pensioner.
To all the Bischopis thair befoir,
He doing daylie his devoir,
He gat allowance, being leill,
Ane pensione of a chalder of meill.
Our to this Bischop now is he gane;
His letter of tak hes with him tane;
Sayand, ye man be gude, my Lord,
And to yor man misericord.
This angle noble in my neife
Vnto yor Lordschip I will gife,
To cause you to renew my tackis.
The vther little answer makkis.
The Angle noble first he tuike,
And syne the letters for to luike:
With y^t hes byknife furth hes tane,
And maid him tuētie tackis of ane,
In litle crownes began to cut them;
The vther gaid hame backwards but them,
Sichand, and durst say no mair,
And left his angle noble thair.
With thir, and mony sic lyke trickis,
The haill coūtrie this coūtrie cōvictis.
The pure men plentis y^t duellis besyde him,
How creipis in a hoill to hyde him,
And barris them fast w^tout the yettis,
When they come there to crave there debtis;
For kaill, candle, and knocked beir,
Herbis to the pot, and all sic geir,
He never payis ane pēny he takkis.
To heir the mone the pure folk makkis,
What malisones are to him gevin,
Cryand a wengance from the hewin,
Come doun on this deceatful Lowrie;

I wald not for the carse of Gowrie
To be a bischop in his esteat.
To heir, when he gangis throw the gait,
How everie wyffe on vther puttis,
Bidding the bischop pay for his guttis,
And cryis, gar pay me for my eall,
Ane vther for candle, the thrid for caill:
The fourt cryis out for knocked beir,
How dar this dastard hud our geir?
A vengeance fall his feinzit fay^t,
For poinding of the pure folkis graith.
Efter my Lord this larwme ringis,
For this and mony sic lyke thingis,
Suppose it stude on all thair lyffis,
He will not get amongis the wyffis
Ane pynt of aill in all the tovne,
Except the silver be laid down.
Then gif ze knew his duble tackis
Amonges the coūtrie men he mackis;
With feinyeit seillis and antideatis,
And tuentie vther tryme cōceatis,
Setting the coūtrie be the earis,
And takis no tho^t of ny^{t}bo^{r}is weiris,
Se he be sure to fill his hand,
How meikle blood be in the land.
Gif siclyk bischopis be admittit,
Grit God and all the warld sall wit it;
This makis his trickis, his feinyeit toyes,
What clocked knaverie he cōvoyes.
His wattir drincking, his seiknes feinyeit,
Fearand the kirk shuld on him pleinyeid.
It cōes to licht now, at the last,
Fra tyme the ministers are past,
The trick of Guisians devysit,
He hes bene ane to interpryse it;
Ane waikrife devill daylie to wirk,
To saw seditione in the kirk,
Learning a lessone at ald Frogmortene,

As he cōfessit at his departing.
To conterfute that fals cōceat,
And speik the Quenis Grace be the gait,
He fand his seikness was so sair,
Throw all his bodie heir and thair,
That nathing my^t his panes repell,
Except it were some sacred well
In Lorane, or the well of Spaa :
Bot his cōmissione na man saa :
Which text cōtenit na vther thing
Bot cōmendationes fra our Kyng
Vnto the Quene of Englandis Grace,
Beseikand hir to help his case,
And to send new support aganist him.
Mortone, sayis he, the lawis hes slaine him,
And Gowrie hes gottin a cōdigne syse,
Conformīg to his interpryse,
With sindrie vtheris that loves thair factione,
That daylie dois mentene y^t actione :
As Anguse, Mar, and Maister of Glames,
Tak thir thrie for na saikles lambes,
But proude ambitious bangesters,
With some seditious ministers,
Cōtempneris of our authoritie,
Subscryvit aganist our Maiestie,
For to destroy our realme and regione,
Without respect of true religione ;
Beleivand we should bring hame the mess ;
Luke what religione ye profess :
I salbe būde therby to byde,
Under grit God ye salbe guyde,
My tutrix in my tendir yeiris,
Sen none in earth to me so deir is
As ye my kindlie cusines.
Gif I had gritter bussines,
I think ye aucht for to defend me,
With succo^r and support to send me.
To bring this mater to ane end,

My sacred bischop I have send,
As Semple sayis, ane subtile tod,
To bring me hame the word of God
From Italie and Almainie,
In Geneva and Germanie,
To seik the trew experiēce,
For libertie of cōscience.
Give ye think gud, I hald it best
That bayᵗ our realmes myᵗ live in rest.
With this and vther siclyk wairis,
Befoir the coūsal he declairis
A fals, deceatfull, feinyeit taill,
Bot alwayis for thair awin availl.
Bot yit, or he bound to the read,
How that his packmātie was mead,
I thing it best for to declair.
His blew clock beand worne so bair,
He causit an talyeoʳ turne it and mak it
Into wich maill; a frind he packt it.
His sarkis, his schone, his ganging gowne,
Ane fitt case for a feinyeit lowne;
Na dentie geir this Doctor seikis;
Of tottis russet his ryding breikis;
Ane hamelie hat, a cott of kelt,
Weill beltit in ane lethrone belt;
A bair clock, and a bachlane naig,
His ruffe curfufled about his craig;
The one end to his belt hang doun,
The vther stude above his crovn.
Thair was a brave embassadoʳ
Befoir so noble ane auditoʳ,
The Quene of Englandis Maiestie,
Hir coūsall and nobilitie.
In hir triumphand palice placit,
May sic fellowis be defacit.
Allace, that Scotland had no schame,
To send sic howfing carles from hame!
Now oʳ embassadoʳ is boune,

With bag and bagag off the toun,
All ny^t in Seytoun he remaned,
Whair wyne and aill was nothing hayned;
And fra my Lord he gat a letter,
To cause him to be treat the better,
To Monsier, to mak him speid,
The Frenche embassado^r indeid,
That daylie yit in Londoun lyis,
Wha can an evill turne weill devise;
And syne to Berwick on the morne,
Whair all men leuch my Lord to scorne;
Na mulettis thair his cofferis caries,
Bot lyk a court of auld cashmaries,
Or cadyers cūig to ane fair;
And yit some honest men gaid thair,
For fewis and takkis y^t he sic sett thame,
Beleivand in y^t towne to get thame,
Bot may gaip lang or he get them;
As they have sped, ye may speir at them.
Tuiching his awin tryne, ye shall heir,
The vicar of   on a meir,
That wonder weill can turne a can,
A ganeand maister for sic a man,
With vthere fellowis tuo or thrie;
Gude Robert Melwene of Carnebie,
I shuld not racken in with thea;
Of honest men he had na mea.
But he may ruse him of his ryding,
In Londoun for his longsome byding.
Thair Holieglas begane his gaidis,
As he was learned amangis the laidis.
To Maist: Hanam sone he past,
And sowmes of silver fra him him ast
In borrowing while he come bak.
The man beleivand it he spak,
Vnto this sophist sone cōsentit;
But he had efterward repentit,
Were not a man amongis thē sell,

Whose cōscience causit him to tell,
And quyetlie his coūsall gave him,
That Holieglas wald sone deceave him.
The man perceaving it was sua,
Gave him the gek, and lute him gea,
Thankand his God, and gud men baith,
For his delyvering of y^t skeath.
O Holieglass! thought thou no schame,
And thou but laitlie come frome hame?
Vpon the secund day at morrow,
Suld our embassado^r gea borrow,
And Want or ever he wyn ower Tweid?
Bot God be praisit he come no speid.
To Londoun Lowrie tuke the geat,
With traine my^t staik for his estait,
His wantone vicare on a meir,
Twa vther fellowis to turse his geir;
Bot never ane honest man had he,
Save Robert Melwene of Carnebie,
That with that bischop went about,
To sett his feinyeit falsett out;
Bot als gude he had sittin idle,
As there ower land to leid his brydle,
Considering what reward he gatt,
Still on his owne cott taill he satt,
As salbe tauld you or we tuyne,
In loco quo it shall come in.
To tell all ludgene whair he lay,
And ay on be the brek of day,
Wald be ower langsome to collect;
I wilbe brief in that respect.
Bot yit the menstrallis and the bairdis,
Thair trowand to obtene rewardis,
About his ludgene loudlie played;
Bot menstrallis, serving man, and maid,
Gat Mitchell in an auld pocke nucke,
Save dira adew his leive he tuik.
He be the gait with murmo^r passis,

Allace, I have forget the lasses !
Bot yit thay shall not want a plak ;
Will God give I returne abak.
This was to cloik his waine cōceat,
For he come home ane vther gait ;
As Culen Kyngis that Christ adorned,
Per aliam viam he returned.
In Londone he ane ludgene tuike,
A inkeiper, a cōmon cuike,
Ane tapster bay^t of aill and wyne,
That weill my^t staik for sic a tryne.
Vnto the court the word is gane,
That he had sic ane ludgene lane.
Little they said, what evir they thought.
Vnto this bischop there was brought
Ane new-maid coische for to decore him ;
Ane serving gentlemā send for him,
That stude ane long ho^r at his yeatt,
Or he could ony entres geatt,
While he was grathed into his geir,
Siclyke as he was wont to weir,
As I befoir have specifeit,
And Maister Willie will verefeit.
The man that was his messinger,
The Quenis Grace Latin secretare,
Being eschamit fra ever he saw him,
Said to himself, a vengeance faa him.
To this our brave embassado^r,
Whome to we doe sic hono^r,
That I am send for to hir Grace,
A cowe bust in a bischops place :
Yit in the cosche he lap at last.
Into the palice are they past,
Which callit is the fair White hall,
     the palice wall
      and wald no^t spair,
Which is a thing inhibit thair.
Ane porter sone did him persave,

And to the bischop his blissing gave
Betuixt the schoulders a royall route,
Turning him wodderschins about.
To scape the fray he was so fane,
He put vp club in scheath agane.
Cüing to presence of the Quene,
Becaus he had not sic thingis seine,
He wist not weill how to behave him,
Bot as some vthers counsall gave him ;
And that was of a semple sort,
As I can tell by true report
Of gentlemen that stude besyde him,
That he had na mair grace to guyde him ·
Nor it had bene ane hieland quow,
Lurcane and lowring I wat not how.
Then his cōmissione being red,
Out of the palice he was sped,
Then to the wall agane gois he,
To   part of honestie.
The portars publictlie reprovit him,
And doubtless they had thair mischevit him,
Were not the gentle men excuset him,
And thame forbade to stryke a stranger.
He beand scapit of that danger,
Hame through the past, and wald not spair ;
Thay maid a midwyfe of him thair ;
They bring thame farre on ābeling foiles,
Bot send thame hame throw on thair soilles.
Tuo moneth he tareit efter that,
But never presence agane he gat.
With bischops he began to fleich,
Desyring licence for to preich.
Of his auld sermon he had perquier,
Bot they had never hard thame heir.
Of omnigatherene now his glose,
He maid it lyk a Wealchmā hose ;
Tempora mutantur, was his text.
The bischops vicar being vext

To ruse his maister, and set him out,
Sayand to thame y^t stude about,
Gif ye his preiching could persave,
My maister is a lerned knaif:
Placebois part behind his bak,
Vnto the people this he spak:
The preiching done, the chapter red,
They baith gaid fow aneuch to bed.
This poysoned preicheo^r of Godis word
Is not vnlyk a suple suord;
For in the fyire when ye have heat it,
To ony syde you lyk to sett it,
It will go worth and stand therto,
So will this duble docto^r doe.
For greid of geir, and warldly graith,
On baith the gaitis he grūds his fayth.
For daylie we may se his dress,
When Monseir gaid vnto his mess,
Into ane gallerie neir besyde;
Thair wald this halie bischope byde,
Saying, forsuith, it was not smittel.
I think he weyit the mater litle,
How mony messis there was done,
Sa he wer packed weill at none;
For daylie thair he gaid to dyne,
To gett his fill of gude white wyne.
The denner done, he wald not spair,
Downe to a house, tuo myle and mair,
To Lambeth. bischope of Canterberrie,
Vpon his feit, but not to ferrie;
For archness to had in a grote,
He had no will to fie a bote;
Bot or he come neir hand the yeatt,
Vpon ane dyke doun was he sett
Into a secreit out of sicht,
And sat thair till his schone wes dicht.
He gave thame leive to dicht his schone;
To sponge his cloak durst not be done.

It hurt the woole, and wrought it bair;
Puld off the mottes, and did no mair;
He had na will to weir his cleathis;
Then to that bischop in he geas.
With mony flattering taill and fals,
He held that bischop in the hals,
Seiking the secreit of his wittis,
And ay besydis he fillis his guttis,
Wachting the wyne, for it was wycht.
Then, when this turn cott tuke gude ny^t,
Half way hameward vp the calsay,
Said to his servandis for a quha say.
Alace, the porter is foryett,
But sorrow mair the men my^t gett.
Then to a sowters chope he past,
And for a pair of schone he ast.
Bot or he sperit the price to pay thē,
His thovmbis was on the soillis to say them;
Then with his knockles he on them knockit;
Eftir that he had long tyme blockit,
With grit difficultie he tuik thame,
And pat thame on; ewill mocht he bruik them.
With Monsier then he moyen maid,
Lamēting sair his lang abaid,
Thinking to borrow a hundreth pundis,
And oblist him for to be bund
To pay or he past off the toun.
The vther, na dowt, had laid it downe,
Were not bechance he had a man,
That with his maister roundit than:
My Lord, I kend yone lowne in Parise,
He weill betydis that sometymes careis;
And cōdigne docto^r to all townes,
My mother lent him fyftene crownes;
Besydes some vtheris nychbo^ris thair,
Some lent him less, some lent him mair.
Work what we willit was in vaine,
We uald nevir gett a grote agane.

The vther said nothing for schame,
But held his toung while he turned hamc.
Ten pundis slidling furth he tuike,
And knit it in a neapkin nucke,
Saying, forsuith, I have no mair
Now at this present I may spair.
But when he gettis y^t geir agane,
Thair will na river ryse for raine,
And porter, porter of hellis yeattis,
That day this docto^r payis his debtis.
This wald not serve his turne he tho^t;
Some vther moyen sone he socht.
The Scottis merchandis were lyand thair;
I find he maid thair baggis all bair,
And promised, vnder pane of schame,
To pay so sone as he come hame.
Bot as he payit, ye may speir,
Gif Gilbert Donaldsone were heir;
Or Patrick Quhyt, he weill can tell,
Sayand, thair is no devill in hell
Could find sic falset for to deceave him,
As he, when ever he come to crave him.
Ane vther London paik he playit,
Sending some letters, as he said,
With Patrick Quhyt, as he declairis,
Bearing the wecht of grit affairis,
To come in Scotland to the King.
The man mensueris he saw sic thing.
Suppose the teale be fals and feinyeit,
Yit to the Kingis Grace he has pleinyeit.
Havand the court at his cōmand,
He gart the pure mā leave the land :
For all the fyve bairnes and the wyffe,
This Metropolitane of Fyiffe
Is enterit on his hous and geir;
But how this happened, ye sall heir,
Thought it be tedious for to tell.
The mā duellis in St Androis sell,

He lent this lowne thrie hundreth mĕk;
Bot when he craveth Cok his clerk,
He culd not find ane vther gait,
Bot fred him with this fals cōceat.
Gif this be weill, the warld shall ken
To raise sic schiftis on saikles men.
Than Robert Melwin hame to gang,
On his awin charges lyand lang,
Sayand this burgh I may not bruik,
His precept of pensione furth he tuike,
Biddand my Lord subscryve ane letter,
And swa he did, but not the better.
Hame to the prowest he was directit;
But ye shall heir whow he was geckit.
Hame to the prowest when he past,
It greived him, and he was agast;
Who tuke him by the lap, and lewch,
Ye ken his knaverie weill aneuche.
Of all his teyndis, both meill and beir,
I have discharges for a yeir;
He gart me pay thame or I ledd thame:
The vther tuke thame vp and redd thame.
He sayned him, but he said no mair:
Tak up his Londone wsayage thair.
Ane burges man there beand bound,
Having a trvme schop in the toun;
Vnto this Bischope sone he socht,
To get a licence gif he mocht,
For fortie last of Inglis beir:
Said, ten pund Stirveling I have heir,
And mair, when misteris you cōmand.
The Bischop tuke it weill on hand:
To Secretare Welschingame gois he,
The pearle and flowre of courtasie;
With signato^r in neif alreddie,
He send him to his Soverane Ladie
For fourtie last of Englis beir.
Bot what ane leesing made he heir?

He said, to serve his house at hame,
But it was sauld in want of schame;
And not with him that he began,
He happened on ane vther man,
And tuentie pund Stirveling fra him tuke:
The first merchant he cleane forsuike;
Gave him the geck, and lat him gea;
Gud threttie pundis he cōqueist sea.
Amongis the Bischopis of the towne,
He played the beggar vp and downe,
Without respect of honestie,
Or office of embassadrie.
Ane scaffing warlot, wanting schame,
Thrie of thair haikneis he tuik hame.
He beggit buikis, he beggit bowis;
Tacking in earnest, asking in mowes;
As Maister Jhone Dowglass weill can tell,
How slealie he deceavit him sell;
Borrowing ane coffer to keip his claythis,
Bot with this baggage hame he geas.
This turn cott now returnīg bak,
Trowand some great reward to tak;
Bot Englis men are not so daft,
Bot they perceaved his clocked craft.
They knew him for a sembling baird,
Whome to they wald give no rewarde;
Considering as he sett him furth,
They gave him mair then he was worthe.
Seing his copburde come to nocht,
Tua leathering bosses he hes bought;
Thay will not brek, albeit they fall,
Thir strapis of trie destroyis vs all,
They brek so mony, I may noᵗ byde it;
Heir all the inspraich he provydit.
Returnīg hame, as ye hard tell,
He baid behind a day him sell,
The simple servantis to beguyle,
Sayand, he wald ryde furth a whyle,

To seay a bow that was sūthing wicht;
Syne come agane, and tak gud nycht;
Bot on lap he, and went to wair;
Fairweill; adewe; they gat na mair.
Gif this be honest, ye may ken,
And, namelie, to sic honest men,
Our Legat Lord in primacie,
Besydis his grit embassadrie,
To vse swa in vncouth places;
Litle merwell, in tēporall cases,
He had na will to give reward,
That to his saule had no regard.
For, lying *in periculo mortis*,
Tua of the Kirk to him resortes;
Balcanquhall, as ane Christiane brother,
And Maister Andro Melwill was the other:
Both being fayᵗfull, fearing God.
Went to persuade this subtile tod,
Lascivous maneris to amend,
Sen na man knawis the hoʳ nor end.
This, at the lenth, he lent them eiris,
And brusted out in a blus of tearis.
Brother, he sayis, I schame to tell
Sa oft as I misvsit my sell,
In guyding of the giftis of grace;
Gif God wald lend me tyme and space,
Tua hoʳis in pulpit to deploir it,
My synfull lyfe sall noᵗ be smorit:
With this agane began to greit.
The bretherene, seing him cōtreit,
Gave thankis to God for his repentence:
But now, for all his auld acquētance,
He playit the turnecot for to deceave them,
Denyand plane that ever he spak them.
To George Durrie he played a juike,
That will not be foryet this oulke:
Foure hundreth merkis he gart him get him,
For tackis of kirkis he hecht to set him,

15

And syne set vther men the teindis.
The vther, having forse of freindis,
Concludit schortlie for to slea him,
For vyling of his syluer fra him :
As they had done, no dout, in deid,
Were not he sped him there with speid,
And fand sic moyen for to meis them,
Promissand profeit for to pleis them.
Whairto it turnes I can no^t tell :
But sua the sophist savit him sell.
To him I can find na copair ;
Save anes in France, when I was there,
Gud Clemet Marit had a lowne,
A knaif that cubart all the towne ;
With spreitis employed to everie vice,
As whoredome, drincking, cartis and dyce ;
To sweir, to ban, to steill and tak,
Ane never my^t trow a word he spak :
In everie ludgene whair he wald licht,
Taking his leive without gud nicht ;
Garring the wyfis sing wallaway,
Lyk to the Bischop of Galloway :
But he was sum thing pure and needie ;
And this is feinyet, fals and griedie.
Galloway with no mater meld him,
Except necessitie copeld him :
Taking the warld as God wald send it,
Having ane noble hart to spend it.
Bot ay the mair this smatcher gettis,
The closser garris be keip the yettis ;
Feiding his bellie and his bryde,
Begging and borrowing ay besyde.
Galloway was a man of gude,
Discendit of a noble blude ;
Franck with his freind, fordward and stout,
Having gude maneris to set them out :
And this is but ane cairle, ye sie,
Ane baxteris son of bas degrie ;

Feable and fleid, and nothing worth,
Wanting a face to set him furth.
What suld I lyble of this lowne ?
Not all the paper of this towne,
And blek it baith vnder and abone,
May had the half that he hes done.
Wha could cleirlie descryve his cases
In Parise, and in vther places,
Gif men my^t tyme and laser get ?
Some thingis, indeid, I have forget :
Parceaving that he was scant of clathis,
To Londone Bischop sone he geathis,
Desyring the borrowing of a gowne,
He said, to preich in through the towne.
The Bischop, obeying the first cōmand,
Send for his wardrop man fre hand.
Tuiching that part I mā cōmend him ;
Ane diligat gowne indeid he send him :
Bot when that gowne comes hame agane,
Winter salbe butt wind and raine.
Albeit I was not there to see,
He weiris it yit, to verefie ;
Growgraine of silk, bot it is gray,
When ever ye see it, siris, ye may say,
He gat that gowne, with this ingyne,
Weill lyned with costly furringis fyne.
How he beguylit Jhone Harper of York,
Ane Scottis tailyeo^r, lives on his work,
Aff fra a merchant he gart him tak
New brekis and dowblat, for to mak,
Of Turkie taffatie, na war geir ;
Bot as he payeth him, ye sall heir.
This turne cott with his trickis begane,
Growand familiar with the man,
Sayand forsuith my silver is done ;
But Londone will me releive sone :
For in that toun I tak na cair ;
The Scottis merchants will meit me thair,

With monie, als mekle as I will tak.
Whairfore, to my returnĩg bak,
Ye wald doe weill gif ye wald thrist me,
And at this present not molest me.
Ye salbe payit ; tak ye no thought :
Your tristene sall not be for nought
At our nixt meiting.   What suld mair ?
The vther saw him speik so fair ;
To crave him forder he thoght schame.
Bot turne cott, now returnĩg hame,
Fand out some vther gait to gea :
Sewin pund he payit this pure mã sea.
Some sayes he played ane fouller thing,
Bespewed the pulpit befoir the king ;
Or ever the preiching was midpart done,
He neither held vnder nor abone.
Na ferlie ; his cõtagious stomack
Was sa owersett with Burdeous drũmake ;
And George Gipsones iskie bae
Had all the wyte he womit sae.
Sone after that, for sowmes of debt,
A meas^r vpon the gait him mett,
Gewing him charges to obey,
To enter in warde, or els to pay.
This lowrie little ans^r mackis,
Bot on a gray bonnet he tackis ;
A scheip hewit clock to cover his cleathis ;
But lad or boy to Ley^t he geathis ;
Lapp in a bott, and maid him boun ;
Sen syne he come not in the toun.
Ane vther trick, as I remember ;
The threttene day of this November,
Vnto his bed he bownit so fow,
Sleipping and snoring lyk a sow ;
Dreamand some devill he had sene,
Out of the bed he wald have bene ;
But on the flure he gat a fall,
While doun came Cannabie and all

Vpon his bellie, with sic a brattle,
The houshold, hearing sic a rattle,
Mervelit mekle what it suld be ;
Lychtit candles, and came to sie,
And fand him lyand lyk a swyne,
Bayth bak and syde bespewit with wyne.
Seeing it rid, they waxt so red,
Believing it had bene blood he bled ;
Cryand out, harmesay, he was stickit ;
While ane pat doun his hand and lickit.
This is not blude, thot it be hewit,
But Burdeous wyne, that he has spewit,
With schame and lack I will not lane,
They laid him in his bed agane.
Therefore I wald ye vnderstude,
We have na tyme for to cōclude :
For ay the longare Lowrie leivis,
As fassione is of feinyit theivis,
They wilbe daylie for doing ill.
Ewin sa I will augment my bill,
As I gett witt in mair and mair
Of his proceidingis heir and thair.
I sall leive blankis for to imbrew thame,
That he a nosebitt my beleive thame,
Whome to my buik salbe directit.
Being in Paris lait suspected
For art and part of mūbling messis,
Thought he hypocrysie professis :
Albeit this be not weill set furth,
Becaus the mater was not worth,
Desyre the Bischope to be cōtent,
Becaus I am not eloquent.
I have tane trawell for his saik,
And ryme may for a raipfull staik.
Mind ye thir heidis that I rehers ;
I sall not faill to mend my vers.

Quod R. S.

FINIS.

XXXVI.—Followis the Ballat maid vpoun Margret Fleming, callit the Flemyng bark in Edin=burght.

[GEORGE BANNATYNE'S Manuscript Collection of Poems, 1568, No. 164, preserved in the Library of the Faculty of Advocates, Edinburgh.—The Evergreen: Being a Collection of Scots Poems, wrote by the Ingenious before 1600. Published by Allan Ramsay, Edinburgh, 1724.— Chronicle of Scottish Poetry; from the Thirteenth Century, to the Union of the Crowns. Edited by James Sibbald, Edinburgh, 1802.]

HAIF a littill Fleming berge
Off clenkett wark bot scho is wicht
Quhat pylett takis my schip in chairge
Mon hald hir clynlie trym and ticht
Se that hir hatchis be handlit richt
With steirburd, baburd, luf and lie
Scho will sale all the wintirnight
And nevir tak a telzevie

With evin keill befoir the wind
Scho is richt fairdy with a saill
Bot at ane lufe scho lyis behind
Gar heise hir quhill hir howbands skaill
Draw weill the takill to hir taill
Scho will nocht miss to lay zour mast
To pomp als oft as ze may haill
Zeill nevir hald her watter-fast.

To calfet hir oft can do non ill
And talloun quhair the flud-mark flowis
But gif scho lekkis gett men of skill
To stop hir hoilis laich in the howis
For falt of hemp tak hary towis,
With stane-ballest withowttin vder

In moneless nichtis it is na mowis,
Except ane stowt man steir hir ruder

A fair vesschell abone the watter
And is bot laitly reiket to
Quhairto till deif zow with tome clatter
Ar nane sic in the floit as scho
Plvm weill the grund, quhat evir ze doo
Haill on the fick-sheit and the blind
Scho will tak in at cap and koo
Withowt scho ballast be behind

Nae pedderis pak sho will ressaif
Althocht hir travell scho sowld tyne
Na coukcald karle nor carnlingis pet
That dois thair corne and caitell tryne
Bot quhair scho findis a fallow fyne
He wilbe frawcht fre for a souss
Scho kareis nocht bot men and wyne
And bulzoun to the counze-houss

For merchandmen I may haif mony
But nane sic as I wald desyre
And I am layth to mell with ony
To leis my mater in the myre
That man that wirkes best for his hyre
Syne he salbe my mariner
Bot nycht and day mon he nocht tyre
That sailis my bony ballinger

For anker-hald nane can be fund
I pray zow cast the leid-lyne owt
And gif ze can nocht get the grund
Steir be the compas and keip hir rowt
Syne treveis still and lay abowt
And gar her top twiche wind and waw
Quhair anker dryvis thair is na dowt
Thir tripand tyddis may tyne ws a

Now is my pretty pynnege reddy
Abydand on sum merchand blok
Bot be scho emptie be our leddy
Scho will be kittill of hir dok
Scho will ressaif na landwart Jok
Thocht he wald frawcht hir for a croun
Thus fair ze weill, sayes gude Johne Cok
Ane nobill telzeour in this toun.

FINIS Q. SEMPILL.

XXXVII.—Heir followis the defence of Crissell Sandelandis For vsing hirself contrair the Ten Commandis; Being in ward for playing of the loun with every ane list geif hir half a croun, etc.

[GEORGE BANNATYNE's Manuscript Collection of Poems, 1568,
No. 165, preserved in the Library of the Faculty of
Advocates, Edinburgh.—The Evergreen: Being a Collection of Scots Poems, wrote by the Ingenious before
1600. Published by Allan Ramsay, Edinburgh, 1724.—
In this Expostulation with the Magistrates of Edinburgh
on account of some harsh measures which they had
adopted against Mrs. Crissel Sandelandis and her frail
family, in whose company one of the Protestant Clergy
had been discovered, Sempill introduces the names of
some distinguished characters of the time.]

ERNITIOUS peple perciall in despyte
Susanis judges saweris of seditioun
Zour cankert counsale is the causs and wyte
Bowstert with pryd and blindit with
ambitioun
Fyndand na cryme nor havand na commissioun
To hurt Dame Venus Virgenis as ze do

Gif ze sa raschlie rin vpoun suspitioun
Ze may put vthiris on the pannell to

To Sandelandis ze wer our sair to schame hir
Sen ze with counsale mycht quyetlie command hir
Grit foulis ze wer with fallowis to defeme hir
Havand na causs bot commoun voce and sklander
Syne findand no man in the houss neir hand hir
Except ane clerk of godly conversatioun*
Quhat gif besyd Johne Dureis self ze fand hir
Dar ze suspect the holy congregatioun

Zour fleslie conscience garris zow tak this feir
Beleif ze virgynis wilbe win so sone
Na god forbid Bot men bourd als neir
And wemen nocht the wor quhen that is done
Had scho bene vndir and he hobland abone
That war a perellous play for to suspect thame
Bot laddis and lassis will meit eftirnone
Quhair Dick and Dvrie dow nocht bayth correct thame

Sen drunkardis gluttonis and contentious men
Schedderis of blude and subiectis gevin to greid, †
May nocht possess the hevinly gloir ze ken
As in the bybill dalie do we reid
Lat thir be wyit allyk till every leid
Syne fornicatioun plasit amangis the laif
Exemp zour self throw all the toun in deid
Than luke how mony ze onmerkit haif

Gif ze beleif nocht Betoun be his word
In hir defenss it can nocht be reffusit
Latt him that fallowis fecht it with ye sword
Ane ancient law quhen ladeis ar accusit
Is ministeris sic men to be abusit
That knawis the scripteur and the ten commandis
Albeit he and scho wor in ane houss inclusit
He sew na seid in to hir Sandelandis

* *On the margin*—" The Minister Betoun."   † " Viz., Covetyce."

As for the rest I knaw nocht thair vocatioun
Thair lyfe thair maneris Bot I heir mony mene thame
Catholik virgenis of the holy congregatioun
Syn wer to tyne thame gif ze cowld obtene thame
Quhat can ze say except that ze had sene thame
With rein in ra all nakkit but adherance
Than tak a bowstring and draw it doun betwene thame
And gif it stickis it hes ane evill apperance

Catitois clerkis quhois college ze frequentit
Quhen ye wor wanfleris of hir wantoun band
Now ze ar lamit fra labour I lamentit
Zour pistolis twinit and bak sprent lyk a wand
Snapwark adew fra dagmen dow nocht stand
And worss than that ze want zour morsing powder
Than cumis conscience with crukit staf in hand
Greitand for byganis bowand bak and schowder

Remembir first zour former qualitie
And wrak na virgenis with zour wilfull weir
Gif ze will nocht Than our regalitie
Hes power planely to replege thame heir
Mycht thay win to the girth I tak no feir
Doun by the Canno Croce I pray zow send thame
Quhair Patrik Bannatyne hes promeist to compeir
With lawfull ressonis reddy to defend thame

On causs thair is thay can nocht be convict
Ze had na power fra the sone wes sett
The provest gaif na power to Gilbert Dick
The speciall thing that sowld nocht bene forzett
Thay war nocht theivis nor zit condempt in dett
Nor ridhand tane quhilk was na causs ze knaw
Bot ze latt rukis and ravynis rin throw the nett
And saikles dowis makis subiect to ye law

Zour perciall Juge we may declyne him to
Bot sett me doun the persone Pennycuke

Or Sanderis Guthrie lat see quhat he can do
He kennis the caice and keipis zour awin court buke
For men of law I wat nocht quhome to luke
Auld James Bannatyne wes anis a man of skill
And gif he cumis nocht thair I wald we tuke
To keip oure dyet Maister Dauid Makgill

Quhat cummer castis the formest stane lat see
At tha peure winchis ze wranguslie suspect
For sklenting bowttis Now better war lat bee
Nor to begin to gett zour selffis ane geck
The grittest falt I find in this effect
Ze baith tuke money and put thame selffis to schame
Bot quhen the court cumis to the toun quhat reck
We sall restoir thame to thair stok agane

In zour tolbuth sic presouneris to plant
Wilbe ressauit weill ze may considder
Gud Captane Adamsone will nocht lat thame want
Bedding howbeit thay sowld lig all togidder
As for his wyf I wald ze sowld forbid hir
Hir eyndling toyis I trow thair be no denger
Becauss his lome is larbour groun and lidder
But vndirstanding now to treit ane strenger

The grittest greif I find ze haif defament
Thir leill trew luvaris and done their freindis bot lack
Becauss thair bandis wer reddy to be proclamit
The pairteis mett and maid a fair contrack
Bot now allace the men ar loppin aback
For oppin sklander callit ane speikand devill
In grit effairis ze had nocht bene sa frack
Concernyng the rewling of zour commoun weill

To pvneiss pairt is parcialitie
To pvneiss all is hard to do in deid
Bot send thame heir to oure regalitie
And we sall see gif we can serve thair neid

This rurall ryme quha sa lyk for to reid
To Dict and Dury is directit plane
Quhair I offend thame in my landwart leid
I salbe reddy to reforme agane

FINIS Q. SEMPLE.

XXXVIII.—Followis the Ballat maid be Robert
Semple, of Jonet Reid, Ane Violet, and Ane
Quhyt. Being slicht wemen of lyf and conver-
satioun, and tabernaris.

[George Bannatyne's Manuscript Collection of Poems, 1568,
No. 166, preserved in the Library of the Faculty of
Advocates, Edinburgh.—The Evergreen: Being a Col-
lection of Scots Poems, wrote by the Ingenious before
1600. Published by Allan Ramsay, Edinburgh, 1724.—
Chronicle of Scottish Poetry, from the Thirteenth Cen-
tury, to the Union of the Crowns. Edited by James
Sibbald, Edinburgh, 1802.]

OFF cullouris cleir quha lykis to weir
Ar sindry sortis in to this toun
Grene zellow blew and mony hew
Bayth Pareis blak and Inglis broun
Lundoun sky quha lykis to by
Bit Cullour de Roy is clene laid down
Dundy gray this mony a day
Is lychleit bayth with laid and loun

Stanche my fyking and stryd my lyking
Ar semely hewis for sommer play ;

Dundippit in zello For mony gud fallo
As Will of Quhit-hawch bad me say
I will nocht dennyit till nane that will by it
For silver nane salbe said nay
Ze nocht to plenzie my clayth will nocht stenzie
Suppois ze weit it nycht and day

And I haif Quhyt off grit delyt
And Violett quha lykis to weir
Weill werand Reid quhill ze be deid
Quhilk sall nocht failzie tak ze no feir
The Quhyt is gude and richt weil lwid
Bot zit the Reid is twyis als deir
The Violet syne bayth fresche and fyne
Sall serve zow hosyng for a zeir

The Quhyt is twiche and fresche ennewche
Soft as the silk as all men seis
The Reid is bony and socht of mony
They hyve abowt the house lyk beis.
With Violet to gif ze haif ado
It meitis lyk stemmyne to zour theis
Seure be my witting not brunt in the litting
Suppois baith laidis and lymeris leis

Off all thir thre hewis I haif left clewis
To be oure court-men wintter weid
Twynit and small, the best of thame all
May weir the claith for woll and threid
Bot in the walk-mill, the wedder is ill
Thir ar nocht drying dayis indeid
And gif it be watt I hecht for that
It tuggis in hoilis, and gais abbreid

Zit it is weill walkit cairdit and calkit
Als warme a weid as weir-the-deule
Weill wrocht in the lwmis, with wobster gwmis,
Bayth thik and nymmill gais the spwle

Cottond and schorne, the mair it be worne
Ze find zoursel the grittar fule
Bot bony forsuth cum byit in my bwth
To mak zow garmentis agane zule

Bot mixt thir togidder, zourself may considder
Quhat fyner cullour can be fund
And namely of breikis, gif ony man seikis
Sall haif the pair ay for a pund
Howbeid it be skant, na wowaris sall want
That to my bidding wilbe bund
Weill may thay bruikit thay neid nocht to lukit
Bot graip it marklynis be the grund

Zour court-men heir has maid my claith deir
And raisd it twell-pennies of the ell
Zit is my claith seuver, for sadills to ceuver
Suppois the sessioun raid thamesell
The Violet certane wes maid Dumbartane
The Reid wes walkit in Dumkell
The Quhyt hes bene dicht in mony mirk nicht,
But tyme and place I cannot tell

Now gif ze wirk wyislie and shaip it precyslie
The elwand wald be grit and lang
Gif the byess be wyd gar lay it on syd
And sa ze cannocht weill ga wrang
And for the lang lest it wald be schewid fast
And cair nocht by how deip ze gang
Bot want ze quyht threid ze can nocht cum speid
Blak walloway mon be zour sang

Bot thocht it be auld and twenty tymis sawld
Zit will the freprie mak zow fane
With vlis to renew it and mak it weill hewit
And gar it glans lyk Dummygrane
Syne with the sleik stanis that serveis for the nanis
They raise the pyle I mak zow plane

With mony grit aith thay sell this same claith
To gar the byeris cum agane

Now is my wob wrocht and arlit, to be bocht
Cum lay the payment in my hand
And gif my claith felzie ze pay nocht a melzie
The wob salbe at zour command
The market is thrang, and will nocht lest lang
Thay by fast in the bordour land
Albeid I haif tynsell zit mon I tak hansell
To pay for buth-maill and my stand

My claith wald be lwd with grit men of gud
Gif lawdis and lownis wald latt me be
Zit mon I excuse thame how can I reffuse thame
Sen all menis penny makis him free ?
The best and the gay of it myself tuk a fay of it
A wylie-coit I will nocht lee
Quhilk did me no harme bot held my cost werme
A symple merchant ze may see

This far to releif me that na man repreif me
In Jedburgh at the Justice air
This sang of thre lassis was maid abone glassis
That tyme thot thay wer tapstaris thair
The first wes ane Quhyt a lass of delyt
The Violett bayth gud and fair
Keip the Reid fra skaith scho is worth tham baith
Sa to be schort I say na mair

Finis Q. R. Semple.

Appendix.

I.—POEMS ASSIGNED TO SIR JAMES SEMPLE OF BELTREES.

(Born 1566.   Died February 1625.)

[The following Poems, NOW FOR THE FIRST TIME PRINTED, are preserved in a small Quarto Manuscript Volume, written before 1598 and 1610, in the Library of the Faculty of Advocates, Edinburgh.   They dwell much on the beauty of his Mistress, with the constancy and fervour of his attachment, whilst he calls on all that " Heeris these Amorous Tragicke Playes" to condole with him on his want of fortune, since the Fates have ordained that his love should go unrequited.]

I.—Loues Lament.

Y Loue allace is Loathsum wnto me : restles I liue
in absence of my sweete
The harde mishapis I have incurred latelye : hes
with dispaire ourquhelm'd my
weerie spreit : O the Loyell saul is this the fates decreete :
may I noucht haue your presens as befoir
Adew contentment till thow me intreit, so sall be sene ay till
thow me restoir
Knew I allace the way I might deploir not to the world but
to thy self my teers
Onlie by the may cuirit be my soir, ten thousand heartes may
not sustene sic weeres
No worldlie pleesure can expell my paine ; but presence of my
deerest deer agane.

16

II.—Ane Dyor.

QUHEN Diaphantus knew, the destanyes decreete
    Quhenn he was forcet for to forgoe, his deere and Loving
      sweit
Ouervoited with the vailles of balme-rebaiting trees
Ourgazeinges grouflings on the gronde : with death prent in
    his eyes
Oft precisit hee to speeke : Ohe quhile hee did assaye
The agonizing dread of deathe : his wrastling voyce did stay
At last as ane quho stryues : aganes both woe and shame
Diere charridora can hee crye : myne ay adoirit dame
ffirst I attest thy name : syne nixt the godds aboue
But cheefe of thes, that boy that beeris the staitely stile of Loue
Let thoese recoirds with me, what was my constante pairt
And giue I did noucht honour the ! with ane weell hallowit
    hairt
To sacreefice to the : my secreete chaist desyres
Vpoun thy bewties alter brunte ! with neuer quenching fyeris
Thow was that idole still : quhoes Image I adoirit
The sanct to quhome I made my vowes : quhoes pities I
    imploirit
The stare which saued my schipe · from tempest of dispair
Quhen the horizoun of my hoipe ! ou'rcloudit was with cair
Thow was that soueraigne balme · that sweet catholick saw
Quhilk couerit me of all my ills · that did my heart ourthrow
But now suche strange events : hes interveinit sensyne
That I dare not avow to saye : nor think that thow art myne
Quhilk makes me to insert : in thois my sorrowing songes
The histories of my mishaps : my miseries and wronges
Noucht that I can accuise : my charidora no
I onlie execrate the wierds : cheefe workeris of my woe
Sould schoe quhom I haue seruit : sua mony lothsum zeeris
ffor quhom my dew distelling eyes hes sched suche storme of teirs
Sould schoe I say be made : ane pray to suche a one
Quho for her saike he never gave : not ane vntymely grone
No suirelie swrelie no ? the weirdes may doe me wrong
And mak her by there bade decreete : to quhom schoe suld belong
Because the heavin dothe blenke on sum : moir blyther then on
    me
And giue them giftes moir plawsible : to charme a churles eye

Zet dare I weell compair : yea peraduenture vaunte
That schoe is myne by richt of loue : thoucht luck in loue I
    wante
Albeit my horoscope · Invaide my worldlie thinges
Zit into Loue it gaue me liue : for to compair with kinges
ffor giue I knew there were : beneathe the starrie skye
That durst avow to loue my Love moir faithfullie then I
I would ryue out this heart : which interleanes my breathe
And cast it doune befoir her feete : and dye a schamefull breath
But sen boith tyme and schoe : hes tryit me to be trew
And hes founde such faithfullnes in me : as salbe founde in few
I.rest secuire in that : and care noucht wha pretend
The mae presoome the mair my pairt proues perfit to the end
And wtheris faithles faythe : in ballaunce put with myne
Sall mak my treuth for to triumphe : and lyke a sunne to schyne
There sall no change of tyme : of heavin of soile noir ayre
Inforce me to forgett my vowes : maide to my fairest fair
Quhilk now I heere renew : In solemne forme againe
That to witnes as I beganne : so sall I suire remayne
I sweere by thy tuo eyne : my onlie dearest deare
And by the stageoun stankes of hell : by which the gods do siveir
That thow arte onlie schoe : quhois countenance I crave ·
That I salbe in Lyfe and death : thy best affected slaue ·
That I sall neither sighe nor sobe : nor zit sall greit nor grone ·
ffor one that euer sall tak Lyfe : saif the evin the allone ·
That there sall no deceit of Lovelye Laughing ene
Nor charmeing sounds of syriou songes : nor fare fetchit sighes
    betuene
Deface out of my mynde : whiche are so suire Imprest
Thy wordes soe wyse, thy Luikes so grave : thy maneris so
    modest
That day sall nevir daw : nor sunne sall never schyne
Sall quarrell me for appostate : for nought remayneing thyne
And that which heere I sweere : Least sylence suld it smoir
The verie trees sall testiefie : quhilk onlie are befoir
And cheefe and aboue all : this holeine sade and grene
Into the quhilk thy name and myne : in graven may be sene
O happie happie tree : quhoes euer blessit barke
Sall ludge the trophie of our loue for thy Immortall worke
Quhilk hes the force to caus : the memorie remayne
Sequestrate from the bastard soirt : of trees which are prophane

And quhenn the rest salbe : ouerpast with cairles eye
Zet sall thow be adorit and kist : for charidorais trei
Ze peraduenture to : ffor diaphantus saike
Sum rectles bodie cuming by : will homage to the make
Thus blisst sall thow remayne : quhenn I salbe agast
Into quhat corner of the eirth : poore wretch I salbe cast
Indeid all is in doubt : saue this we mone depairt
The bodye must in pilgrime be : and shee must haue the hart ·
The thoucht of quhilk exyle : and dolorous devoirce
Breedes sorrow sorrow heer in me : this eloquence perforce
ffor quhill I was resoluit : to thesaurize my greeife
Becaus that it sould move in men : moir mervell nor beleef
The never ceassing feide · of melancounterous faites
Ouer haistnit this abortiue birth : of Importune regrates
To witnes to the world : that my mishaps are suche
That thoucht I murne lyke man half mad : I cannot murne
    too much
ffor giue of all mishaps : this be the first of all
To haue bene happie happie anes : and fra that hap to fall
I wote I may weell say : that diaphantus name
Is the sournyme of all mishaps : and signifies the same
ffor giue there wer no hell : but out of heavin to bee
Considder what her wante would worke : whois sight wes
    hevin to me
I think all thois that speekes : of sorrow sould think schame
Quhenn diaphantus salbe heard : for charidorais name
Her bewtie was but bloote · her treuth wes vnreprovit
The ane deseruit for to liue, the vther for to be Lovit
Zit hes this deuilishe dame : of destanies ordanit
That he sall Lois baith Lyfe and Loue : and schee a faythfull
    frende
Quherefoir all zee that heeris : these amorous tragicke playes
Bestow on me ane world of plantes : on her a world of prais

SEMPLE

III.—Craiges passionado:

QUHY did the gods ordaine : ane michtie monarchis mynde
    Within the presoun of my corps : to be inclo'sd and pynde
Quhy did they predecrec : suche intestine debate
Suche euill weeris to be betuixe : my calling and conceite
Giue as sum say there be : ane transfiguratiounc thenn
Evin at sum princes fall or death : my baleful birth began
And as he dyit his saull and spirit : hes flowin into me
Quhilk maks my munting mynde so fare : aboue my fate to flec
Zit doubt I giue or no : my predecessoures gone
That vmquhile prince hes iuster caus : or I for to bemone
Hee pleanes perhaps becaus : within a worlde so wylde
His princelie and heroike thouchts suld daylie be defylde
I murne againe becaus : my founde conceatie thoucht
Doune weyit allace be my wnwoorthe: resolues and turns to
    noucht
Giue ane or bathe be plagued : I cannoucht weell defyne
The punishment may weell be his : but all the pane is myne
Zit thinke secuirelie think ; tho thow be baslie borne
Suppois the shell be cast away ; zet will the perle be worne
But heere ane freesche alarum : my heart does now assaill
To think and noucht reveele my thouchtis : me thinks cannot
    availl
ffor quhereto can they serve : be they from her obscuired
ffor quhom my present and my past : displeasures I indured ·
Sen schee evin lyke the foule : quha liftes within her beake ·
The schellfische heiche into the air : that it may fall and breake
Sen schee I say hes heysit : myne hearte aboue the skyes
Sall schoe not knaw quhat's in my mynde : I murmure and
    devyis
Zis suirelie zes but how : be word by wryte or baith
Sall I reveell my hidin harmes : my long conceillit skayth
By none of thois for quhy : my rivell for I see
Hes made ane dullfull interdyte : betuix my dame and me
O happie happie hee : to liue in suche estaite
He come in tyme curst be the tyme : allace I come to late
Zet let him beere with this : sence funncie maks me fonde
He sall noucht Louc her him allone : and he hade sworne vpound
My richt's salbe alsgoode as heeis : I sweere by Jove aboue

Althoucht hee war me fare in Lucke : he wares me noucht in
    Loue
He Loues (allace) and findes : In Loue rewairde agane
I wate I Loue alsweell as he : and finds no thing but pane
I ade this meikle mair that breids my hart releif
Quhen schoe her bewtie doeth behold : in glasses of my greif
My Lynnes may schaw my Loue : my Loue may schow my pane
And schoe within my panes may spye : her bewties force agane
ffor giue I soucht rewairde : schee wold replye I knaw
It wer ane great disgrace to her : for to descend sua law
To Loue or reaffect ane wretche ane puissante power
By birth and bloode Ignoble borne ; inglorious and obscuire
Zet were it noucht eneuche : I sould Leive of to Loofe
Ore from the worlds miracle : my mynde for to remove
All thinges againe deformed ; In chaos masse shalbe
Befoir ane retrospiciante I : sall ceas from Loving the
First let omeriane blacke · eternall mixt ourvaill
The earthis circumference befoir my fixit faithe sall faill
Thes monomathicke Jarris : betuix my selff and the
Out of my mynde sall nawayes make my fixit Idea dee
My Loue quhere it is laid : sall grow and floorishe greene
And suche apostasie in me : at no tyme shalbe seene
ffor how came I from Loue : or from my thoughts refraine
And how cann I but Loue my thouchtes : and thinke on loue
    agane
Tuyse am I now reduceit : to my pretendit theame
And giue my selffe my thouchtis or her I wate not quhat to
    blame
Giue her I wer vnwise : or giue my thouchts or me
O thenn are na caus for a caus : but caus sould quarrellit be
But ohe as sum alledge Loue harboures aye the heart
There is na plague beneth the pole : of quhilk I haue na pairt
And all the duillefull dintes that in despaire cann duell
Conglomerat's in armes hudge : my pleesures to expell
Zit giue as I haue saide : ane transfiguratioune be
Quhy doe noucht these my raging thouchts : tak journey now
    and flee
And seek sum saifer schoire ; quherein at large to fleit
ffor I have deyed ten thousand deids : sen they and I did meit
Wald god I anes had dyed : thenn hade my fanncies flede
But in suppoised death's Lyfe : by thoucht susteint and fede

Thenn sall I saye I liue : or sall I saye I dee
I am noucht dead and giue I sould alledge I liue I lie
The babell of my mynde : hes drevin me soe awaye
That as I wate noucht quhat I think : I wate not quhat I saye
Zit weell I wate I Loue : and zit shee wates noucht this
Thus if wyteles of my woe : and still bereav's my bless
Ane paradoxe I graunte : and zit ane theame must trew
Quhois certane groundes breeds suirest greefes : quhilk I can-
    noucht eshew
And zit giue trew Loue might : trew Loues rewarde obtene
Thenn weell I wote my waiting on : wald not be wair't in vane
But while my sanct espyis : in saddest songes my syte
Sehee thinkes I haue na mynde of Loue : but wryt's becaus I
    wryte
But zet while schee on me : for to conferre wald call
Oft haue I sworne by heavin and eirthe : my mistres warrs
    them all
And oft haue wee discouerit boith quhy quhairefoir and how
I Lou'd my dame and oft wald schee : baith loue and all allow
Zet durst I not behold : her to her self to sohow
But thesawriz'd my hiddin harmes : and ay conceallit woo
And as the fearefull babe : quho knawes his task perqueir
And sett's the buike asyde befoir : the appoynted hour draw neir
And ou'r and ou'r againe : his Leassoune doeth repeate
That hee may satisfie and pleis : the maister quhen they meit
Zit quhen ane compt is tane : all fleis from out his thoucht
And quhat he knew he quyte forezet's : feir setts his mynde
    alloucht
Evin sua it faires with me : my harong clearlye cunde
Hes presence hes obliterate : befoir I haue begunde
And oft haue I determened : my passiones to displaye
And zit Immediatelie : I weiping went awaye ·
O in my Loveing Lines : O blind with brusit teares
Hes schee espyit my passiones strong, my stryving hoips and
    feirs
Oft hes schoe sweetlye said : thy mistres were to blame
Gif cruell schee, to the that soe : her praises doeth proclame
And ware thow myne said schoe : I suirelie wald be loath
Thy Loue thy hoip : thy faithe sould finde ; or raip rewarde
    of wrath
Thus cannoucht I but thinke : and half perswade my sell

Schee knawes I Loue her best of all : suppois I dare not tell ·
Zit Leist my name sould be : transsumpt heir and theire
Inrol'd with foolische soulls who feides : on apprehensions bair
I shaipe with spidie haist : to sett asyde all shame
And by sum meanes to manifest : my dule vnto my dame
Quhois must renouned name : for me sall nevir be knowne
But in my mynde sall still remayne : in bloodie figures drawne
So sall my Loue to her : and with my Loue my paine
May ather by my presence be : or poesie maid plaine
I cease regraiting still : that wicked weirds hes wrocht
Suche annalogicke descrepannce : betuix me and my thoucht
Quhilk maks me thus allace : but pietie to be pyn'd
Quhenn I beheld suche monsterous : greit greefs within my
      mynd ·
And still sall I bewaill : till thouchts there actions breid
And mak ane ramigratione there : from quhence they did proceid
And sua till vengit tyme : my wiste contentment bring
I end and on the heichts of hoip : in hovering thouchtis sall hing

Semple.

IV.

LET not the world beleive : the accuising of my fate
      It tendis to alluirit to condole with me my tragicke state
Nor that I haue sent furthe : these stormie teeris of rage
So by disburding of my breast : my sorrowes to assuage
No no that serues for noucht : I craue no suche releef
Nor will I zeild that any sould : be partiners of my greef
My fantassie to feid : I onlie spend thois teares
My plaintes playes me no musick sound's : so sweetlie in my
      eares
I wish that from my birth : I had acquanted beine
Still with mishap's and never had : but noyes and horrours seine
Then ignoraunte of Joyes ! Lamenting as I doe
As thinking all menn did the Lyke : I micht content me to
But ohe my fate was worse : for it is in ane glas
Schow me throw Lytle blenks of bles : the state quherein I was
Quhich wnperfyted Joyes : scairce constante for ane hour
Was Lyke but to ane watteriesoonne : that schynes befoir a
      schour

ffor giue I euer thoucht : or rather dreem'd of Joyes
That Lytle Lichtning but foirshewde : a thunder of annoyes
It was but Lyke the fruite : that tantalus tormentes
Quhich whill hee sies and not attanes : his hunger but augments
ffor sua the shaddow of : that but Imaginit mirth
Cald all the crosses to recoirde · I suffered since my birth
Quhich are to be bewaill'd : but hard to be redresst
Quhois strange effect's may weill be felt : but cannot be exprest
Judge what the feelling was : whenn thinking on thinges past
I trimble at the torment zit : and stande ane tyme agast
Zit doe I noucht repent : but will with patience pyne
ffor thoucht I murne I murmure not : Lyke men that doe repyne
I grante I waile my Lote : zit I approve her will
Quhat my suill oracle thinkes gude : I never sall think ill
Giue I had onlie sought : ane saluo to ease my paines
Long since I hade bewailled my Lote : alongst the illisian planes
Zit mynde I noucht in this : selff Louer Lyke to dyee
As ane that cair't not for her Lois : so I my self wer free
No may ten night's annoyes : mak her ane nicht secuire
Ane day of dolour's vnto her : ane momentes mirth procure
Ore may ane zeeres Lament's : rejoyce her half ane hour
May seavin zeir's sorrow's mak her sade : I sall not think them
        sour
And gif shee doeth delychte : to heere of my desecis
Thenn O bleast I quho soe may haue : the occasioun her to pleas
ffor now the caus I liue : is noucht for lufe of Lyfe
But onlie for to honour her : that holds me still in stryfe
And ore these vowes I mak : doe vnperformit escaipt
This world sall anes agane renverst : resoome her shaples shape
But what : what haue I vowed my passiones wer too strong
As giue the myldest of the world delighted to doe wrong
As schee quhom I aduire : with so devoite ane mynde
Could rest content to see me sterve : be glade to see my pynde
No no schee wailles my state : and wald appays my caires
Zet interdytit to the faites : confirmes her will to theris
Thenn O vnhappie man : whom evin thyne sanct wold saue
And zit thy crewell destanie ; doeth damne the to thy grave
This sentence thenn may serve : for to confound my fear's
Quhy brust I not my breist with sighis : and droune my eyes
        with teirs
Ohe I haif murnit so muche : that I may murne no moir

My miseries pas numbring now : plaintes perisch in their stoir
The meanes to vnloade my breast : does quyte begin to faill
ffor being drunk with too much doole : I wate not how to waill
And since I wante ane way : my anguishe to reveell
Of force contented with my faite : I'le suffer and conceell
And for to wishe the world : evin as my Loue wish'd me
I vse ane countenance Lyke to one, quhois mynde from greif
        wer free
ffor quhenn shoe did disdaine : shee schew'd ane smylling face
Evin quhen that schoe denunc'd my death : schee sem'd to
        promieis grace
So sall I seeme in shaw : my thoughtes for to repois
Zit in the centure of my saull : sall shrow'd a world of woes
Thenn wofull breast and eyes : zour restles cours controule
And with na outward signes betraye : the anguishe of my soule
Eyes rayne zour shoures within : arrouze the eirth no moir
Pas doune with a deludge of tear's : the breast ze burnd befoir
Breast arme zour seelf with sigh's, giue ou'r waike to defend
Then perishe by zour proper fyres : and mak ane honest end

                              ANE DYOR.

Ʋ.

EVIN as the dying swayne almost bereft of breath
        Soundes dulefull songes and dririe notes a presage of
        her death
Sua since my date of lyfe almost expyr'd I find
My obsequeis I sadlie sing as sorrow toonnes my mynd
And as the rairest bird ane pyle of wood doeth frame
Quhich being fyred by Phebus rayes scho falls into the flame
So by tuo sunnye eyes I giue my fauncies fyre
And burne my self with bewties rayes evin by my awin desyre
Thus the angree gods at lenth begin for to relent
And anes to end my dathefull lyfe for pietie are content
Forgiue th'nfernall poweres the dampned saulls wold pyne
Thenn let them send them to the light to leid a lyfe lyke myne
O giue I could receaue the crosses and the cairs
That from my cradle to my bears conduct me with despairs
Then hungrie Tantalus pleas'd with his lote wald stand
I famishe for ane sweeter foode quhilk still restes in my hand
Lyke Ixiones restles wheelle my fancies rule about

And lyke a gwest that stoue heavin's fyres they tare my bowells
    out
I worke ane endles task and lois my labour still
Evin as the bloodye sisteris doe that emptie as they fill
As Siciphus stone returnes his ghoist guiltie to appaill
I euer rais my hoip sua heiche they bruse me with there fall
And giue I could in sume my seuerall greefes relate
All wold forget there proper harmes and onlye waill my state
So greivous is my greef and paine so panefull is my greef
That death whiche doeth the world affright wold zeild me to releef
I haue mishaps sua lang as in ane habite hade
I think I luik not lyke my self but whenn that I am sade
As birds that flee but in the aire fishes in sea doe diue
Sua sorrowis lyke as element by which I onlie liue
Zit this may be admired as moir then strange in me
Altho' in all my horoscope not one point cleir I see
Aganest my knowledge zit I manye a tyme rebell
And seek to gadder groundis of hoip ane hevin amids a hell
O poysoune of the mynde that doeth the wittis bereave
And shrew'd it with ane cloake of loue does all the world deceave
Thow arte the rocke on which my comfoirts schip didst dashe
It's thow that's daylie in my woundes thy hookit heids does
    washe
Blinde tyrante is O thow by whome my hoips lye deid
That whylls thraws furth a dert of gold and whils a lump of leid
Thus oft thow woundes to but in tuo differente states
Quhich treuth a strange antipathie ye one loues and the vther
    heats
O but I ere I graunte I sould noucht the vpbraid
It's I to passiones tyrannie that haue my self betrayed
And zit this cannocht be my iudgement aymes amiss
Ahe deere Aurora it is thow that ruyn'd hes my bliss
Ane fault that by thy sex may pairtlie be excuised
Quhich still does lois quhat profer'd is affects quhat is refuised
Quhills my distracted thoughtes I stryu'd for to controill
And with fain'd gestures did disguyis the anguishe of my soull
Thenn with inveiting lookes and accents stampt with loue
The mask that was vpoun my mynde thow labourst to remove
And whenn that once ensnair'd thow in thois nets me spy'de
Thy smylles were shaddowit with disdaines thy bewties cloth'd
    with pryde

To reateane thy grace I wate noucht how to goe
Sall I once fall befoir thy feete to pleid for favour soe
No no I'le proudlie go my wraith for to asswage
And liberallie at last enlardge ye raines vnto my rage
I'le tell what wee were ones our chast zit fervent loue
Quhill in effect thow seam'd to affect the which thow didst
    disprove
Quhill once to ingrave thy name vpoun a rock I sate
Thow vowed to wryte myne in a mynde more firme by fare then
    that
The marble stane then stampt reteanes that name of thyne
But ah thy moir then marble mynde it did not sua with myne
Swa that whiche thrawt me first sall set me free againe
Thois flames to which thy loue gave lyfe sall die with thy
    disdane
But ahe quhere am I now how is my iudgement lost
I speik as it were in my power lyke ane that's free to boast
Haue I evin sauld my self to be thy bewties slaue
And quhen thow taks all hoip fra me thow taks but quhat yow
    gave
That former loue of thyne did sua posses my mynde
That for to harbour vther thouchts na roume remaynes behinde
The onlie meanes by which I mind to avenge this wrong
It is by making of thy prais the bourding of my song
Thenn quhy sould thow suche spyte for my gude will returne
Vas euer god as zit sua made to make his temple burne
My breast the temple was quhence insens thow receaued
And zit thow sets the same afyre which otheris wald haue saued
But quhy sould thow accuis Aurora in this gyise
Shee's als fateles as shoe is fair als innocent als wyse
For it is but throuche my misluckt giue any fault ther be
For shee who was of nature mylde was cruell made by me
And since my fortoune is in woe to be bewrapptt
I'le honour her as of befoir and hate my awin mishaptt
Her rigourous cours sall serue my loyell pairt to prove
And as ane tuichstane for to trye ye vertew of my love
Quhich whenn her bewtie fades salbe als cleir as now
My constancie it salbe knowne when wrinckled is her brow
Sua that suche tua againe sall in no age be found
Shee for her face I for my fayth baith worthie to be croun'd

SEMPLE

VI.

WILL thow remorsles fair, still laughe whill I lament,
    And sall thy cheefe contentment be, to see me malle-
        content?
Sall I Narcissus lyke, ane flying shade still chaise
Or lyke Pigmaleon straine a stone, quhilk bare no sence of grace
No ! no, my blind loue now, must burrow reassonnes eyes
It was thy fairnes made me sounde, zour wrong name [now] mak
    me [wise]
My just desert's disdaines to loue ane loveles dame,
The lyfe of Cupidis fyre confides, Into ane mutuall flame
[For] gaue thow but a looke, or gaue thow but a smyle
Ore sent thow furth but ane sweit siche, my sorrow to begyle,
My captiues thouchts perhaps myght be redeem'd from pane
And thois my mutineris malecontents, mycht freinds with hoip
    agane
But thow as it appears, still cairles of my gude
And as it seem's wald eternize, thy bewtie with my bloode,
Ane great disgrace to the, to me ane monstrous wrong,
Quhilk tyme will teache the to repent, befoir that it be long,
Then, to prevente thy schame, and to abraidge my woe,
Becaus thow will noucht loue thy freinde I'le cease to lufe my
    foe.   SEMPLE.

VII.

LET him whois hapeles state : is as it aye hes beine
    And hes bene euer as it is : ane caue caires to conteine
Still strampld doune with sturte : let him the weird's Imploir
That they may fill his dayes with zeir's : nor zeer's with days
    no moir
I clame no right to Lyfe : tho' Lyfe acclame to me
The comfoirt that my Lyfe impoirt's : Is that it liue to dye
Zit by constran'te of Loue ill : my pennance sall furth proue
That tho' I doe not Loue to liue : zit doe I liue to Loue
Her with whom I'is be ay : in absence present bee
Quhois matchles nevir dying worth : I sall adoiring dye
Goe then zee pliders power : of never purchast peace
Resigne my Loue her awin disdaine : liue me with my disgrace
 . Tell to her secrecte sight : since better could noucht bee

Lang haue I foughtin with my fate : and now am forcit to flee
Sall neuer Loue dissolue : the Lyfe that loue beganne
How Lang sall Langour be the lord : the louer be the man
The darkeest cloudes will cleir : ill storme will sumtyme ceas
And everie battell sumtyme hes : ane day perfixt for peace
But where Loue Lyis intrinch't : within a breist of feares
Na kynde of comfoirt claer's there croce : nor joy dryis vp there
    teer's
Reid thenn remorseles fair : quha knawes nor it may be
That pittie pitticles befoir · prove pittiefull to me
My tempted hee attempt's : slow soiring out of sight
My mounting mynde clume did allace : but came not to the sicht
Thy face the field wheerein : my Loue and thy disdaine
Vnreconceild compeditouris : vowes euer to remayne
Sen so it is allace : giue her gudenicht and goe
Devoirc't from weell espousit to wrong : and interteinit with woe
Rit nether contrair cace : nor prosperous event's
Sall mak my pen Leive of to blote : the Lynnes of my Lament's
And for thy worth I vow : In forrand lands to fair
Thy [inter]dyti[d] pilgrime puire : for euer heir and thair
And as thow was that one : to quhome I faith profest
Looke in quhat corner of the eirth thy Loouer poore sall res[t]
There be assuir't sweet saull : sum sonnet salbe sung
And sowst with sorrow for thy saik : tald with a truthfull tung
Hade I als manie hearts : as my harte thouchts commands
And euerie harte of all these hearts : I sweere als manye hands
Eache hand sould hold a pen : to wryte thy worthie rair
As post's of thy eternal prais : to tell the world thour't fair
Let it suffice the pen : puire saull her sicht to flee
Since thow hes founde thy marterdome : remedyles to bee
Rest zee in thy vnrest : and murray be thow still
The maike where meneles miseries directes there endles ill
Giue her ane long gudenicht : and seeke vnto thy soir
Sum hermitadge where broken herts · are heipit in stoir
And there releefles dead : vpgaue the ghoist and all
That woorthie famē may fetche of thee, a fate memoriall
That as thow Loueing Liued : her Louer poore and trew
Sua at thy Letter dying breathe : thow bade her last adew
Thus sall thy ending bee · begging vnto her prais
Her prais whilk neuer sall haue end : sall end my wretchit dayes

                                                    SEMPLE.

FINIS AMEN.

II.—POEM ON SOME OF THE AULD MAKARS OF BALLATES, SANGIS, AND TRAGEDIES, BY ALLAN RAMSAY [1724].

[Originally printed as a Broadside, in double columns, without date, and Reprinted in the "MEMORIALS OF GEORGE BANNATYNE, 1545-1608." Edited by DAVID LAING, ESQ. for the Bannatyne Club, Edinburgh, 1829.]

SOME FEW OF THE CONTENTS.

HEIR mighty JAMES the First, the best of Kings,
Imploys the merry Muse, and smyling sings.
Grave BALANTYNE, in verse divinely wyse,
Makis Vertew triumph owre fals fleechand Vyse.

And heir DUNBAR does with unbound ingyne,
In satyre, joke, and in the serious schyne.
He to best poets skairslie zields in ocht ;
In language he may fail, but not in thocht.

Blyth KENNEDIE, contesting for the bays,
Attackis his freind DUNBAR in comick layis,
And seims the fittest hand (of ony then)
Against sae fell a fae to draw his pen.

Heir LETHINGTON the Statisman courts the Nyne,
Draps politicks a quhyle, and turns divyne ;
Sings the Creation, and fair Eden tint,
And promise made to man, man durst not hint

To rouse couragious fyre behald the field,
Quhair Hardyknute, with lanss, bow, sword and scheild,
With his braif Sonis, dantit the King of Norss,
And cleithed the plain with mony a saules cors.
At Harlaw and Redsquire, the sonis may leir,
How thair forbeirs were unacquaint with feir.

Quhen frac the dumps ze wald zour mind discharge,
Then tak the air in smiling SEMPLIS Berge :
Or heir him jyb the carlis did Grissy blame,
Quhen eild and spyte takis place of zouthheids Flame.

Licht skirtit lasses, and the girnand wyfe,
FLEMING and SCOT haif painted to the lyfe.
SCOT, sweit tungd SCOT, quha sings the Welcum hame
To MARY, our maist bony Soverane Dame ;
How lyflie he and amorous STUART sing !
Quhen lufe and bewtie bid them spred the wing.

To mend zour morals, with delyt attend,
Quhyle HENRYSON dois guidness recommend ;
Quhyle Truth throw his transport Fablis schynes,
And all the mynd to quhat is just inclynes.

Amangst these starnis of ane immortal bleis,
MONTGOMERY's quatorsimes sall evir pleis ;
His eisy sangs, his Cherry and the Slae,
Sall be esteimd quhyle sichs saft lufe betray.

LINDSAY the Lyon, hardly here is sene,
But in the third Apartment of the Grene, *
He sall appeir as on the verdant Stage ;
He towind the vyces of a corrupt aige.

Thair Warkis I've publisht, neat, correct, and fair,
Frae antique manuscriptis, with utmost cair.
Thus to their fame, a monument we raise,
Quhilk sall endure quhyle Tymis telld out be days.

---

* Ramsay announced his intention to publish a third and fourth volume
of the Evergreen.

Glossary

[NOTE.—In the old spelling *i* is often used for *j*; *u* for *v*; *v* for *u*; *y* for *i*; *ui* for *oo*; *z* for *y*; *y* for *th*; *quy* for *wh*. *Is* forms the termination of the plural; *and*, of the present participle; *it*, of the preterite tense.]

A

A, page 231, *all*.

Abaid, 207, *abode*.

Abandoned, 194, *brought under absolute subjection*.

Abbreid, 237, *abroad, asunder*.

Abon, 50, *above*.

Absconse, 162, *hide*.

Abufe, 101, *above*.

Aby, 75, " Faynd aby we set her," *devil a bit did we regard her*, aby, *for by*.

Acht, 30, *ought*.

Acknawledgeing, 58, *acknowledging*.

Actit, 175, *acted, enacted*.

Admiratioun, 1, *wonder*.

Adorned, 218, *used for adored*.

Affeir, 16, *warlike preparations*.

Affeiring, 165, *belonging*.

Agane, 114, *against*.

Agast, 50, *aghast*.

Ainis, 51, *once*.

Air, 109, *early*.

Air, 239, *eyre*.

Aire, 191, *heir*.

Airt, 68, *quarter*.

Airt and pairt, 116, *art and part*.

Aithis, 125, *oaths*.

Alaw, 108, *low*.

Albeit, Albeid, 7, *although*.

Ald, 213, *old*.

Aleuin, 59, *eleven*.

All and sum, 119, *everything, everyone*.

Almaist, 53, *almost*.

Als, 228, *as*.

17

Alswa, 39, *also.*
Alsweill, 5, *as well.*
Althocht, 81, *although.*
And, 4, *if.*
Ane, 1, *a, one;* war ane, 21, *were united.*
Anes, 198, *ones,* 226, *once.*
Aneuch, anew, 190, *enough.*
Angle noble, 212, *angel noble, a coin.*
Anker-hald, 231, *anchorage.*
Ans, 155, *once.*
Anterous, 99, *adventurous.*
Apperandly, 72, *apparently.*
Appost, 126, *dispose, settle.*
Archness, 220, *anxiety.*
Arlit, 239, *earnest given.*
Asay, 239, *trial.*
Assailzeit, 50, *assailed.*
Asswetit, 2, *accustomed.*
Ast, 216, *asked.*
Asteir, 12, *rouse, excite.*
Ather, 164, *either.*
Athort, 181, *about, across; far and wide.*
Attoure, 8, *above.*
Aucht, 18, *ought.*
Aucht, 50, *eight.*
Auentuire, 13, *chance.*
Auld, 2, *old.*
Aver, 208, *cart-horse.*
Awin, 28, *own.*
Ayre, air, 204, *oar.*

B

Bable, 116, *a bauble was a short stick, with a head carved at the end of it like a poupée or doll, carried by the fools or jesters of former times.*

Baburd, 231, *the larboard, or left side of a ship.*
Bachlane, 215, *shambling.*
Bade, 124, *stayed, withstood.*
Baid, 157, *help, remedy.*
Bailfull, 107, *baneful, grievous.*
Baill, 143, *sorrow.*
Baird, 224, *railer, lampooner.*
Bairdrie, 186, *bawdrie.*
Bait, 152, *boat.*
Baith, 8, baitht, 185, *both.*
Bald, 187, *bold.*
Ballates, 1, *ballads.*
Ballinger, 231, *a kind of ship.*
Balme, 197, *mild, sound.*
Ban, 226, *curse.*
Bands, 83, *bonds.*
Bane, 105, *King of Bane, the same with King of the Bean.*
Bane, 128, *ready, prepared.*
Baneis, 53, *banish.*
Bangesters, 214, *brawlers.*
Bargane, 127, *combat, fight, contention.*
Barnage, 66, *baronage.*
Barne, 145, *child;* barnis, *lads, men.*
Barnetyme, 148, *brood of children.*
Barret, 71, *contention, grief, trouble.*
Bastianes brydell, 183, *the marriage of Bastian, one of Queen Mary's attendants; to be present at which the Queen left Darnley on the night of his murder.*
Battellis, 190, *battle array, division of an army.*

Bauch, 71, *abashed, out of countenance.*

Bauldlie, 180, *boldly.*

Baxters, 200, *bakers.*

Be, 55, *by, against.*

Bedene, 82, *forthwith.*

Bedreidis, 109, *dreads.*

Beforne, 64, *before.*

Begouth, 25, *began.*

Behauld, 25, *behold.*

Behufe, 102, *behoof.*

Beild, 38, *shelter.*

Beinly, 168, *snugly.*

Beir, 152, *noise, disturbance.*

Beir seid tyme, 71, *time of sowing barley.*

Beis, 74, *is.*

Beit, 167, *to mend by making addition.*

Belive, 5, *soon, quickly.*

Bellie Blind, 132, *the person blindfolded in Blind Harie.*

Beltit, 75, *girded.*

Ben, 204, *towards the inner apartment of a house.*

Bent, 126, *earnest.*

Bent, 127, *keen.*

Bergane, 87, *strife, quarrel, fight.*

Beriall, 139, *burial,*

Bescik, 111, *beseech.*

Bestiall, 60, *cattle, horses, sheep.*

Besy, 179, *busy.*

Bet, 109, *struck.*

Betraissand, 117, *betraying.*

Be war with, 174, *beware of.*

Be witcheit, 30, *bewitched.*

Bide, 124, *wait, stay.*

Bigging, 170, *building.*

Bill, 59, *writing, complaint.*

Bird alane, 170, *alone, the only one left of a family.*

Bittis, 109, *rug in b., tear to pieces.*

Bladis, 180, *pieces, fragments.*

Blaiknit, 50, *blackened.*

Blasnit, 65, *blazoned.*

Blawne, 130, *blown.*

Ble, 50, *black and blue, livid.*

Bleir, 109 *obscure.*

Blek, 227, *blacken.*

Blekkit, 199, *deceived.*

Blockit, 221, *bargained.*

Blok, 232, *bargain, scheme.*

Blude, 50, *bloody.*

Blumis, 77, *blooms, flowers.*

Blus, 225, *flood.*

Blyithlyke, 77, *gay, gladsome.*

Bobbis, 130, *gusts, blasts.*

Bocht, 175, *bought.*

Boide, 130, *a billow agitated by the wind.*

Boire, 141, *perhaps for bower.*

Boistit, 163, *bragged.*

Bonatris, 187, *bonnets ; Dalyell reads bonattis.*

Bony, 231, *fair, beautiful.*

Bordall, 201, *brothel.*

Borrowing, 177, *loan.*

Bosses, 197, *bottles.*

Bot, 74, *but, that ; without.*

Botis and hummis, 137, *buts and hums,*

Bouistrit, 116, *bolstered.*

Boun, 228, *ready, gone.*

Bourd, 233, *jest.*

Bowdin, 30, *swollen.*

Bowit, 179, *enlisted.*

Bowstert, 232, *bolstered, lifted up.*

Braics, 194, *braes.*

Brak, 181, *broken.*

Brasche, 181, *an assault, an attack.*

Brast, 44, *burst.*

Brattle, 229, *clatter.*

Braulis, 175, *brangles, menaces.*

Brawlit, 171, *marbled, also explained as fine.*

Breid, 64, *breadth.*

Breif, 104, *write.*

Breikis, 183, *breeches.*

Breiris, 77, *briars.*

Breistand, 194, *springing up.*

Brent, 3, *high, steep* ; browis brent, *high forehead.*

Brether, 168, *brethren.*

Brig, 167, *bridge.*

Brint, 153, *burnt.*

Brintstane, 160, *brimstone.*

Britheringis, 4, *brethren's.*

Brod, 104, *prick.*

Broderit, 117, *fraternized.*

Brouin, 167, *brewed.*

Browne, 80, *brewed.*

Bruik, 164, *enjoy.*

Brukill, 130, *brittle.*

Brunt, 79, *burnt.*

Brusted, 225, *bursted.*

Bryde, 226, *damsel.*

Budding, 71, *bribing.*

Buddis, 121, *bribes, gifts.*

Buft, 179, *stuffed.*

Buithis, 122, *booths, shops.*

Buk heid, 126, *a sort of game, perhaps Hide and Seek.*

> "And for dreddour that he suld bene arreist
> He playit buk hude behind, fra beist to beist."—*Henryson's Fables.*

Bule, 183, *Dalyell reads bufe.*

Burrio, 11, *a hangman, Fr. bourreau.*

Burrowis towne, 169, *borough.*

Burrow rudis, 71, *lands belonging to a borough.*

Bus, 58, *bush.*

Buschment, 177, *ambush.*

Bust, 218, *apparently for busked, dressed.*

But, 102, *unless;* butt, 227, *without.*

Bute, 206, *help, remedy.*

Butiene, 182, *booty.*

By, 29, *against, beyond.*

By, 117, *buy, pay for.*

Byde, 64, *endure.*

Byde or gang, 64, *go or stay.*

Bydis, (*original,*) 181, *Dalyell reads hydis.*

Byganis, 284, *bygones.*

Byke, 23, *hive.*

C

Cail, 103, *cabbage.*

Caird not by, 137, *recked nought.*

Cald, 115, *cool.*

Calf, 176, *chaff.*

Calfet, 230, *to caulk, for calfuter.*

Calk, 176, *chalk.*

Calsay, 221, *causeway.*

Campioun, 65, *champion.*

Canker, 132, *ill-humour ;* cankert, *peevish, cross.*

Cannabie, 228, *cor. of canopy.*

Carle, 168, *churl, countryman.*

Carling, 210, *old woman, witch.*

Carpe, 158, *sing.*

Cartes, 226, *cards.*

Caryit by thy senses, 116, *out of thy wits.*

Cashmaries, 216, *fish carriers.*

Cassin, 167, *cast.*

Castelliuir, 181, *Dalyell reads Castell suir.*

Cat harrows, draw the cat harrows, 100, *they thwart one another.*

Chaip, 136, *cheap.*

Chaipit, 66, *escaped.*

Chaisson, chessoun, 80, *blame, accuse.*

Chapmen, 157, *pedlars.*

Charr, 152.

Cheis, 75, *choose.*

Chereist, 28, *cherished.*

Chesit, 8, *chose.*

Chope, 221, *shop.*

Claif, 37, *clave.*

Clair, 191, *clear.*

Clairis, 158, *maltreat.*

Clais, 151, *clothes.*

Claith, 237, *cloth.*

Clap, 147, *pat, fondle.*

Claver, 208, *clover.*

Clawbackes, 193, *supporters.*

Cleathis, 221, *clothes.*

Cleik, 91, *to catch as by a hook.*

Clengit, 67, *cleanse, give proof of innocence.*

Clenkett, 230, *hammered.*

Cline, 177, *clean.*

Cloik, 84, *cluck.*

Close, 70, *passage, entry.*

Coische, cosche, 218, *coach.*

Coist, 135, *changed sides.*

Cokadraill, 159, *crocodile.*

Combure, 92, *burnt, blew up with gunpowder.*

Come, 50, *came.*

Commendis, 110, *commendation.*

Commouit, 87, *moved.*

Compair, 116, *comparison.*

Compeiris, 67, *presents one's self in court in consequence of being summoned.*

Complene, 203, *singing.*

Condescend, 130, *agree, specify*

Conding, 33, *severe, merited, proper.*

Confidder, 166, *assemble, confederate.*

Conqueist, 224, *acquired.*

Consait, 8, *conceit.*

Consauit, 11, *conceived.*

Conuene, 82, *meet.*

Conuict, 158, *convict.*

Convoy, 202, *a trick;* convoyit, *conveyed, accompanied.*

Copout, 203, " to play copout," *to drink off all that is in a drinking cup or drinking vessel.*

Corbeis, 78, *ravens.*

Corenothe, 158, *coronach.*

Cor mundum, to cry, 118, *to confess a fault.*

Cose, 70, *exchange.*

Cost, 239, *the side.*

Counnand, 132, *engagement, contract.*

Counze houss, 231, *mint.*

Courche, 170, *a covering for a woman's head.*

Cousing, 116, *cousin.*

Couth, 4, *known.*

Cow, 75, *to cut down, cut the heads off;* cowit, *closely shorn.*

Cowe, 218, *a scarecrow, hobgoblin.*

Cowsauly, 71.
Crackis, 207, *talk.*
Craig, 215, *throat.*
Craw, 77, *crow.*
Cro, 118, *pigsty.*
Croce, 64, *cross.*
Cronall, 180, *colonel.*
Crounis, 73, *crowns.*
Crous, 17, *brisk.*
Cuire, 12, *cover.*
Cumbart, 226, *cumbered.*
Cumin, 18, *come.*
Cummer, 235, *gossip.*
Cunning, 188, *skill.*
Curage, 67, *courage.*
Curfufled, 215, *discomposed.*
Cvre, 40, *care.*

D

Da, 2, *doe.*
Daft, 35, *mad.*
Dalyday, 1, *Dalilah.*
Dang, 178, *beat.*
Danter, 192, *conqueror, subduer.*
Dantonit, 70, *daunted.*
Daw, 75, *dawn.*
Debait, 191, *protection.*
Deceissit, 208, *died.*
Decoir, 70, *adorn.*
Decreittit, 105, *decreed.*
Deddy, 165, *dad, father.*
Defacit, 215, *confounded, disgraced.*
Defendit, 85, *prohibited.*
Deflorand, 175, *deflowring.*
Deid, 58, *death.*
Deif, 231, *deave.*
Deill, 117, *diel, devil.*
Deir, 151, *hurt, harm.*

Delatouris, 205, *accusers.*
Deloyaltie, 129, *disloyalty.*
Delt, 82, *divided.*
Delyte, 116, *delight.*
Demereitis, 193, *merit.*
Demylance, 116, *a light lance. a short spear.*
Deneir, 66, *a small Scots coin.*
Deplane, 146, *plaine, show.*
Descriue, 99, *describe.*
Det, 186, *duty,*
Detreitis, 198, *so in the original ; obviously intended for decreitis.*
Detrusaris, 121, *a violent opposer.*
Detrusit, 126, *thrust out.*
Deuoir, 178, *devour.*
Deuoir, 184, *service.*
Deuyne, dewyne, 4, *divine.*
Devoir, 198, *duty.*
Dicht, 238, *dressed, handled.*
Ding, 36, *beat.*
Ding, 111, *worthy.*
Ding doun, 16, *overthrow.*
Dintis dowse, 16.
Dirtin, 109, *defiled.*
Dispaired, 120, *desperate.*
Dispone, 91, *dispose.*
Disprysis, 92, *condemn.*
Dissait, 9, *deceit.*
Dissaitfully, 117, *deceitfully.*
Dissave, 151, *deceive.*
Dit, 167, *close up.*
Doables, 44, *duplicity.*
Doand ane quhyle, 174, *go on for a time.*
Docht, 178, *could.*
Dolent, 142, *mournful.*
Done, 113, *used as an expletive.*

Dontane, 159, *throbbing.*
Dotit, 51, *endowed.*
Douchtaly, 194, *doughtily.*
Doughtie, 73, *doughty.*
Douke, 6, *bathe, dive.*
Dour, 175, *stiff, hardy.*
Dout, 143, *regard, fear.*
Dow, 5, *is able to.*
Dowbill, 1, *double.*
Dowie, 194, *doleful.*
Dowis, 234, *doves.*
Dowkand, 189, *diving.*
Downe, 165, *dare.*
Draffen, 126, *the castle of Draffen.*
Dram, 50, *sad, melancholy.*
Drapping, 198, *dropping.*
Dred, 130, *dreaded.*
Dreggers, 170, *loiterers.*
Dres, 121, *assuage;* 160, *prepare.*
Drest, 53, *treated, prepared, chastised.*
Drie, 156, *endure.*
Drug, 168, *to pull roughly or forcibly; Dalyell reads drag.*
Druken, 35, *drunken.*
Drummake, 238, *meal and water mixed in a raw state.*
Dryftis, 108, *drifts, schemes.*
Dryue of the tyme, 79, *put off.*
Dude, 106, *do it.*
Duire, 12, *hard.*
Dule, 75, *grief.*
Dung, 78, *overcome.*
Dussie, duschet, 205, *a musical instrument.*
Dustifit, 109 *a pedlar, revelry; perhaps the name of a dance.*
Duvill, 132, *for devil.*
Dykis, 180, *stone walls.*

Dysartis duschet, 202.
Dysartis pype, 106.
Dytone, 149, *motto.*
Dyver, 207, *bankrupt.*

E

Eall, 213, *ale.*
Easter, 207, *eastern.*
Edder, 110, *adder.*
Ee, 10, *eye.*
Effeiris, 193, *is fit, is becoming.*
Effrayit, 67, *affrighted.*
Efter syne, 21, *afterwards.*
Efterwart, 102, *afterward.*
Eftir-claip, 132, *evil consequence.*
Eik, 136, *augment;* eikit, *added.*
Eik, 160, *also.*
Eild, 91, *age.*
Eine, ene, 162, *eyes.*
Eith, 194, *easily.*
Ellis, 175, *otherwise.*
Elphe, 208, *elf.*
Elphyne, 210, *elfland.*
Els, 67, *also.*
Elvasche, 200, *elfish.*
Endlang, 133, *along.*
Ennewche, 237, *enough.*
Enorme, 130, *lawless.*
Entres, 196, *entrance.*
Erie, 159, *affected with fear.*
Ethnik, 182, *heathen.*
Euend, 187, *event.*
Evill win, 210, *ill won.*
Exame, exem, 146, *examine.*
Excambion, 147, *exchange.*
Exemp, 233, *exempt.*

Exerce, 20, *exercise.*
Eyndling, 215, *jealous.*

F

Faa, fa, 218, *befall, betide.*
Faceles, 30, *frontless.*
Face ocin, *(original)* 186, *Dalyell reads fatt oxin.*
Factis, 99, *deeds.*
Faid, 2, *a company of hunters.*
Faill, 4, *fault.*
Failzie, 237, *fail.*
Fair, 10, *appearance.*
Fairdy, 230, *swift, expeditious.*
Fais, 18, *foes.*
Fais, 143, *falls.*
Fallow, 54, *fellow.*
Falset, 164, *falsehood.*
Falt, 230, *want.*
Fand, 226, *found.*
Fane, 5, *feign.*
Faug, 2, *to grasp, lay hold of.*
Farnzer, 75, *last year.*
Fas cast, 201, *scheme.*
Fassoun, 98, *fashion.*
Faucht, 71, *fallow.*
Faucht, 193, *fought.*
Fauldit, 109, *folded.*
Fauldit neif, 109, *fist.*
Faultouris, 4, *transgressors.*
Fecfullest, 131, *most powerful.*
Feche, 105, *fetch.*
Fecht, 75, *fight.*
Feddrum, 77, *wings.*
Fegges, 157, *figs.*
Feid, 163, *enmity.*
Feill, 85, *understanding.*
Feinzeit, fenzeit, 2, *feigned.*
Feinzeit fair, 10, *feigned countenance.*

Feir, 2, *companion; associate.*
Feir of weir, 151, *a warlike expedition.*
Feirit, 145, *afraid.*
Feirs, 94, *fierce.*
Feit, 61, *fee'd, hired.*
Fell, 159, *the hide.*
Felloun, 66, *fierce, cruel.*
Fellounly, 140, *cruelly.*
Felterit, 11, *entangled.*
Ferand, 2, *affeirand, becoming.*
Ferlie, 228, *wonder.*
Ferynes, 144, *vigour, pith.*
Festin, 152, *fasten.*
Feycsit, 131, *fetched.*
Fidder, 24, *lot, crowd.*
Find, 177, *fiend.*
Firrat, 6, *ferret.*
Fist, 32, *first.*
Flaine, 2, *arrow.*
Flait, 74, *scolded.*
Flaw, 100, *blast, storm of snow.*
Fle, 167, *frighten.*
Fleich, 219, *flatter.*
Fleid, 207, *frightened.*
Fleid, 227, *timid.*
Flemit, 92, *banished.*
Fleslie, 233, *fleshly.*
Fletche, 5, *flatter.*
Fleyit, 180, *afraid.*
Fling, 83, *kick.*
Flit, 152, *remove.*
Floit, 231, *float, fleet.*
Flycht, *(original)* 179, *Dalyell reads slycht.*
Flyte, 27, *scold, wrangle.*
Fo, 55, *foe.*
Focke, 198, *folk.*
Foirspeik, 154, *predict.*
Forbears, 155, *forefathers.*
Forbure, 148, *forbore.*

Force, 132, *for foirse, foresee.*
Forcie, 66, *powerful.*
Forde, 37, *for it.*
Forder, 228, *further.*
Forethocht, 100, *forethought.*
Forfault, 40, *forfeit.*
Forgaif, 55, *forgave.*
Forloppen, 198, *fugitives.*
Formois, 3, *fair.*
Forsuik, 148, *forsook.*
Forte, 183, *forty, brave.*
Forthink, 89, *rue, repent of ;*
pret. forthoght.
Forwereit, 7, *wearied.*
Forzet, 31, *forget ;* foryet, *forgot.*
Foul fall, 150, *woe betide.*
Fow, 220, *drunk.*
Fra, 3, *from.*
Fra ainis, 8, *from the time*
that.
Fraer, 157, *freare, a basket.*
Frahand, 150, *presently.*
Frak, 59, *ready, active.*
Fraklie, 68, *hastily.*
Franke, 193, *so in the original,*
but it may perhaps be an
error for fracke, active.
Fray, 73, *be afraid.*
Frayit, 88, *affrighted.*
Frawcht, 232, *freight.*
Frawcht fre, 231, *freight free.*
Frear, 74, *more free, more*
ready.
Freik, 180, *a stout fellow.*
Freiris, 193, *friars.*
Freis, 58, *freeze.*
Freith, 113, *free, liberate.*
Fremitnes, 164, *strangeness.*
Freprie, 238, *frippery.*
Frere, 141, *friar.*
Fristit, 83, *delayed.*

Fruster, 92, *frustrate.*
Fuilzeit, 131, *got the better of.*
Fules, 130, *fowles.*
Full, 3, *very.*
Furnissit, 108, *furnished.*
Furringis, 196, *furs.*
Furthe, 11, *out.*
Furtherit, 136, *furthered, sped.*
Furthschawin, 39, *shown forth.*
Fute, 16, *foot ;* 39, fittis ; fute
the field, *take the field.*
Fyk, 153, *vex, perplex.*
Fyking, 236, *such a degree of*
intimacy as suggests the
idea of courtship.
Fyle, 35, *defile, sully.*
Fyne, 9, *end.*

G

Ga, 19, *go.*
Gaid, 220, *went.*
Gaidis, 216, *tricks.*
Gaif, 6, *gave.*
Gaip, 216, *gape.*
Gaist, 139, *guest.*
Gaist, 139, *ghost.*
Gait, 214, *way.*
Gallous, 69, *gallows.*
Gan, 41, *began.*
Gane, 71, *gone,*
Ganeand, 216, *suitable.*
Ganestand, 125, *withstand.*
Gang, 146, *go ;* gangand, 215,
going, walking.
Ganzell, 100, *recompence.*
Ganzelon, 173, *Ganelon. the*
celebrated traitor of the Ro-
mances of Charlemagne, the
person that took a bribe to
betray the French army to
the Saracens.

Gar, 36, *make*.
Garisone, 120, *garrison*.
Gartane, 82, *garter*.
Gat, 125, *got*.
Gaw, 128, *the mark left on the skin by a stroke or pressure; a sore*.
Gayth, 149.
Gea, 217, *go*.
Geathis, 227, *for geas*.
Geck, 235, *mock, befool*.
Gedds, 145, *pikes*.
Gein, 31, *given*.
Geir, 20, *wealth, substance*.
Gek, gave him the, 217, *gave him the slip*.
Gent, 170, *neat*.
Gers, 169, *grass*.
Gersom, grassum, 168, *premium for a lease*.
Get, 35, *brat*.
Geue, 186, *if*.
Geuen, 185, *given*.
Gien, 182, *Dalyell reads greit*.
Gif, 4, *give*.
Gif, 22, *if*.
Gild, 183, *clamour*.
Giltles, 70, *guiltless*.
Gird, 109, *stroke*.
Girnell, 160, *a large chest for holding meal*.
Girth, 234, *sanctuary*.
Giue, 173, *if*.
Glaikis, get the, 122, *be gulled*.
Glaikrie, 195, *idle wantonness*.
Glamer, 35, *noise*.
Gled, 135, *kite*.
Gleib, 197, *a piece or part of anything*.
Gleims, 67, *flames*.
Gloir, 63, *glory in*.

Glorie, 39, *gloried*.
Glore, 191, *glory*.
Gluiffis, 162, *gloves*.
Glystryng, 78, *glistering, glittering*.
Goishalk, 2, *goshawk*.
Goldspink, 77, *goldfinch*.
Gormondis, 154, *gluttons*.
Gorring, 175, *goring, killing*.
Gospellar, 140, *gospeller*.
Gowanis, 76, *daises*.
Graip, 238, *grope*.
Graith, 135, *apparatus of whatever kind, gear, money*.
Granges, 118, *buildings belonging to a corn-farm*.
Grank, 159, *the groaning of a wounded hart*.
Grathed, 218, *dressed*.
Gre, 132, *step*,
Gre, 153, *agree, reconcile*.
Greance, 185, *agreement*.
Greinis, 78, *greens*.
Greis, 173, *in greis, degree*.
Greit, 225, *cry*.
Grenis, 73, *longs*.
Gripit, 183, *gripped, seized*.
Grit, 173, *great*.
Grof, 171, *having harsh features, unpolished, vulgar*.
Grome, 15, *man, bridegroom*.
Gros, 171, *gross, course*.
Growgraine, 227, *grogram, a sort of cloth*.
Gude, 136, *good*.
Gude lyke, 164, *good looking*.
Gudeman, 166, *master of a family*.
Gude, men of, 32, *men of property*.
Gudschir, 66, *grandfather*.

Guldis, 65, *gules.*
Guse, 168, *goose.*
Guthorne, 135, *a guitar.*
Guyding, 33, *conduct.*
Gwmis, 237, *for gome, or guym, a man.*
Gyding, 83, *rule.*
Gymps, 153, *taunts.*
Gyrth, 118, *sanctuary.*
Gyse, 152, *a mask, a dance.*
Gysours,173, *guisers, maskers.*

H

Ha, 3, *ha! benedicite;* 160, *ha! treason.*
Had, 227, *hold.*
Haif, 152, *have.*
Haill, 8, *whole, all.*
Haillely, 140, *wholly.*
Hait, 9, *hot.*
Haitrent, 11, *hatred.*
Halden, 67, *held.*
Hallous, 69, *saints.*
Hals, 174, *throat, neck.*
Halsit, 55, *embraced,*
Haly, 4, *holy.*
Hame, 52, *home.*
Hamelie, 215, *homely.*
Hane, 146, *spare.*
Hank, 88, *to tie tightly, so as to leave the mark of the cord.*
Hansell, 239, *first money received in payment of goods.*
Happit, 196, *covered.*
Harbrie, 199, *harbour.*
Hardiment, 195, *hardihood.*
Harkit, 204, *whispered.*
Harlat, 206, *scoundrel.*
Harmesay, 229, *alas.*

Harne, 141, *hardin, coarse.*
Hartlie, 188, *heartily.*
Hartsum, 4, *merry, courageous.*
Hauld, 112, *hold.*
Hautie, 105, *haughty.*
Hayned, 216, *spared.*
Hear, 74, *higher.*
Hecht, 75, *promised, engaged.*
Heich, 28, 156, *high.*
Heill, 91, *cover.*
Heirfoir, 67, 192, *herefor, for this.*
Heis, heise, 67, *raise, lift.*
Heith, 179, *for heich.*
Hele, 49, *he'll.*
Helterit, 138, *roped, pinioned.*
Herreat, 202, *harried, plundered.*
Heuch, 138, *crag.*
Hewit, 229, *coloured.*
Hichit, 141, *panted.*
Hicht, 168, *heighten.*
Hie, 52, *high.*
Hiest, 174, *highest.*
Hing, 117, *hang.*
Hint, 164, *laid hold of.*
Hoiplost, 109, *hopeless.*
Hole, 199, *whole.*
Holiglas, 205, *a character in the old romances. Belg. Uylespegel, i.e., Owlglass.*
Holk, 185, *dig.*
Holkis, 84, *a disease of the eye.*
Holtis, 78, *forests, woods, high and barren ground.*
Hosted, 204, *coughed.*
Hosyng, 237, *hosen.*
Houshald, 168, *household.*
Howbeid, 238, *howbeit.*
Howfing, 215, *spunging.*
Howis, 230, *hollows.*

Howlets, 78, *owlets.*
Hud, 213, *hoard.*
Hudefull, 204, *full of a hud,
the trough used by masons
for carrying mortar.*
Hudge, 27, *huge, great.*
Huif, 134, *heaved or lifted at
baptism, named.*

"Or gyf a man have hove a chylde,
God hyt ever forbide and shylde."
                          Halliwell's Dict.

Huiking, 93, *regarding.*
Huirdome, 10, *whoredom.*
Hunder, hundreth, 126, *hun-
dred.*
Hure, 141, *whore.*
Hy, 170, *haste.*
Hycht, 8, *high, highly.*
Hynd, 169, *hind, ploughman.*
Hyntit, 69, *laid hold of.*
Hyntworthe, 208, *an herb.*

I & J

Iaip, 182, *mock.*
Ile, 144, *isle.*
Ilk, 28, *each.*
Imates, 190, *emmets.*
Imbraist, 135, *embraced.*
Imbrew, 229, *engross.*
Implorde, 30, *implore it.*
Impriving, 206, *disproving.*
Impung, 119, *impugn.*
Impyre, 103, *empire.*
In, 54, *into.*
Inbringis, 88, *brings in.*
Inbrocht, 146, *imported.*
Incastrat, 190, *for incarcerat.*
Incluse, 74, *enclose.*
Incontinent, 204, *immediately.*

Indeuoir, 167, *devote ;* 38,
indeuorde, *devoted.*
Inding, 117, *unworthy.*
Indyte, 103, *write, capacity.*
Infame, 53, *infamy.*
Infekit, 179, *infected.*
Ingraitly, 192, *ungratefully.*
Ingyne, 129, *capacity, genius.*
Iniure, 112, *injury.*
Inspraich, 224, *furniture of
a house.*
Intak, gers, 169, *plow up the
commons.*
Inteir, 129, *entire, true.*
Interup, 103, *interrupted.*
Intill, 130, *into.*
Intreit, 57, *entreat, treat*
Inuyfull, 87, *envious.*
Johne Vpaland, 23, *a name
applied to a rustic.*
Jonet flouris, 77, *marsh mari-
gold.*
Iskie bae, 228, *usquebaugh,
whisky.*
Ithand, 97, *busy.*
Ithandly, 101, *busily.*
Juike, 225, *trick.*

K

Kankirt, 116, *ill-natured.*
Karle, 231, *fellow.*
Kedzochis seid, 71, *Cadzow,
the Hammiltounis.*
Keik, 158, *peep.*
Keill, 163, *kill.*
Kelt, 215, *cloth with the nap,
generally of native black
wool.*
Ken, 16, *know, pret. kend.*
Kenely, 111, *keen.*

Kep, 149, *receive in falling.*
Kinred, 25, *kindred.*
Kist, 152, *chest.*
Kittie vnsell, 165, *a light wench.*
Kittil, 130, *ticklish*, 232, *tickle.*
Klynclene, 203, *clinking.*
Knaif, 205, *knave.*
Knapscall, 169, *a headpiece.*
Knat, 95, *knit.*
Knaw, 152, *know.*
Knocked beir, 212, *a preparation of barley.*
Knoxis, 199, *knock.*
Kyith, 91, *show.*

L

Labeis, 195, *flap or skirt of a man's coat.*
Lack, lak, 28, *reproach, blame.*
Laich, 230, *low.*
Laidis, 216, *either people, or languages* ; 237, *lads.*
Laif,. 233, *rest.*
Lair, 108, *lore, learniny.*
Laird, 33, *landholder.*
Lais, 162, *lace.*
Lait and aire, 123, *late and early.*
Laith, 5, *loth.*
Lamber, 288, *amber.*
Lane, 229, *lie.*
Lang by, 135, *by a concubine.*
Lang, thocht greit, 103, *longed much.*
Langsum, 194, *tedious.*
Langsyne, 84, *long ago.*
Lap, 157, *leapt.*

Larbour, 235, *sluggish.*
Larwme, 213, *larum.*
Laser, 227, *leisure.*
Lashe, 19, *remiss, faint.*
Lattin, 56, *let.*
Lattouce, 211, *lettuce.*
Lauche, 141, *laugh.*
Lauchfull, 127, *lawful.*
Law, 53, *low.*
Law, 192, *bring low.*
Lawers, 170, *lawyers.*
Lawrie, lowrie, 200, *the fox.*
Lawtie, 129, *loyalty.*
Leave, 206, *rest.*
Leesing, 223, *lie.*
Leid, 2, *language, a lay.*
Leid, 70, *person.*
Leid, 71, *for reid.*
Leill, 212, *loyal, faithful.*
Leir, 30, *to teach, to learn* ; leird, *learned.*
Leit, 82, *delay.*
Leitches, 208, *physicians.*
Len, 162, *lend.*
Lendis, 75, *loins, buttocks.*
Les, 52, *unless.*
Lesingis, 71, *lies.*
Lest, 28, *please, be pleased.*
Lest, 51, *last.*
Lethrone, 215, *leathern.*
Leuch, 216, *laughed.*
Levit, fore, 208, *four leaved.*
Lewrand, lowring, 200, *lurking.*
Lich, for licht, 115, *light.*
Lidder, 235, *sluggish.*
Lig, 235, *lie.*
Limmer, 237, *rogue.*
Lippin, 106, *trust.*
List, 66, *like to.*
Lither, 46, *lazy.*

270 GLOSSARY.

Litils, 197, *so in original, but probably a misprint for litill.*
Litting, 237, *dyeing.*
Live, 199, 200, *leave.*
Lochis Lin, 134, *compare Meg Lochis get, p. 96.*
Locket, 204, *what is belched.*
Lois, 90, *loss.*
Loppin, 235, *leapt.*
Lothsum, 14, *loathsome, hateful.*
Lounrie, 35, *villainy.*
Loup, 132, *flee the country for debt, &c.*
Lowiner, 204, *calmer.*
Lowitt, 129, *loved.*
Lowne, 30, *fellow.*
Lowreis, 3, *see Lawrie.*
Lude hir, 152, *loved her.*
Luf and lie, 230, *a sea phrase; both on the windward and on the lee side.*
Lufe, 230, *luff, also love.*
Luid, lwid, 8, *loved.*
Luiffis, 183, *palms.*
Luifsum, 77, *lovely.*
Lusty, 123, *handsome, pleasant, agreeable.*
Lute, 217, *let.*
Luyf, 142, *love.*
Lwmis, 237, *looms.*
Lyart, 157, *the French coin called a liard.*
Lychtit, 229, *lighted.*
Lychtlit, 28, *despised.*
Lymmeris, 75, *scoundrels.*
Lyncbus, 209, *a jail; perhaps erratum for limbus, or limbo.*
Lyre, 159, *flesh.*
Lyth, 14, *joint.*

M

Ma, 50, *more.*
Mache vilian, 43, *Machiavellian.*
Maddie meinis, 3, *harlot's lamentations.*
Magistrat, 133, *magistracy.*
Mahoun, 138, *Mahomet, the devil.*
Maik, 92, *match, equal.*
Maikles, 173, *matchless.*
Maills, 168 *rents.*
Mailzeis, 162, *plates or links of which a cout of mail is composed.*
Mainsworne, 117, *mansworne, perjured.*
Mair, 50, *more.*
Mair, 113, *mayor.*
Mairouir, 171, *moreover.*
Maisson, 60, *house, family.*
Maist lyke, 80, *most likely.*
Mak, 75, *make; mak to, set to; mak cair, 76, for may cair.*
Makaris, 69, *bards, poets.*
Maling, 26, *malign.*
Malk, 124, *see maik.*
Man, 20, *must.*
Manassing, 128, *menacing.*
Manesworne, 171, *perjured.*
Manged, 41, *confounded; 123, maimed.*
Markis, 72, *aims.*
Marklynis, 238, *in the dark.*
Marrow, 2, *mate, companion; 147, match.*
Marynes, 144, *merriness.*
Mea, 216, *more.*
Measer, 226, *macer.*

Meffan, 141, *Paul Meffen (Methven).* See *Knox's Historie, Lib. IV. p.* 364.

Meg Lochis get, 96, *compare Lochis Lin,* 134.

Meine, 9, *method.*

Meinis, 104, *complain.*

Meir, 202, *mare.*

Meis, 9, *mitigate.*

Mekill, 157, *much.*

Mell, 125, meddle.

Melzie, malze, 239, *a coin of small value.*

Mendis, 75, *amends, compensation.*

Mene, 19, *lament, complain.*

Menez, 100, *followers of a chieftain, crowd.*

Menss, 35, *honour.*

Mensueris, 222, *perjures himself.*

Mesure, 86, *moderation, measure.*

Met, 171, *measure.*

Me think, 79, *methinks.*

Midding, 65, *midden.*

Midpart, 228, *half.*

Minnie, 165, *mother.*

Mirk, 238, *dark.*

Mischant, 102, *wicked.*

Mischevit, 219, *hurt, injured.*

Miscuikit, 104, *miscook it.*

Misericord, 103, *merciful.*

Misgyde, 166, *abuse, spoil.*

Misknaw, 100, *to be ignorant of.*

Missit, 8, *for mis-set, displeased.*

Mist, 202, *lost.*

Misteris, 223, *there is need.*

Mistraisting, 60, *mistrusting.*

Mo, 5, *more.*

Mocht, 223, *might.*

Mold, 73, *mould, earth.*

Montanis, 179, *bulwarks.*

Moriane, 53, *swarthy.*

Morsing powder, 234, *apparently powder used for priming.*

Mot, moit, 5, *may.*

Mowes, 224, *jests.*

Moyane, moyen, myance, 153, *means, interest, a fee.*

Mulettis, 216, *great mules.*

Mum, 99, *mutter.*

Murdreist, 28, *murdered.*

Myndis, 87, *intends.*

Myne alone, 119, *alone.*

Mynt, 187, *attempt.*

Myrk, 30, *darkness.*

Myrrenes, 187, *Dalyell reads inclinit to meiknes.*

Mys, 85, *fault, mischief;* 115, *miss.*

Myschantly, 66, *wickedly.*

Myster, 93, *need.*

N

Nan, 178, *none.*

Nane, 31, *none.*

Nanis, 238, *purpose.*

Nascence, 90, *childhood.*

Necessair, 23, *necessary.*

Neif, 223, *fist, hand.*

Neist, 145, *next.*

Nochttheles, 64, *nevertheless.*

Nois, 55, *nose.*

Nor, 146, *than.*

Nosebitt, 229, *anything that acts as a check or restraint.*

Nother, 91, *neither.*

Nouells, 119, *news.*

Nouther, 18, *neither.*
Noy, 159, *annoyance.*
Noysum, 65, *giving annoy-
ance.*

O

Obeysant, 67, *submissive.*
Oblist, 221, *obliged.*
Oche, 1, *oh!*
Ocht, 19, *ought.*
Of tyme, 22, *oft times.*
On, 234, *one.*
Ones, 161, *once.*
Onmerkit, 233, *unmarked.*
On slane, 96, *unslain.*
Ony, 5, *any.*
Opone, 168, *oppose.*
Or euer, 57, *ere.*
Ouer, 9, *too.*
Ouerblawin, 39, *overblown,
gone.*
Ouer cast, 99, *glance over.*
Ouer hand, 114, *upper hand.*
Ouerharld, 63, *oppressed.*
Ouerlay, 74, *beat severely, op-
press.*
Ouerluikit, 82, *overlook it.*
Ouirgang, 175, *overrun.*
Ouirhaill, 125, *break through.*
Ouirsyle, 151, *circumvent,
covered.*
Ouirthraw, 145, *overthrow.*
Oulke, 225, *week.*
Our harrill, 131, *oppress.*
Ourlaid, 186, *beat severely.*
Ourset, 187, *overcome.*
Ourthrow, 187, *overthrow.*
Outher, 59, *either.*
Ovirthrawne, 130, *overthrown.*
Owerganc, 207, *overrun.*

Owersett, 228, *overcome.*
Oyne, 208, *oven.*

P

Pace, 126, *pasch, Easter.*
Packmantie, 215, *portmanteau.*
Packt it, *perhaps erratum for
packit,* 215, *packed.*
Paik, 207, *trick.*
Paikis, 122, *a drubbing.*
Paine, 33, *punishment.*
Pairt, 34, *party.*
Pallartis, 203, *rascals.*
Pallat, 86, *crown of the head.*
Palmsoneuin, 137, *Palm Sun-
day even.*
Palyard, palzart, 36, *rascal,
lecher.*
Palzardrie, 108, *whoredom.*
Pance, 86, *muse;* panst, 86,
was careful.
Pand, 131, *pledge.*
Pansand, 1, *musing.*
Papingaw, 77, *parrot,*
Pasche, 121, *Easter.*
Pasendlang, 96, *pass along.*
Pat, 58, *put.*
Patlis, 72, *pattles, sticks with
which the ploughman clears
away the earth from the
plough.*
Paun, 87, *peacock.*
Pech, 159, *pant.*
Pedderis, 231, *pedlars.*
Pegrall, 4, *paltry.*
Peirtly, 68, *briskly, boldly.*
Peirtryks, 172, *partridges.*
Pellettis, 180, *bullets.*
Pellottis, pellets, 196, *skin of
a sheep without the wool.*

Peloure, 38, *thief.*
Perfyte, 8, *perfect.*
Perigall, 3, *quite equal.*
Perqueir, 144, *accurate.*
Persaif, parsaue, 112, *perceive.*
Phareis, 210, *fairies.*
Pieteous, 434, *piteous.*
Pietie, 170, *pity.*
Placebo, 220, *a flatterer.*
Plaine, 194, *show.*
Plat, 25, *set, place.*
Pleinyeid, 213, *complained.*
Pleit, 194, *maintained in de-bate.*
Plentis, 212, *complaints.*
Plenzies, 168, *complain.*
Plesoure, 12, *pleasure.*
Plewche, 140, *plough.*
Pluck up fair, 187, *ready to pluck up everything by the roots* At p. 183, line 1, *Dalyell reads, maid them pluk up lair.*
Pluk at the Craw, 109, *a kind of game.*
Plumis, 183, *feathers.*
Plunted, 197, *perhaps erratum for painted.*
Pocke nucke, 217, *corner of a sack.*
Poinding, 213, *distraining.*
Pois, 202, *treasure.*
Porteris (*original*) 191, *should be potteris.*
Potgun, *cannon or musket.*
Pow, 81, *pull.*
Practicques, pretticques, 208, 209, *practices.*
Praisit, 8, *prized.*
Preforme, 21, *perform.*
Preif, 64, *prove.*

Preist, 86, *exerted himself strenuously.*
Prenis, 157, *pins.*
Prenit, 162, *pinned.*
Prentise, 117, *apprentice.*
Preuene, 74, *prevent.*
Pringnant, 144, *pregnant.*
Prolong, 68, *delay.*
Promouis, 142, *promotes.*
Propone, 64, *propose, set forth.*
Propyne, 161, *present.*
Proterue, 23, *froward.*
Prothogall, 71, *prodigal.*
Pruise, 12, *Dalyell reads pruife, proof.*
Pryse, 8, *praise.*
Pryse, 167, *appraise.*
Puir anis, pureanis, 8, *the poor.*
Puneis, 3, *punish.*
Puttis, on vther, 213, *gives a gentle push, as a hint.*
Pvneiss, 225, *punish.*
Pynand, 198, *oppressing.*
Pyne, 72, *agony, pain.*
Pyned, 54, *pained, racked.*

Q

Quarrell, 20, *quarrel, cause.*
Quat, 178, *quit.*
Queutance, 35, *acquaintance.*
Quha, 5, *who.*
Quhairfoir, 12, *wherefore.*
Quhairfra, 159, *wherefrom.*
Quhaitfoir, 135, *for which.*
Quha say, 221, *sham, pretence.*
Quhat, 54, *what.*
Quhat reck? 235, *what matters, exclamation of indifference.*
Quheill, 152, *wheel.*

18

Quheit, 147, *wheat.*
Quhen, 5, *when.*
Quhidder, 134, *whether.*
Quhilk, 2, *which.*
Quhinger, 128, *a short hanger used as a knife at meals, and as a sword in brawls.*
Quhip, 126, *whip.*
Quhissill, 84, *whistle.*
Quhois, 234, *whose.*
Quholpis, 10, *whelps.*
Quhome, 23, *whom.*
Quhomlit, 9, *whelmed.*
Quhow, 131, *how.*
Quhy, 146, *why.*
Quhyle, 134, *time.*
Quhylis, 134, *whiles, sometimes.*
Quhyte, 169, *white.*
Quod, 51, *quoth.*
Quow, 219, *cow.*

R

Raid, 143, *road ;* 187, *rode.*
Raid, 204, *roadstead.*
Raip, 33, *rope.*
Rais, 85, *rose.*
Rak, 71, *stretch.*
Rakles, 9, *careless, rash.*
Rang, 68, *reigned.*
Rank, 107, *row.*
Rapfow, 34, *ropeful, gallows-bird.*
Rasche bus, 58, *bush of rushes.*
Rashe, 88, *dash.*
Raungard, 200, *renegade.*
Ray, 9, *break ray, to go into disorder.*
Rayne, 219, *perhaps roe or kid.*
Read, 215, *road.*

Rebald, 143, *a low worthless fellow.*
Red, rad, 73, *afraid.*
Red for wyuis, 183, *afraid of the women.*
Reft, 211, *bereft.*
Regiment, 204, *government.*
Reheirs, 171, *rehearse.*
Reif, 78, *to rob ;* 156, *robbery.*
Reikit, 7, *reached, handed.*
Reikit, 231, *fitted out.*
Reil, 91, *reel, swagger.*
Reill, 152, *whirl.*
Reingat, (Renigat?) 34, *forsworn.*
Reist, 164, *arrest.*
Remeid, 75, *remedy.*
Remord, 110, *feel remorse for.*
Renigats, 104, *renegades.*
Replege, 234, *replevin.*
Ressaif, 231, *receive.*
Ressauit, 235, *received.*
Rest, 211, *perhaps erratum for reft.*
Restorde, 38, *restore it.*
Reteir, 183, *withdraw.*
Retreit, 72, *repeal, reverse, retract.*
Retyre, 45, *return.*
Reuer, 39, *robber.*
Reuth, 157, *ruth, pity.*
Reuthfull, 16, *pitiful.*
Reving, 197, *stealing.*
Rewolk, 198, *revoke.*
Rid, 152, *rede, counsel.*
Riggein stanes, 179, *stones forming the ridge of a house.*
Ring, 34, *prevail ;* 151, *reign.*
Ring, 111, *kingdom.*
Rokket, 135, *rochet, a little blue cloth cloak.*

Rome, 104, *kingdom.*
Rome-raikeris, 135, *those who pretended to bring relics from Rome.*
Rouch, 119, *rough.*
Roundit, 221, *whispered.*
Roupand, 136, *croaking.*
Rowme, 166, *room, possession, places.*
Roy, 159, *king.*
Rubiatouris, 104, *robbers, ragamuffins.*
Ruffyis, 104, *ruffians.*
Ruffyis, raggit, 107, *Dunbar has ruffy ragmen, seems a name for the devil.*
Rug, 109, *pluck, pull about.*
Ruggars, 104, *depredators.*
Ruse, 192, *praise, a boast.*
Ruttery, 30, *lechery.*
Rycht, 101, *good, excellent.*

S

Sa, 1, *so.*
Saa, 214, *saw.*
Sace, 155, *cease.*
Saces, 174, *sauces.*
Sacke, sact, 122, *destroy.*
Saikles, 11, *guiltless.*
Sake, 193, *sack, ruin.*
Salbe, 10, *shall be.*
Sall, 145, *shall.*
Samin, 186, *same.*
Sangis, 2, *songs.*
Sanit, 134, *made the sign of the cross, blessed.*
Sar, 181, *serve.*
Sark, 135, *shirt, surplice.*
Sat, 55, *set.*

Sauch, 71, *sallow, willow;* rak ane sauch, *crack hemp.*
Saucht, 68, *at ease.*
Saule, 51, *soul.*
Saw, 171, *sow.*
Say, 166, *so.*
Say, 239, *trial.*
Sayit, 75, *assay it.*
Scaffing, 224, *spunging.*
Scellat, 7, *small bell.*
Schalde, 204, *shallow.*
Schavellis, 120, *schavellings, priests.*
Schawis, 61, *shows.*
Schent, 91, *confounded, to destroy.*
Scherat, 185, *chariot.*
Schewed, 238, *sewed.*
Schill, 37, *shrill.*
Schir, 162, *sir.*
Scho, 73, *shoe.*
Schorde, 37, *threatened.*
Schot, 183, *pushed, shot.*
Schouris, 37, *throes, pangs.*
Schowder, 234, *shoulder.*
Schyre, 161, *territory, shire.*
Sclander, 120, *slander.*
Se, 99, *for ze, ye.*
Sea, se, 228, *so.*
Sect, wyne, 208, *wine called sack.*
Sedull, 149, *schedule.*
Seik, 169, *sick.*
Seinzeour, 54, *signor.*
Seir, 64, *several.*
Seis, 96, *for ceis, cease.*
Seller, 168, *cellar*
Semblie, 211, *assembly.*
Sembling, 224, *deceitful.*
Sempill, 195, *simple; commonly a pun upon the author's name.*

Sen, 65, *since.*
Sensours, 148, *censers.*
Sensyne, 55, *since then.*
Seriand, 96, *sergeant, servant.*
Seruis, 107, *deserves.*
Settin by, 30, *esteemed.*
Sew, 233, *saw, sowed.*
Sey, 151, *assay, trial.*
Seyis, 165, *seas.*
Shent, 19, *confounded.*
Shoir, 4, *threaten.*
Shone, 141, *shoes or sandals.*
Shrewit, 92, *accursed, wicked.*
Sic, 8, *such.*
Sicernes, 13, *security.*
Sich, 14, *sigh.*
Sicht, 161, *see.*
Sicker, 33, *fast, sure.*
Siclyke, 105, *such ;* 148, *so.*
Sillie, 211, *weak, foolish.*
Sillubs, 210, *potions.*
Sinderit, 88, *sundered.*
Sindill, 131, *seldom.*
Sindrie, 54, *sundry.*
Sit, 30, *for zit, yet.*
Sith, 48, *since.*
Sith, 158, *for site, grief ; or
   sich, sigh.*
Skaill, 170, *disperse.*
Skaith, 57, *hurt.*
Skalit, 178, *broke up.*
Skar, 115, *take fright.*
Skeich, 156, *apt to startle.*
Sklander, 235, *slander.*
Sklenting, 235, *oblique, de-
   noting immoral conduct.*
Sklenting bowtis, 235, *mal-
   practices.*
Sla, slea, 15, *slay.*
Slealy, 224, *slyly.*
Sleuth, 52, *slothful.*

Slidder, 24, *unstable, slippery.*
Slokin, 106, *quench.*
Slycht, 6, *slight.*
Smaikrie, 205, *roguery.*
Smaiks, 146, *rogues.*
Smatcher, 226, *a contemptu-
   ous term for a man.*
Smittel, 220, *infectious.*
Smorit, 33, *smothered.*
Smuire, 13, *smother.*
Snadoun, 37, *poetical name
   for Stirling.*
Snapwark, 234, *a firelock.*
Snaw, 58, *snow.*
Sogeouris, 118 ; Soiouris, 180,
   soldiers.
Somzeit, 188, *Dalyell reads
   soinzeit, cared.*
Sorrow mair, 221, *not a whit
   more.*
Sou, 188, *Dalyell reads sen.*
Soupit, 59, *supped.*
Sous, souss, 100, *a sou,
   French halfpenny.*
Soutar, 141, *a shoemaker.*
Sow, 134, *for zow.*
Sowld, 235, *should.*
Sowseyis, 179, *Dalyell reads
   fowseyis, fosses.*
Sowsit, 11, *plunged.*
Sowt, 180, *assault.*
Spaird, 39, *spare it.*
Spald, 117, *shoulder.*
Speciallis, 190, *particulars.*
Speill, 138, *climb.*
Sperand, 178, *asking.*
Sperit, 221, *asked.*
Spill, 44, *kill.*
Splene, 121, *heart.*
Sprent, bak, 243, *bent back.*
Spring, 205, *a quick and
   cheerful tune.*

Spuilze, **183**, *spoil.*
Spwle, **237**, *weaver's shuttle.*
Stack, **204**, *stuck.*
Staik, **217**, *fit, suit.*
Staikit, **205**, *settled.*
Standfulis, **179**, *tubfuls.*
Stangear, **187**, *for strangear.*
Stangis, **110**, *stings.*
Stark, **21**, *strong.*
Steik, **108**, *shut.*
Steikis, **183**, *stitches.*
Steir, **16**, *to meddle with so as to injure.*
Steir, **55**, *disturbance, trouble ;* **178**, *rule.*
Steirburd, **230**, *starboard.*
Steir my tyme, **135**, *lay hold on an opportunity.*
Stemmyne (*or stenning*) **233**, *a species of fine woollen cloth anciently worn in Scotland.*
Stickit, **174**, *stabbed.*
Stirk, **172**, *bullock or heifer.*
Stoundis, **87**, *ache, keen shooting pains.*
Stoup, **58**, *stoop, bow.*
Stourt, **54**, *trouble.*
Stouth, **4**, *theft.*
Stowen, **209**, *stolen.*
Straik, **190**, *stroke.*
Strais, **84**, *straws.*
Strang, **92**, *by violence.*
Strease, **208**, *straws.*
Strukin, **147**, *struck.*
Strynd, **109**, *kindred.*
Stur, **20**, *see sturre.*
Sturdie, **88**, *sturdy, violent.*
Sturely, **175**, *strongly.*
Sturre, **31**, *be in ill humour with.*
Sturtsum, **15**, *cross.*

Styme, **79**, *the faintest form of any object.*
Sua, **193**, *so.*
Subscryue, **168**, *subscribe.*
Subumbragit, **191**, *overshadowed.*
Suddartis, **181**, *soldiers.*
Suddrone, **121**, *southern.*
Suid, **95**, *should.*
Suire, **19**, *sure.*
Suld, **15**, *should.*
Suldarts, **50**, *soldiers.*
Suppone, **201**, *suppose.*
Supposts, **169**, *supporters.*
Sur, **210**, *an expletive or augmentative.*
Susseis, **84**, *scruples.*
Susseit, **63**, *hesitated.*
Swa, **20**, *so.*
Swaits, **169**, *new ale or wort.*
Swarfit, **181**, *fainted, swooned.*
Sweingeour, **85**, *sluggard.*
Sweir, **127**, *swore.*
Sweyning, **50**, *sleeping, dreaming.*
Swidder, **99**, *swither, hesitate.*
Swinge, **15, 17**, *swing, sway.*
Swoumand, **152**, *swimming.*
Swoumit, **3**, *swam.*
Swyne, **229**, *sow.*
Swyre, **187**, *pass of a mountain.*
Syc, **25**, *such.*
Syce, **165**, *raise.*
Syiss, sysc, **211**, *assise.*
Sylit, **9**, *blindfolded, betrayed, covered.*
Syluer, **226**, *money.*
Syne, **73**, *then.*
Syte, **5**, *grief, disgrace.*
Sythment, **72**, *assythment, compensation.*

T

Ta, 159, *toe.*
Ta, 195, *to.*
Tailzeouris, 158, *tailors.*
Taine, 11, *taken, conceived.*
Taine, 27, *the one.*
Takin, 148, *token.*
Talloun, 230, *to cover with tallow or pitch, to caulk.*
Tane, 7, *than.*
Tane, 197, *taken.*
Tas, 200, *cup.*
Tees, 208, *toes.*
Teichit, 59, *taught.*
Teill, 171, *till.*
Teindis, 197, *teinds, tithes.*
Teine, 120, *sorrow.*
Teinfull, 65, *wrathful.*
Telzeour, 232, *tailor.*
Telzevie, 230, *a perverse humour.*
Tenc, 3, *sorrow, vexation.*
Tene, 105, *mad with rage.*
Tent, 22, *heed.*
Tentyue, 113, *attentive.*
Teoch, 122, *tough.*
Tha, thay, thea, 68, *they;* 235, *those.*
Thairout, 170, *in the open air.*
Thappoyntment, 55, *the appointment.*
Theikit, 167, *thatched.*
Theis, 237, *thighs.*
Thigging, 170, *to beg in a genteel way.*
Thir, 5, *these.*
This, 102, *thus.*
Thocht, 11, *though.*
Thoill, 12, *bear.*
Thoull, 110, *thou wilt.*

Thovmbis, 221, *thumbs.*
Thrall, 11, *enslaved;* 124, *thraldom.*
Thrawart, 11, *froward.*
Thre, 50, *three.*
Threttene, 184, *thirteen.*
Threttie, 50, *thirty.*
Threw, 3, *for drew.*
Thrid, 149, *third.*
Thring, 23, *to press, thrust oneself forward.*
Thring doun, 95, *thrust down.*
Thrist, 118, *thirst.*
Thrist, 228, *trust.*
Throne, 98, *tron, instrument for weighing heavy wares.*
Throuchly, 166, *thoroughly.*
Thyne furth, 127, *thenceforth.*
Till, 24, *to.*
Tine, 193, *lose.*
Tinklaris, 158, *tinkers.*
Tint, 70, *lost.*
Tit, 191, *a quick pull, a jerk.*
To, 30, *too.*
Tod, 71, *fox.*
Todlyar, 142, *more fox-like.*
Togidder, 175, *together.*
Tokis, 142, *for takis.*
Tome, 33, *book.*
Tome, toome, 231, *empty.*
Top ourtaill, 140, *head o'er heels.*
Tother, 145, *other.*
Tottis, 215, *refuse of wood.*
Toung, 9, *tongue.*
Tow, 160, *rope.*
Traine, trane, 12, *a road, path,* 29, *a blind, a fetch, deception,* 173, *train of gunpowder.*
Traist, 5, *trust ;* 53, *trusty.*

Tranc, 114, *draw, entice.*
Trapit, 178, *caparisoned.*
Tratling, 114, *tattling.*
Tratorie, 69, *treason.*
Trauell, 78, *labour.*
Tray, 3, *trouble.*
Traytorie, 63, *treason.*
Tred, 59, *tread, track.*
Treit, tret, 145, *treated.*
Trest, 90, *trust.*
Treveis, 231, *sail backwards and forwards.*
Trewis, 150, *truce.*
Trinfauld, 104, *threefold.*
Tristene, 228, *trusting.*
Tristsum, 10, *sad.*
Trowth, 49, *truth.*
Trumpe, 142, *beguile, deceive.*
Tryne, 216, *train, retinue.*
Trystis, 97, *appointments to meet.*
Tuggis, 237, *pulls by jerks.*
Tuilzeour, 122, *one addicted to broils, a slight fighter.*
Tuix, 99, *twixt.*
Tulchin, 198, *a calf's skin stuffed with straw.*
Turse, 217, *pack in a bundle.*
Tuyne, 217, *part.*
Twa, 7, tway, 87, *two.*
Twell-pennies, 238, *twelve-pence.*
Twiche, 237, *tough.*
Tyde, 85, *tide, season.*
Tyke, 38, *dog, cur.*
Tykit, 173, *tied, bound.*
Tyne, 9, *lose.*
Tynsall, 55, *loss.*
Tyritness, 73, *tire.*
Tythance, 175, *tidings.*

U

Uane, 181, *vain.*
Ugsum, 5, *frightful.*
Unduchtie, 117, *undoughty.*
Unlefull, 92, *unlawful.*

V

Vagabounds, 88, *wanderers.*
Vaiage, 9, *voyage.*
Vaikit, 135, *became vacant.*
Vaill, 85, *avail, end.*
Vanlatit, 2, *unlatit, destitute of proper breeding, unkind.*
Vder, 230, *other.*
Veildaris, 86, *weilders, causers.*
Venenianis, 120, *mercenaries.*
Venerial, 196, *mercenary.*
Vepe, 76, *weep.*
Vinqueist, 86, *vanquished.*
Visioun, visorne, 197, *mask, or visor.*
Vlis, 238, *oils.*
Vmquhile, 8, *the late, erewhile.*
Vncouth, 125, *strange, foreign.*
Vndoutit, 81, *undoubted. cowardly.*
Vnfauld, 197, *unfold.*
Voce, 70, *voice.*
Volatill, 174, *wild fowl.*
Volt, vult, 190, *face, look.*
Vpaland, 23, *in the country, rustic.*
Vprychteousnes, 59, *uprightness.*
Vpthrow, 72, *up through.*
Vther, 25, *other ;* mony vther ma, *many others.*

W

Wa, 15, *woe.*

Wa worth, 15, *woe betide, beshrew.*

Wachting, 221, *quaffing.*

Waif, 160, *wave.*

Waik, 93, *is vacant.*

Waill, 143, *choose.*

Wair, 147, *spend.*

Wair, went to, 225, *meaning uncertain.*

Wairit, euill was it, 136, *ill bestowed.*

Wais me, 70, *woes me.*

Wait, 60, *wot, knows.*

Wait, 88, *wot.*

Waithman, 181. *hunter.*

Wak, 162, *moist.*

Wald, 54, *would, wouldst.*

Walis, 180, *walls.*

Walkane, 3, *awake.*

Walkit, 237, *fulled.*

Walk-mill, 237, *fulling-mill.*

Walkryfe, 144, *wakeful.*

Wallaway, 1, *well-a-day.*

Wallis, 133, *waves.*

Wallow, 77, *fade.*

Walterars, 168, *overturners.*

Wan, 57, *won, got to.*

Wander, 120, *see wandrethe.*

Wandrethe, 108, *misfortune.*

Wanhaip, 132, *ill luck.*

Wanluks, 130, *misfortunes.*

Wanrest, 108, *unrest, disquiet.*

Wapis, 174, *tosses.*

Wappin, 91, *weapon.*

War, 71, *outdo.*

War, 191, *were.*

War, be war, 9, *beware.*

War, wars, 176, *worse.*

Wardlingis, 51, *for world-lingis.*

Wardrop, 227, *wardrobe.*

Wareis, 159, *execrate.*

Warin, 100, *growing.*

Warld, 9, *world.*

Warr, 152, *aware.*

Waryit, 134, *cursed.*

Warysoun, 6, *reward.*

Wat, 10, *wot.*

Watt, 237, *wet.*

Watter caill, 169, *broth made without meat in it.*

Watter-fast, 230, *watertight.*

Wauflers, 234, *danglers.*

Waw, 130, *wave.*

Wawis, 117, *walls.*

Way, 1, *wo, woful.*

Wear anew, 67, *for we are enow.*

Wed, 153, *pledge.*

Weddir, 130, *weather.*

Wedset, 158, *to alienate heritable property under reversion.*

Weid, 133, *herb.*

Weid, 237, *weed, clothing.*

Weill war I, 136, *happy was I.*

Weill was her, 3, *happy was she.*

Weir, 2, *war, dispute.*

Weird, 143, *fate.*

Weirdis, *the Fates.*

Weltred, 131, *overturned.*

Weskan (*orig.*), 88, *we skail?*

Weyit, 192, *weighed.*

Wich, 215, *which.*

Wicht, 230, *stout, strong.*

Wichtnes, 117, *strength.*

Widder, 77, *wither.*

Widdie, 71, *a halter.*

Wirriare, 200, *a swiller.*
Wirryit, 71, *worried, strangled.*
Without, 23, *unless.*
Withouttin, 101, *without.*
Witten, 80, *known.*

> For had I witten that I wait,
> Allace is Scotts wisdume.

i.e., *wise behind-hand.*

Witt in, wittin, 229, *knowledge.*
Wittis, 32, *wits, wisdom, senses.*
Wo, 92, *woful.*
Wob, 239, *web.*
Wobster, 237, *weaver.*
Wod, 6, *mad.*
Wodderschins, 219, *against the course of the sun.*
Woll, 179, *well.*
Wondie, 187, *windy.*
Wont shone clout, 4.
Wor, 140, *were.*
Wor, 233, *worse.*
Worssand, 187, *Dalyell reads worsland, scrambling.*
Wowaris, 238, *wooers.*
Wox, 170, *waxed.*
Wrang, 71, *wrong.*
Wrangous, 136, *wrongful.*
Wreik, 160, *do vengeance on.*
Wrestis, 86, *screws, twists.*
Wretheit, 12, *wroth, angry.*
Wroken, 106, *revenged.*
Wsayage, 223, *usage, practice.*
Wylie-coit, 239, *under-petticoat.*
Wylit, 9, *enticed.*
Wyn, 157, *gain.*
Wyritt, 130 *wearied.*
Wyse, 113, *manner.*
Wyssit, 29, *wished.*
Wyte, 93, *blame.*
Wyuis, 183, *women.*

Y

Y, *used for the original letter for Th.*
Ya, 35, *those.*
Yai, 56, *they.*
Yair, *there.*
Yame, 35, *them.*
Yan, 35, *than, then.*
Yat, 35, *that.*
Ye, 35, *thee.*
Yead, 209, *went.*
Yeattis, 196, *gates.*
Yire, 198, *ire.*
Yis, 36, *this.*

Z

Z, *used for the old form of Y.*
Zaik, 164, *ache.*
Ze, 2, *ye.*
Ze, 96, *see.*
Zea, ze, 31, *yea.*
Zeid, 53, *went.*
Zeill, 230, *ye'll.*
Zeir, 26, *year.*
Zell, 6, *yell.*
Zello, 237, *yellow.*
Zeman, 169, *yeoman.*
Zet, 59, *gate.*
Zing, 90, *young.*
Zis, 53, *for zit.*
Zisterday, 58, *yesterday.*
Zit, 2, *yet.*
Zone, zond, 71, *yonder, that.*
Zoung, 22, *young.*
Zour, zoure, 3, *your.*
Zout, 6, *cry, scream.*
Zoutheid, 22, *youth.*
Zow, 3, *you.*
Zow, 168, *ewe.*
Zule, 238, *yule.*

Errata.

[NOTE.—Notwithstanding an earnest desire to insure accuracy a few errors have been discovered, which are here corrected. In publications of this kind such will occur ; but it is hoped they will be considered of no material importance.]

Page 6,	line 1,	*for* flycht	*read* slycht.
... 8,	... 27,	... chefit	... chesit.
... 12,	... 25,	... pruise	... pruife.
... 12,	... 33,	... plesosre	... plesoure.
... 13,	... 3,	... conse rue	... conserue.
... 19,	... 4,	... suie	... suire.
... 22,	... 12,	... sportlie	... shortlie.
... 23,	... 29,	... horint	.. hornit.
... 24,	... 13,	... stidder	... slidder,
... 25,	... 10,	... begonth	... begouth.
... 39,	... 17,	... als wa	... alswa.
... 46,	... 19,	... neake	... make.
... 63,	... 17,	... suffeit	... susseit.
... 63,	... 17,	... saithles	... saikles.
... 67,	... 28,	... carage	... curage.
... 68,	... 1,	... fauchs	... faucht.
... 71,	... 2,	... by	... ly.
... 71,	... 15,	... leid	... reid.
... 73,	... 2,	... placc	... place.
... 73,	... 21,	... cronnis	... crounis.
... 77,	... 15,	... friutfull	... fruitfull.
... 87,	... 16,	... commonit	... commouit.
... 88,	... 15,	... weskan (*orig.*)	we skail ?
...108,	... 7,	... fall .	... full.
...114,	... 1,	... sulk	... suld.
...115,	... 18,	... lich	... licht.
...116,	... 24,	... consing	... cousing.

Page 125, line 23, *for* sweit   *read* sweir.
... 127, ... 32, ... hirn ... him.
... 128, ... 13, ... cpmmands ... commands.
... 132, ... 30, ... losrt ... lost.
.. 135, ... 23, ... begonth ... begouth.
... 138, ... 26, ... connict ... conuict.
... 144, ... 34, ... walkryse ... walkryfe.
... 145, ... 20, ... fall ... sall.
... 154, ... 28, ... thau ... than.
... 158, ... 26, ... flowne ... stowne.
... 179, ... 22, ... sowlit ... fowlit.
... 182, ... 19, ... sleyit ... fleyit.
... 191, ... 10, ... porteris (*orig.*) potteris?
... 192, ... 5, ... dauter ... danter.
... 202, ... 37, ... promtione ... promotione.
... 215, ... 16, ... thing ... think.
... 236, ... 23, ... bit ... bot.
... 239, ... 15, ... fay ... say.
... 239, ... 22, ... thot ... that.
... 241, ... 19, ... O the ... Oche.
... 241, ... 28, . . deer ... deere.
... 242, ... 8, ... precisit ... preeisit.
... 243, ... 9, ... breath (*orig.*) deathe.
... 243, ... 21, ... siveir ... sweir.
... 246, ... 23, ... came ... cann.
... 247, ... 6, ... if ... is.
... 248, ... 21, ... tendis ... endis.
... 249, ... 14, ... suill ... saull.
... 250, ... 4, ... sinco ... since.
... 250, ... 11, ... promieis ... promeis.
... 253, ... 8, ... sounde ... founde.
... 253, ... 11, ... confides .. consistis.
... 254, ... 11, ... slow ... flew.
... 254, ... 12, ... sicht ... hicht.

R. SYME AND SON, PRINTERS, EDINBURGH.

www.ingramcontent.com/pod-product-compliance
Lightning Source LLC
Chambersburg PA
CBHW021034030726
47496CB00006B/1532